$\mathcal{B}iographies$

IN AMERICAN FOREIGN POLICY
Joseph A. Fry, University of Nevada, Las Vegas
Series Editor

The Biographies in American Foreign Policy Series employs the enduring medium of biography to examine the major episodes and themes in the history of U.S. foreign relations. By viewing policy formation and implementation from the perspective of influential participants, the series seeks to humanize and make more accessible those decisions and events that sometimes appear abstract or distant. Particular attention is devoted to those aspects of the subject's background, personality, and intellect that most influenced his or her approach to U.S. foreign policy, and each individual's role is placed in a context that takes into account domestic affairs, national interests and policies, and international and strategic considerations.

The series is directed primarily at undergraduate and graduate courses in U.S. foreign relations, but it is hoped that the genre and format may also prove attractive to the interested general reader. With these objectives in mind, the length of the volumes has been kept manageable, the documentation has been restricted to direct quotes and particularly controversial assertions, and the bibliographical essays have been tailored to provide historiographical assessment without tedium.

Producing books of high scholarly merit to appeal to a wide range of readers is an ambitious undertaking, and an excellent group of authors has agreed to participate. Some have compiled extensive scholarly records while others are just beginning promising careers, but all are distinguished by their comprehensive knowledge of U.S. foreign relations, their cooperative spirit, and their enthusiasm for the project. It has been a distinct pleasure to have been given the opportunity to work with these scholars as well as with Richard Hopper and his staff at Scholarly Resources.

Volumes Published

Lawrence S. Kaplan, *Thomas Jefferson: Westward the Course of Empire* (1999). Cloth ISBN 0-8420-2629-0   Paper ISBN 0-8420-2630-4

Richard H. Immerman, *John Foster Dulles: Piety, Pragmatism, and Power in U.S. Foreign Policy* (1999). Cloth ISBN 0-8420-2600-2 Paper ISBN 0-8420-2601-0

Thomas W. Zeiler, *Dean Rusk: Defending the American Mission Abroad* (2000). Cloth ISBN 0-8420-2685-1   Paper ISBN 0-8420-2686-X

Edward P. Crapol, *James G. Blaine: Architect of Empire* (2000). Cloth ISBN 0-8420-2604-5   Paper ISBN 0-8420-2605-3

David F. Schmitz, *Henry L. Stimson: The First Wise Man* (2001). Cloth ISBN 0-8420-2631-2   Paper ISBN 0-8420-2632-0

Thomas M. Leonard, *James K. Polk: A Clear and Unquestionable Destiny* (2001). Cloth ISBN 0-8420-2646-0   Paper ISBN 0-8420-2647-9

JAMES K.
POLK

JAMES K. POLK

A Clear and Unquestionable Destiny

THOMAS M. LEONARD

Biographies
IN AMERICAN FOREIGN POLICY

Number 6

A Scholarly Resources Inc. Imprint
Wilmington, Delaware

Scholarly Resources Inc.
104 Greenhill Avenue
Wilmington, DE 19805-1897
www.scholarly.com

All photos have been reproduced from the collections of the Library of Congress.

Library of Congress Cataloging-in-Publication Data

Leonard, Thomas M., 1937–
James K. Polk : a clear and unquestionable destiny /
    Thomas M. Leonard.
        p. cm. — (Biographies in American foreign policy ; no. 6)
    Includes bibliographical references (p.) and index.
    ISBN 0-8420-2646-0 (alk. paper)—ISBN 0-8420-2647-9 (paper :
alk. paper)
        1. Polk, James K. (James Knox), 1795–1849. 2. United States—
Foreign relations—1845–1849. 3. United States—Territorial
expansion. 4. Presidents—United States—Biography. I. Title.
II. Series.

E417 .L4   2000
973.6'1'092—dc21
[B]   00-032961

For those who helped along the way—

Richard Dean Burns,

Jules Davids,

John Finan,

Lester Langley, and

Ralph Lee Woodward, Jr.

About the Author

Thomas M. Leonard is Distinguished Professor and Director of the International Studies Program at the University of North Florida. He has been a Fulbright Lecturer at Instituto Juan XXIII Argentina and the Institute for Advanced Studies in Mexico. His most recent publications are *United States and Latin America, 1850–1903: Establishing a Relationship* (2000) and *Castro and the Cuban Revolution* (1999). In addition to a Fulbright research grant, he received other research awards from the National Endowment for the Humanities, United States Department of Education, and the Andrew Mellon and Ford Foundations.

Contents

Introduction

Writing in 1845, New York journalist John O'Sullivan asserted that it was the "manifest destiny" of the United States to expand across the continent and spread the blessings of its liberty to all of those swept up in its path. O'Sullivan reflected the confidence that Americans had in their egalitarian and democratic society, at least in comparison to the remainder of the world at the time: Great Britain, continental Europe, and Latin America. The American society provided greater opportunity for economic and social advancement and participation in a more representative government, while Great Britain and continental Europe continued to endure monarchical political structures and stratified societies. The Latin Americans appeared as victims of Spanish imperialism, the imposition of the Catholic religion, and the presence of mixed-blood peoples, all of which made them inferior to the North Americans. O'Sullivan's positive description of the United States was not new. Tom Paine had made the claim at the time of the Revolutionary War, and as recently as the 1820s President John Quincy Adams did the same. All three men believed that the United States served the world as the beacon of liberty, that all peoples aspired to be like the Americans, and that God had chosen the United States to spread its wings of freedom, at least across the continent from the Atlantic to the Pacific. Others professed that the United States should take the blessings of its society beyond the continent.

In the atmosphere of expansion that characterized the presidency of James K. Polk from 1845 to 1849, the spirit of Manifest Destiny was used to justify the annexation of Texas and the acquisition of the Oregon, New Mexico, and California territories. Manifest Destiny, however, masked the more pragmatic reasons for expansion—namely, economics and security. The confidence in America's righteousness allowed President Polk to bully the governments in London and Mexico City, not recognizing that internal affairs had a greater influence on their foreign policy decisions than American jingoism. Manifest Destiny also concealed sectional divisions that had significant political ramifications at the national level and influenced the course of national expansion.

Polk's political life spanned the generation that witnessed the development of America's greatness. He participated in Jacksonian Democracy and experienced, for better and for worse, the growing social egalitarianism and greater participatory democracy. In this changing political environment, Polk adhered to the Jeffersonian and Jacksonian principles of a frugal government guided by the strictest interpretation of the U.S. Constitution. His unbending faith in those principles is largely responsible for his mixed record on domestic issues, as witnessed by the congressional battles over tariff revision, the establishment of an independent treasury, and the demand for internal improvements. But those political battles paled in comparison to the arguments regarding continental expansion.

Although the popular quest for Oregon and California sprang upon the nation like a bolt of lightning in the mid-1840s, and the annexation of Texas was handed to Polk by outgoing President John Tyler the day before Polk assumed office, the movement Westward spanned, and in some instances predated, Polk's political career that began in 1822. And the reasons for U.S. continental expansion were many. With the annexation of Texas and the New Mexico, California, and Oregon territories, Americans residing in those areas fell victim to Mexican or British authority, under which they suffered discrimination and were denied the opportunity for self-government. By spreading the U.S. flag over these territories, the new residents would be secure in the benefits of democracy.

In the South and Southeast, plantation owners wished to protect their "peculiar institution" of slavery by acquiring new territories from which slave states would be carved. The addition of new slave states, they reasoned, would ensure their representation in Congress, where sectional interests could be protected. Abolitionists vehemently opposed the expansion of slavery on moral grounds. Elsewhere, residents in the Old Midwest envisioned the new territories to be occupied by a multitude of small farms, not slave plantations. These battle lines became drawn in the debates regarding the admission of Texas to the Union, Southern disinterestedness in the acquisition of Oregon, and the delay until 1850 in admitting California to the Union.

In their euphoria to acquire Pacific Coast ports that opened the door to trade with East Asia, New England merchants apparently overlooked the political consequences of additional agrarian states, either free or slave. These commercial interests feared that war with

England over any of these territories would adversely impact upon the nation's trade. At the same time, commercial interests in the Midwest established a lucrative trading link to Santa Fe in present-day New Mexico, and, farther south, New Orleans became an entrepôt for trade with Mexico. War would only sever those relationships. Each group made its point to President Polk.

Since the independence of the United States in 1776, the American people distrusted the British, and their presence on the U.S. periphery was always viewed as a threat to national security. Polk shared this perspective, which influenced his diplomacy regarding Texas, Oregon, and California. He anticipated every British move as one designed to prevent the United States from expanding to the Pacific, and he suspected the British of going to war over Oregon and providing military support to the Mexicans in their effort to reclaim Texas. At the same time, slaveowners envisioned a British presence in Texas as the first step along a path to interference in the "peculiar institution" in the Southeast.

Just as domestic considerations influenced the course of U.S. diplomacy, internal affairs affected the foreign policies of Great Britain and Mexico. Over time the United States became the beneficiary of these internal dynamics. In the 1840s the British people suffered from severe food shortages, a rebellious Ireland, and fragile relations with France. The London government understood that it could not pursue a bullish policy over distant lands on the North American continent that might result in war because popular support at home was wanting. This consideration prompted the government to compromise on Oregon, permit the Americans to occupy California, and abandon any thought of supporting the Mexicans in the struggle with the United States. For the Mexicans to succeed in any conflict with the United States, they needed foreign support because their government was bankrupt and wracked by dissension that raised the probability of its peripheral states leaving the Mexican union. Despite its haughty nationalism that demanded the return of Texas and refusal to surrender lands on the Pacific Coast, Mexico was in no position to defend itself. Polk benefited from Mexico's weakness when he prosecuted a successful war beginning in 1846.

The reader will be reminded of these separate themes throughout the chapters of this book. Rather than a chronological approach, the volume takes a topical one. The first chapter focuses upon Polk's political career from its beginnings in Tennessee until his election as president in 1844. It also describes his domestic policies and administrative style as well as Polk's ability to govern a conflicted nation on the eve of continental expansion. The chapters that follow focus on the expansionist issues: the annexation of Texas, Oregon, and California, and finally the war with Mexico. Such an approach provides the reader with an understanding of the complexity of continental expansion: it was much more than the moral crusade suggested by the concept of Manifest Destiny.

Words of appreciation go to the series editor, Andy Fry, for giving me the opportunity to undertake this volume and for his insightful suggestions that helped to make the manuscript a better one. Thanks also go to Richard Hopper and his staff at Scholarly Resources for their encouragement and support in bringing the volume to a successful conclusion. Bruce Latimer, head of the Documents Collections at the University of North Florida, remains a good friend as well as an invaluable assistant in tracking down obscure material from distant places. Vernon Payne, a graphic artist in the Instructional Communications Department at the University of North Florida, patiently crafted the maps, and the staff in the Photographic Division of the Library of Congress provided the necessary assistance needed to locate the photographs found in this volume. And again to my wife, Yvonne, who not only keeps a family of six children, five in-laws, and thirteen grandchildren together but also quietly encourages them to pursue their dreams.

T. M. L.
Jacksonville, Florida

Chronology

1778

The British lay claim to Nootka Sound in the Pacific Northwest with the explorations of Captain James Cook.

1792

The U.S. claim to Oregon is made by Captain Robert Gray, who reaches the mouth of the Columbia River • British navigator George Vancouver explores the California coastline.

1795

James K. Polk is born in Mecklenburg County, North Carolina, the first of nine children, to Samuel and Jane Polk.

1796

In his Farewell Address on September 17, President George Washington advises his countrymen to avoid any entangling alliances with foreign nations.

1801

In his Inaugural Address on March 5, Thomas Jefferson warns the nation against joining any permanent international alliances.

1803

The United States purchases the Louisiana Territory from France for $15 million.

1804

Meriwether Lewis and William Clark embark on a journey to explore the headwaters of the Mississippi River and beyond.

1805

The Polk family relocates to Maury County, Tennessee, about sixty miles south of present-day Nashville.

1812

On June 4 the United States declares war on Great Britain for violating its neutral rights, impressing its sailors, and supporting Indians to prevent its westward expansion • The Russians establish Fort Ross in California north of San Francisco Bay.

1814

The War of 1812 comes to a conclusion in December with the Treaty of Ghent, which establishes the U.S. claim in Oregon to territory south of the Columbia River.

1816

In January, Polk enters the University of North Carolina at Chapel Hill. Two years later, he will graduate with highest honors • The Second Bank of the United States is established for a twenty-year period.

1818

The United States and Great Britain agree to the joint occupation of the Oregon Territory between the Columbia River and the 49th parallel.

1819

The onset of "panic" (depression) brings about the popular demand for new political leadership • On February 22, Secretary of State John Quincy Adams completes the Trans-Continental Treaty with Spain, which defines the Texas boundary at the Sabine River. Spain also surrenders its claims to the Pacific Northwest Territory (Oregon).

1820

Polk is admitted to the Tennessee bar and begins to practice law in Columbia • Congress approves the Missouri Compromise, which establishes the southern boundary of the state (36° 30') as the demarcation line for future slave states.

1821

The Mexican government grants Moses Austin a contract that permits him to bring American settlers into Texas. Over thirty thousand Americans will migrate there within the next fifteen years • A permanent trading route is established between St. Louis, Missouri, and Santa Fe in present-day New Mexico.

1822

Polk's political career begins with his election to the lower house of the Tennessee state legislature.

1823

A lifelong friendship with Andrew Jackson begins as Polk breaks ranks with the leadership of Tennessee's Democratic Party to support Jackson's bid for the U.S. Senate • In his Annual Message to Congress on December 2, President James Monroe proclaims the doctrine that bears his name: henceforth, the Western Hemisphere will be off limits to European intrusion.

1824

On January 1, Polk marries Sarah Childress, the daughter of a prominent Murfreesboro merchant and planter • The Russian claims to northern California end with the abandonment of Fort Ross • U.S. merchantmen establish trading houses along the California coast from San Diego in the south to Yerba Linda in the north.

1825

In April, Polk is elected to the U.S. House of Representatives and immediately begins to work against the legislative proposals of President John Quincy Adams. He is reelected for every term until his resignation in 1839 • Mexico rejects President Adams's offer of $2 million for the Texas territory.

1826

Polk speaks out against U.S. participation in the Congress of Latin American states meeting in Panama, fearing that its results might risk war with Great Britain • The first U.S. overland expedition reaches into California's San Joaquín Valley • In a report to President Adams, Boston merchant William Sturgis encourages settlement of the Oregon boundary at the 49th parallel.

1827

The Americans and British agree that their joint occupation of the disputed Oregon Territory can be abrogated by giving a year's notice.

1828

Polk supports Jackson's successful bid for the presidency. Over the next eight years, Polk labors on behalf of the president's legislative program and becomes impressed with his strong leadership style.

1830

Illustrating his strict constructionist view of the Constitution, Polk supports Jackson's veto of the Maysville Road legislation.

1832

Although he opposes high protective tariffs and advocates states' rights, Polk rejects John C. Calhoun's nullification theory that denies the imposition of federal tariffs in South Carolina.

1833

In July, Polk authors the minority report on the Bank of the United States, which asserts that the Bank serves only the interests of the Eastern establishment. Subsequently, Jackson orders the withdrawal of government funds and causes the Bank to collapse.

1835

Polk is elected Speaker of the House of Representatives, a position he holds until leaving Congress in 1839 • Mexico rejects President Jackson's offer to purchase Texas and California.

1836

General Santa Anna overwhelms the American defenders of the Alamo at San Antonio on March 6, only to be defeated by Sam Houston's Texan army six weeks later at San Jacinto • On May 19, Texas declares its independence from Mexico and seeks admission to the United States • Polk supports Martin Van Buren's successful bid for the presidency.

1837

Navy purser William Slacum reports to President Jackson that the British presence in the Pacific Northwest is a threat to U.S. interests • On March 3, the last day of his presidency, President Jackson extends recognition to Texas • The Panic of 1837, which will last for seven years, adversely impacts upon Polk's political career.

1839

Polk leaves the House of Representatives to seek the governorship of Tennessee.

1840

John Sutter establishes a fort on the Sacramento River, which soon becomes an important trading post for Americans entering California across the Sierras • The publication of Richard Henry Dana's *Two Years Before the Mast* alerts the American public to the advantages of California.

1841

President William Henry Harrison dies on April 4, one month after his inauguration. He is succeeded by Vice President John Tyler • In October, Tennesseans elect James Jones governor, marking the first electoral defeat in Polk's political career • Sir George Simpson, manager of the Hudson's Bay Company in the Oregon Territory, encourages the British government to acquire San Francisco Bay before the Americans seize it.

1842

During the negotiations with Lord Ashburton on the eastern U.S.-Canadian boundary and other issues, Secretary of State Daniel Webster proposes a "Tripartite Plan" by which the United States would agree to stay south of the Columbia River in Oregon provided the British convince the Mexicans to let the Americans have San Francisco Bay • In July the United States completes the Treaty of Wanghia, which opens Chinese ports to American merchants and in turn spurs U.S. interest in Pacific Coast ports • Acting on misinformation that war is imminent with Mexico, Commodore Thomas ap Catesby Jones holds the California city of Monterey for a few days in October • John C. Frémont undertakes the first of three exploratory expeditions into California.

1843

The "Great Migration" of pioneers across the Sierras causes Oregon fever to grip the United States. Largely unnoticed at the time is the number of settlers who head for California • In November, Jones again defeats Polk in Tennessee's gubernatorial contest • In December, Robert Pakenham is appointed the new British minister to the United States with the objective of reaching a settlement on Oregon.

1844

On February 24, Secretary of State Abel Upshur, who is willing to compromise on Oregon, is killed in an accident while aboard the USS *Princeton*. His replacement, John C. Calhoun, has no interest in acquiring any part of the Northwest Territory • In the spring, the British government offers to guarantee Mexican control of California if the government at Mexico City will recognize the independence of Texas • On April 1, Secretary of State Calhoun concludes a treaty providing for the annexation of Texas to the United States • At its national convention in Baltimore, the Whigs nominate Henry Clay as their presidential candidate. The party platform makes no mention of expansion • In May the Democratic convention, also meeting in Baltimore, selects Polk as their presidential nominee. The party platform calls for the "re-annexation" of Texas and the "re-occupation" of Oregon • On June 8 the Senate defeats the Texas Treaty of Annexation submitted by President Tyler • In November, Polk wins the presidential election • On December 3, President Tyler calls on Congress to approve a joint resolution providing for the admission of Texas to the Union • In December a clash between local authorities in California demonstrates Mexico's weak hold over the territory and results in calls for the American government to protect its citizens in the region.

1845

On January 25 the House of Representatives approves a resolution providing for Texas's admission to the Union • On February 27 the Senate approves a Texas annexation resolution • Also in February the Senate refuses House legislation that provides for the abrogation of the 1827 agreement with the British for the joint occupation of the Oregon Territory and for the construction of military forts along the Oregon Trail • In his last act as president on March 3, Tyler signs the congressional resolution providing for the admission of Texas to the Union • On March 4, Polk is inaugurated as the eleventh President of the United States • In the late spring, William S. Parrott, Polk's special emissary, fails to persuade the Mexicans to accept the U.S. annexation of Texas and to sell the New Mexico and California territories to the United States • On June 16 the Texas legislature accepts the U.S. proposal to join the Union, which prompts Polk to order General Zachary Taylor to move his troops from Louisiana into Texas • In July, President Polk offers to compromise on the

Oregon question, but he withdraws the offer after Minister Pakenham fails to pass the proposal on to London • In August, Polk informs General Taylor to consider a Mexican crossing of the Rio Grande an act of war • In his influential *Narrative of the United States Exploring Expedition*, Captain Charles Wilkes recommends that the United States seek coastal ports in California because of the treacherous navigation along the coastline in Oregon • On October 17, Polk appoints Thomas O. Larkin, Monterey's most prominent merchant, as his private agent in California. The president orders U.S. naval ships in the area to seize the California ports should war break out with Mexico • On November 10, John Slidell is appointed U.S. minister to Mexico with instructions to have Mexico City accept the U.S. annexation of Texas and to offer up to $25 million for the sale of California and New Mexico. A month later the Mexicans refuse to meet with Slidell because they requested a commissioner, not a full minister • On November 16, Polk appoints Archibald Gillespie as a special emissary to California • In his Annual Message on December 2, Polk calls upon Congress to abrogate the 1827 agreement with Great Britain on Oregon and to extend U.S. control over the entire territory.

1846

Calhoun comes away from a January 10 meeting with Polk convinced that the president will compromise on Oregon • In January, Polk demands that the Mexicans accept Slidell as minister or he will be recalled. The president also orders General Taylor to station his troops on the north bank of the Rio Grande • On February 24, Polk's cabinet agrees to seek a compromise with Britain over Oregon • In late February, with negotiations at an impasse, Slidell relocates from Mexico City to Jalapa, where he receives word from Washington that reaffirms his original appointment and instructions. He demands that the Mexicans agree to negotiate or face a break in relations • Frémont's expedition into California during February and March raises Mexican suspicions about U.S. intentions to seize the territory • On March 31, Slidell departs for the United States after the Mexican government refuses to open negotiations on Texas and the Western territories • In early April, Mexican troops move north to the Rio Grande to demand that Taylor withdraw to the Nueces

River. During the same time, General Taylor cooperates with U.S. naval ships stationed in the Gulf of Mexico to block the mouth of the Rio Grande • On April 16 the Senate approves a moderate resolution providing for the termination of the 1827 agreement on the joint occupation of Oregon • In mid-April, Gillespie finally arrives in Monterey to meet with Larkin and to encourage California's peaceful incorporation into the United States • On April 25, U.S. and Mexican troops, marking the start of the Mexican War, skirmish along the Rio Grande • On May 9, Slidell returns to Washington to report that relations with Mexico have reached an impasse. On that same evening, Polk learns of the military clash at the Rio Grande. In response to these reports the president convenes his cabinet, which agrees to ask Congress for a declaration of war against Mexico • Congress approves a declaration of war on May 12, one day after President Polk's request • On May 13, Polk informs his cabinet that the acquisition of California and New Mexico will be among the war's objectives. The president appoints General Winfield Scott to command the U.S. army, only to be replaced by Taylor twelve days later • Throughout May, Polk devises his war strategy, which includes an attack by Taylor on Monterrey, Mexico; the taking of Santa Fe by General Stephen W. Kearny; and the seizure of San Francisco Bay by Admiral John Sloat and Lieutenant Frémont • British Foreign Secretary Lord Aberdeen's proposed compromise on Oregon is delivered to Polk on June 6 • On June 10, Frémont leads a group of Californians against the local authorities and declares the establishment of the Bear Flag Republic in northern California • On June 18 the Senate approves the British proposal on Oregon. On the same day, General Taylor seizes Matamoros, Mexico • In late June the Polk administration agrees to offer Spain $100 million for the acquisition of Cuba, but it quickly learns that the Spaniards would prefer to see the island sink to the bottom of the sea before transferring it to another nation • On July 7, following a proclamation issued by Larkin that claimed that California was annexed to the United States, a contingent of U.S. Marines raises the American flag over Monterey • In an effort to initiate peace talks, Polk sends a letter to the Mexican government on July 27 • In late July, Congress approves the Walker Tariff and the Independent Treasury

Bill, but Polk, in adherence to Jacksonian political principles, subsequently vetoes internal improvements legislation • With war progress slow, Polk's cabinet on October 17 approves the invasion of Mexico at Veracruz. Reluctantly, the president selects General Scott to lead the assault.

1847

In California on January 10 local authorities sign the Cahuenga Capitulation, which completes the U.S. conquest of the territory • In January, Polk dispatches Moses Beach on a supposed peace mission to Mexico City. The president rejects an offer by the exiled Santa Anna that he be spirited into Mexico from Cuba to negotiate a peace treaty with the United States • Veracruz, Mexico, falls to Scott's army on March 19 • On May 9, Nicholas Trist arrives at Veracruz to accompany Scott to Mexico City, where he is expected to negotiate a peace treaty • In August, Santa Anna returns to Mexico City; but instead of opening negotiations with the United States, he organizes an army to resist Scott's forces • Scott begins his assault on Mexico City on August 13, and exactly one month later takes Chapultepec Castle • Santa Anna is replaced by a provisional government on September 15 as U.S. troops occupy all of Mexico City • Dissatisfied with Trist's diplomatic efforts, Polk orders his recall on October 17 • In refusing Polk's directive, Trist informs the president on December 6 that he will stay on until a peace treaty with Mexico is completed.

1848

On January 26, infuriated at Trist's recalcitrance, Polk orders General William O. Butler to forcibly remove him from Mexico • Butler's instructions to remove Trist arrive in Mexico on February 2, on the same day that Trist completes the Treaty of Guadalupe Hidalgo, which satisfies all of Polk's war objectives in return for $15 million in compensation to Mexico • On March 10 the Senate ratifies the Treaty of Guadalupe Hidalgo • In April, Yucatecans declare their independence from Mexico and seek British protection. Polk explains that circumstances and methodologies may have changed since the 1823 Monroe Doctrine, but its intent to keep Europe from interfering in the hemisphere has not • On May 25 the Mexican congress ratifies the Treaty of Guadalupe Hidalgo • In August,

Congress admits Oregon to the Union as a free state, but the embattled legislature will not come to grips with California until 1850 • In August 1848, Secretary of State James Buchanan finally takes notice of reports from Central America of a growing British presence on the isthmus, but a response awaits the Taylor administration.

1849

On March 6, Polk commences a month-long journey home to Nashville, Tennessee • In ill health, Polk dies in Nashville on June 15.

1

James K. Polk
and His America

I am happy to believe that at every period of our
existence as a nation there has existed, and contin-
ues to exist, among the great mass of our people a
devotion to the Union of the States. . . . To secure
the continuance of that devotion the compromises
of the Constitution must not only be preserved, but
the sectional jealousies and heartburnings must be
discountenanced. . . . Any policy which shall tend
to favor monopolies or the peculiar interests of sections or classes . . . should be avoided.
—James K. Polk, Inaugural Address, 1845[1]

As a steady rain fell upon the steps of the Capitol
Building in Washington, DC, on March 4, 1845, forty-
nine-year-old James K. Polk took the oath of office as the
eleventh president of the United States. The youngest
chief executive until that time, Polk brought with him
twenty-two years of political experience that gave him
the confidence to successfully deal with the national challenges before him. But, could he? Did Polk understand
the immense changes that the United States had under-
gone since 1823 when he began his political career? The
Jeffersonian America into which Polk was born in 1795
differed greatly from the America of 1845 when he assumed the presidency. From the original thirteen states,
the country now numbered twenty-seven, with Texas
awaiting admission to the Union. By the 1840s people had
moved into the Louisiana Territory and many Americans
learned about the wonders of the Far West from their reading of Richard Henry Dana's *Two Years Before the Mast*,

and the reports from the Navy's Charles Wilkes and the Army's Captain John C. Frémont.

The admission of new states and the vision of further westward expansion were not the only changes that occurred in the generation prior to Polk's presidency. The country's economic patterns measurably changed between 1820 and 1840. The economies of the Northeast and Middle Atlantic states became more diversified as agriculture mixed with fledgling industries. During the same generation the South became increasingly dependent upon cotton production for export to mills in the Northeast and in Great Britain. In the Midwest small farms abounded, and riverfront towns such as Louisville, Cincinnati, and St. Louis developed into commercial centers. Railroads, turnpikes, and canals connected these sections, particularly between the Northeast, the Middle Atlantic, and the Midwest.

As the nation's economy developed and changed, so too did the patterns of political behavior. Politics became more democratic, with the rapidly expanding number of people participating in local, state, and national elections. In part, this increase in voter interest resulted from the removal of property-holding and taxpaying requirements from the franchise. The constitutions of newer states such as Indiana, Illinois, and Alabama provided for universal white male suffrage, while older states such as New York, Connecticut, and Massachusetts abolished property requirements. Although women, blacks, and Native Americans continued to be excluded from voting, men flocked to the polls. As the generation advanced, the nation became more democratic, or republican in the eyes of the Jeffersonians, who envisioned a nation of small farmers, artisans, and family-operated businesses.

Other factors that stimulated voter participation included the growing strength in democratic beliefs, the active role of state governments in building roads and canals, the selling of public land, the chartering of corporations, and interactions with Native Americans. Beginning in the 1820s, politicians of every persuasion vied with each other for voters' support. The result was an outpouring of interest in state elections, with voter turnout regularly climbing to over 50 percent and reaching a high of 91 percent in gubernatorial elections. During the same time, interest in presidential contests also increased. Only 27 percent of the eligible voters cast their ballots in the 1824 presidential election, but 58 percent did so in 1828, 55 percent in 1832, 58 percent in 1836, and 80 percent in 1840.

These figures served notice that the common man, not the privileged elite, had a greater voice in the government that served him.

By the 1840s, Americans correctly sensed that the political life of their nation had changed. The old system of politics based on elite coalitions, bound together by ties of family and friendship and dependent on the deference of voters toward their "betters," had largely disappeared. In its place emerged a competitive party system oriented toward the mass electorate, particularly at the state and local levels. In this atmosphere the politicians had to take their message directly to the people. Thus, the major parties grew adept at raising money, selecting and promoting candidates, and bringing voters to the polls. To encourage political participation the parties sponsored conventions, rallies, and parades, catered to popular emotions and ethnic prejudices, and subsidized newspapers that printed scurrilous attacks against opponents. A competitive democratic political system came into being.

In addition to the changing political dynamics, the 1830s ushered in a reformist spirit that contributed to a more egalitarian society. The introduction of public education, the quest for women's rights, the development of labor unions, and the drives for temperance and prison reform all characterized the pursuit of a better America. Compared to the rest of the world, Americans were confident that their progressive society was far more advanced than those in Europe and Latin America. Only in the slaveholding South did the planter class cling to the past in order to preserve its political power and place in the established social order.

For most Americans, the United States had become a true republic in which the supreme power of government resided with the citizens, who were entitled to vote. Their elected representatives, responsible to the people, were to follow the popular will and to govern within the confines of the law. In other words, the common man was at the center of the national political stage. The majority of Americans also benefited from a more egalitarian society, rather than one in which inherited wealth and status bestowed special privilege. The popular belief in the American republic contributed to the nation's self-confidence and the conviction that it was destined to spread its reach across the continent. As explained by journalist John O'Sullivan in 1839, the United States as a "nation of progress, of individual freedom, of universal enfranchisement" was destined for a great future; "its floor shall be a hemisphere—its roof the firmament of the star-studded heavens."[2]

O'Sullivan wrote at a time when Americans living in Texas had already declared the territory an independent republic, and other Americans were trekking across the Rocky Mountains into Oregon and California while still others looked south into Mexico and Central America. After all, they considered inferior the peoples residing on the Great Plains and south of the Rio Grande.

Since the days of colonization, Americans had viewed the Indians as non-Christian savages, incapable of creating a civilized society by themselves or of using land productively. Moreover, by the 1830s, the American people believed that the newly independent Latin American nations, despite their professions of republicanism and democracy, were not democratic at all but rather the victims of Spanish legacies—a centralized government, an established church, and a rigid social structure.[3] Racism entered the equation in Mexico, where the largest segment of the population was mestizo (offspring of an Indian and white union), which made them an inferior people from the American perspective. To improve Mexicans' quality of life, the Americans undertook a moral crusade to justify expansion.

The moral crusade paled by comparison with the hunger for land and markets, with their international overtones. This hunger was most evident with Texas, which was coveted by Southern slave owners for the expansion of cotton plantations and as a source of like-minded political representatives to send to Congress, where they would defend low tariffs and the "peculiar institution" of slavery, the backbone of the Southern economy and social order. At the same time, midwestern farmers and their families crossed into the territories beyond Missouri toward the Pacific. The search for new land brought wagon trains into the Oregon and California territories. New England merchants, aware of the vast potential markets of East Asia, anticipated the need for ports along the California coast. This desire to expand the national horizon brought the Americans into the international arena, where they again met their old nemesis, Great Britain, whom they had long distrusted and whose every move was interpreted as part of a grand plan to thwart American national interests.

As Polk gazed out over the sea of umbrellas at the Capitol on March 4, he was about to inherit an America diverse in its economic, social, and political makeup, and equally divided over the reasons for expansion. Given his personal and political background, was the incoming president prepared to meet the challenge? Did he understand the divisions that characterized his country in 1845?

As indicated in his Inaugural Address quoted above, he clearly understood the nation's sectional and economic differences. But did he understand the republic that he had inherited ?

~

James K. Polk, the first of nine children of a well-to-do family in Mecklenburg County, North Carolina, was born on November 2, 1795, just as the westward trek across the Appalachian Mountains began. Polk's family were part of that pioneering experience. His ancestors came to North America in the seventeenth century from Scotland and Ireland, and their search for farmland took them to Pennsylvania and Maryland before they settled on the North Carolina frontier. By 1770 the Polks had won some economic success and political status among the region's hardscrabble farmers. The family's political prominence was evidenced in May 1775, when Thomas Polk's leadership resulted in the Mecklenburg Resolves, effectively making the Mecklenburgers the first Americans to declare their independence from Great Britain. The American Revolution brought new prosperity to the Polk family, including land warrants (options to purchase) in the future state of Tennessee. With the settlement of the Cherokee Indians' claims in the early 1800s the region of Middle Tennessee opened to white colonization. By 1805 the lure of cheap land and the hope for a new start in life brought American settlers to the fertile land along the Duck River in Maury County, about sixty miles south of present-day Nashville. Polk's parents, Samuel and the former Jane Knox, the daughter of a Revolutionary War hero, were among the migrants into Maury County.

Hard work and perseverance enabled these settlers to transform the Duck River region into a prosperous pastoral economy and its county seat, Columbia, into a thriving country village. As they had in North Carolina, the Polk family found economic, political, and social prominence in Tennessee. For example, when Samuel Polk died in 1827, he left his family several thousand acres of property and fifty slaves.

Young Polk's frailty prevented him from participating in the rigors of frontier life. He spent much of his childhood at home, where his mother instilled in him her Presbyterian faith and taught him to cope with his physical shortcomings through rigid self-discipline. As a result, Polk learned at an early age to control his emotions. Encouraged by his father, Polk briefly pursued a business career, for which he had no interest. Instead, Polk's scholarly inclinations led him to the local Zion Church Academy and then to the Bradley Academy in Murfreesboro. After passing the entrance exams with high scores, the twenty-year-old Polk began his college career as a sophomore in January 1816 at the University of North Carolina at Chapel Hill. Two and one-half years later he graduated with honors in mathematics and the classics. Polk also distinguished himself as a member of the university's debating team, and at his graduation he delivered the salutatory address.

Following graduation, Polk returned to Columbia in the fall of 1818 to pursue a career in law and politics. He clerked under Felix Grundy, a self-educated backwoods attorney who had earned a reputation as one of Tennessee's most famous criminal lawyers. Following his admission to the state bar in 1820, Polk established a law office in Columbia where he continued to practice law throughout his career, primarily as a means to subsidize his political aspirations.

Polk's political career began in 1819, just as America's economic and political landscape began to change. In the years immediately following the War of 1812, the British demand for U.S. cotton accelerated and prompted the rapid expansion of cotton production in the Southern and border states, including Tennessee. The accelerated cotton output was aided by the easy extension of credit by both the Bank of the United States and several state-chartered banks. When the British demand for cotton abruptly plummeted in 1819, so too did the prices for raw cotton and thus the land values of mortgaged farms and plantations. The depression of 1819 (or Panic, to use the nineteenth-century term) set in motion a demand by the laboring classes for the election of new representatives to both the state and national legislatures. In Tennessee, Grundy was among those elected to the state senate on the promise of working for debtor relief, a promise he soon abandoned. The ever-opportunistic Polk seized the occasion to have his mentor secure his own appointment as the senate clerk. In that position, Polk quickly earned a reputation as a diligent record keeper.

Polk also experienced firsthand the political process as he worked closely with many state politicians. At the time, Tennessee was dominated by a group of land-speculating frontier gentry led by John Overton of Nashville and Hugh Lawson White of Knoxville. Their political allies included Governor Joseph McMinn and U.S. Senator John Eaton, and in the state legislature Pleasant H. Miller and Abram Maury. The state opposition faction was led

by Andrew Erwin and included Theoderick F. Bradford and Thomas L. Williams; at the national level were Senator John Williams
and Congressman Newton Cannon. While there was little difference of opinion between them, a significant point of separation was
Andrew Jackson, who had a lengthy association with the Overton
group but was disliked by the Erwin faction. Political feuding
among the landed elite did nothing to relieve the effects of the Panic
of 1819 that were experienced by the majority of Tennesseans. By
1821 economic conditions within the state continued to deteriorate
and led to the election as governor of General William Carroll, a
hero of the 1815 Battle of New Orleans, whose Knoxville mercan-
tile house succumbed to the depression. Carroll blamed the privately owned banks for the depression, a view shared by the
majority of Tennesseans.

Within the milieu of increasing political activism and factionalized state politics brought on by the effects of the Panic, Polk sought
his first elective office. In 1822 he easily won a contest for a seat in
the lower house of the Tennessee state legislature. Although his
family connections proved a valuable asset, the determined Polk
still took to the stump, visiting as many farms as possible in Maury
County to persuade voters to support his cause. Equally important
was his oratory style, which would serve him well in the forthcoming period of popular politics and which earned him the title, Napoleon of the Stump. Interest in the election ran so high that it took
two days to complete the balloting in polling places that often came
close to mob violence. Voters declared their choice publicly before
the officials as candidates and their supporters egged them on. Liquor flowed freely, and Polk reportedly paid for twenty-three gal-
lons of cider and liquor at one polling station. Polk not only won
handily, but he also emerged as a promising star in the firmament
of Tennessee politics.

As a freshman legislator, Polk rejected the conventional wisdom that he join the Overton faction if he were to anticipate a
successful political career. Very few observers expected the Erwin-
Carroll opposition group to long survive. Polk quickly came out
on behalf of Carroll and his program of banking and land reform, a
public school system, internal improvements (infrastructure), the
implementation of a more progressive tax code, and the writing of
a new state constitution, all measures that favored the working and
lower classes.

At the forefront of these issues was the call for banking reform.
As a result of the Panic of 1819, Tennessee's state-chartered banks

had suspended specie payment (hard currency) on their printed banknotes, arguing that they lacked sufficient gold reserves to meet the anticipated demand and that payment in specie would lead to foreclosure of farm mortgages. Polk quickly joined forces with Governor Carroll and frontier legislator Davy Crockett to counter the bankers' claim. On the floor of the legislature, Polk engaged Grundy in a debate over the merits of forcing specie payment. In the end, Polk engineered a compromise in 1824 that provided for phasing in specie payments over a two-year period. Still, the banks were unprepared to meet the hard currency demands when full repayment began in 1826, which forced the state-chartered banks to close their doors.

As equally divisive and emotional as the banking question was the status of government-owned lands in western Tennessee. Beginning in 1822, the University of North Carolina, Polk's alma mater, declared that all unclaimed Revolutionary War land warrants be utilized for the school's benefit. In Tennessee, Grundy struck a deal providing for the division of the land warrants among the University of North Carolina and Tennessee's Cumberland College and East Tennessee College. The warrants quickly fell into the hands of land speculators. When Grundy and the North Carolina agents prepared to strike another bargain in 1823, they found Polk waiting in opposition. He argued that Tennessee was not bound to recognize the forty-five-year-old warrants and that the state's western lands should provide the funds for Tennessee's common school fund, not just for three colleges. Grundy tried to circumvent Polk with still another deal with the North Carolina agents whereby one-half of the proceeds from the western land sales would go to all Tennessee schools. Polk mustered his oratory skills to caution his colleagues "against the charm of Mr. Grundy's eloquence," which contributed to the defeat of Grundy's proposal.[4] Polk also steered through the legislature a memorial to Congress requesting the cession of all federal lands to a state endowment for Tennessee schools, but protests by the Overton land-speculating group and the North Carolinians forestalled action on the Polk memorial. There the issue rested until newly elected Congressman Polk arrived in Washington, DC, in 1825.

On other issues regarding Tennessee's western lands, Polk and his allies met stiff resistance from the speculator-dominated legislature. Speculators continued to gain control of Western District lands on old warrants, although the Polk group forced legislation that allowed occupants to purchase property on which they lived and which they had improved. Moreover, Polk was indignant that much of Tennessee's land was owned by out-of- state speculators who rented it to poor farmers. He wanted the legislature to force these speculators to sell these plots to small farmers who would then "feel an interest in the soil and become endeared to the government."[5] Polk also opposed the state's constitutionally based land-tax policy, which taxed all property at the same rate no matter what the value. But Polk and his colleagues were unable to mount a successful movement for a constitutional convention where the land-tax issue could be addressed. He also called for a reduction in the poll tax, which he considered too high for the state's hardscrabble farmers. Polk emerged from these debates on banking and land issues as a spokesman for the lower socioeconomic groups, particularly for those people residing in Tennessee's frontier Western District.

On matters of government authority, Polk held a "strict constructionist" view. Simply put, the government had no legal authority to perform functions not clearly set forth in its constitution. In fact, the less government, the better. Polk's views became apparent in regard to internal improvements. For example, he opposed the construction of a toll road connecting Nashville and Columbia not only because the road stood to benefit residents more in the former than in the latter, but also because he doubted that the state had constitutional authority to require its citizens to pay tolls to a private company. In contrast, Polk spoke on behalf of a federally sponsored survey for a proposed national road connecting Buffalo and New Orleans and urged Congress to route the road through Tennessee. He rationalized that the U.S. Constitution empowered the government to construct interstate roads and canals to "afford facilities in times of invasion for the speedy transportation of troops and the munitions of war . . . [and] to promote the agricultural, commercial and manufacturing interest of the country."[6] Polk added, however, that the residents of each state affected by any proposed national transportation route had to approve the project. In effect, he understood that the Constitution granted the federal government the authority to undertake infrastructure projects that provided for the defense of the country and contributed to interstate and international commerce.

Concomitant with his strict constructionist view, Polk was an advocate of limited government expenditures. As a state legislator, his fiscal conservatism was evident in his support for local public prosecutors to grant divorces, rather than by a special act of the legislature. He also saw the construction of a state penitentiary as an unnecessary expense.

Although the Tennessee reformers failed to achieve their goals in the early 1820s, the experience helped to shape the parameters of Polk's philosophy and subsequent career. Adhering to the philosophy of Thomas Jefferson, Polk envisioned an agrarian America whose self-reliant citizens expected little from their government, except for the guarantees of individual liberty. He argued that expanded government authority would serve only the elite and result in the corruption that plagued European politics.

Another long-term impact upon his political career was Polk's marriage to Sarah Childress on New Year's Day in 1824. The daughter of a prominent Murfreesboro merchant and planter, Sarah maintained the unbending convictions of Presbyterianism learned during her childhood. At the same time, she had been schooled in the feminine arts of music, needlework, and poetry, which added charm to her quick wit and keen intelligence. While her social skills complemented Polk's aloofness throughout his political career, she shared her husband's belief that worldly goods should come only as a result of honest labor.

Polk's political ambitions were momentarily sidetracked with the emergence of fellow Tennessean Andrew Jackson, a war hero and Indian fighter. Erroneously portrayed as a champion of the people, Jackson had amassed a personal fortune as a frontier planter and speculator. Still, his image as a frontiersman stood in sharp contrast to the Eastern establishment and made him a symbol of the egalitarianism and republican spirit that characterized his generation. Jackson's linkage to Tennessee's economic and political power brokers, who opposed the statewide democratic reform movement in 1823, did not ensure Old Hickory's nomination from the Democratic Party's state caucus to represent Tennessee in the U.S. Senate. Surely, the Democratic reformers, which included Polk, would not support his nomination. But Polk broke ranks and voted with the majority of the legislature in electing Jackson to the U.S. Senate in 1823. Polk found Jackson's views on public policy similar to those of Governor Carroll, and Jackson's image as popular hero fit with Polk's experience in political campaigning. Undoubtedly, Polk was also persuaded by the advice of his old mentor, Felix Grundy, who deserted Tennessee's land speculators to ride on Jackson's bandwagon. Thereafter, until Jackson's death in 1845, Polk remained an unfaltering supporter of Old Hickory and his philosophy regarding limited government, fiscal frugality, and a narrow, or "strict," interpretation of the Constitution.

Polk's political career took another turn with his election to the U.S. House of Representatives in August 1825. During the campaign, Polk engaged his oratory skills and mastery of details on various issues to overcome his apparent stiffness and distance from the common folk who populated the rural Tennessee district. Polk captured 35 percent of the vote in a crowded field of four candidates. Over the next fourteen years, Polk's campaigning skills and commitment to Jacksonian politics served him well as he was continuously reelected until 1839, when he decided to seek the state governorship.

~

When the invigorated Polk went to Washington in the late fall of 1825, he took up residence in a boardinghouse with other members of the Tennessee delegation. Because of a lack of space in the federal buildings, his personal quarters also became his business office. Polk's arrival in Washington coincided with the demise of the Federalist-Jeffersonian party system that set the stage for a new era of politics. The Federalist Party, its reputation damaged by charges of disloyalty during the War of 1812 and its continuing antidemocratic image, lay shattered as a national political force. Even in New England, long the bastion of Federalist strength, the party was in retreat.

The Jeffersonian Republicans, on the other hand, stood triumphant, their ranks swelled by fresh recruits, including former Federalists in the East and, due to the admission to the Union of new states in the West, by small farmers, businessmen, and artisans. By the mid-1800s the Jeffersonians' success proved to be their undoing, for no single party could contain the nation's growing diversity of economic and social interests, sectional differences, and individual ambitions. Increasingly divided among themselves, the Jeffersonians found it more difficult than ever to chart a consistent course.

The final collapse of the Federalist-Jeffersonian party system came with the election of John Quincy Adams as president in 1824. In that year, every wing of the Jeffersonian party competed for the executive office. Of the five candidates, Adams of Massachusetts and Henry Clay of Kentucky advocated strong federal programs that encouraged economic development. William Crawford of Georgia and Andrew Jackson of Tennessee clung to traditionally Jeffersonian principles of agrarianism: limited government, and states' rights. Somewhere in between stood South Carolina's John C. Calhoun, who was just beginning his passage from nationalism to Southern nullification.

When none of the candidates secured a majority of electoral votes, the election moved to the House of Representatives, where an alliance between the Adams and Clay supporters gave the New Englander the victory, even though he trailed Jackson in electoral votes, 84 to 99. The Jacksonians, including Polk, charged that a "corrupt bargain" had been struck, and Adams's appointment of Clay as secretary of state only confirmed the deal. Polk placed responsibility at Clay's doorstep. "I understand the game," Polk wrote Jackson on April 3, 1826, and identified the secretary of state as "the dastardly individual who skulks behind the screen and works the wires."[7] The incident cemented an adversarial relationship between Polk, Adams, and Clay that was subsequently played out in the political arena.

The Adams presidency was the high-water mark of "elite politics" and ushered in "republican politics" at the national level. John Quincy Adams was the last of the so-called Eastern establishment to preside over the nation before the Civil War, and throughout his administration he was confronted by those claiming to be representatives of the people—the Jacksonians. The political skirmishes that followed revealed growing sectional differences. The Adams group subsequently evolved into the Whig Party, led by Clay and Daniel Webster, which advocated a broad interpretation of the Constitution that provided for expanded government activism. In contrast, the Democratic Party that came to include Polk, Jackson, and Martin Van Buren called for limited federal authority and a greater reliance on state and local government to meet the people's needs.

From 1826 to 1830 the Jacksonians fought President Adams at every opportunity. Although one of the youngest members of the Nineteenth Congress, Polk wasted no time in becoming a leader of the Jacksonian partisans, or "factious opposition," who opposed most of the president's programs. Equally motivated by political philosophy and partisan politics, Polk was prominently connected with every leading question. As Polk addressed each issue, he staked out the philosophy that characterized his career.

The "factious opposition" dictated the first order of business for the Nineteenth Congress when South Carolina's Representative George McDuffie proposed a constitutional amendment that would deny the House the power to select a president and vice president and provide for their direct election by the people. Polk concurred. In his maiden speech on the House floor on March 13, 1826, he expressed his full confidence in the body politic: "this is a Government based upon the will of the People; that all power emanates from them; and that a majority should rule." Polk further asserted that Adams's election did not represent the will of the majority.[8] Although McDuffie's proposal fell victim to partisan politics, Polk's congressional colleagues immediately recognized his debating skills and mastery of details in his defense of Jeffersonian republicanism.

In his initial address to Congress on December 6, 1825, President Adams laid out an ambitious program that required federal expenditures for a system of roads, canals, harbor improvements, and fortifications; expansion of the navy; establishment of a naval academy, national university, and astronomical observatory; and support for expeditions to explore various parts of the world. He also called for appropriations to send ministers to the Panama Congress and to the independent nations of Latin America in order to expand commerce. And to effect his program, Adams cautioned the members of Congress not to be "palsied by the will of our constituents."[9] The president claimed that his program would benefit the entire nation rather than any particular interest group.

Adams's program challenged the principles of Polk's political philosophy. As a "strict constructionist," Polk scoffed at the use of federal moneys for education and science and therefore opposed the president's call for a national university and national observatory to be funded by the protective tariff. In 1827, when Adams anticipated a Treasury surplus, Polk authored a special committee report denying the constitutional power of Congress to collect moneys beyond the essential needs of government. Moreover, Polk objected to federal taxation policies that encouraged economic development on the grounds that it would lead to a self-serving and corrupt elite. He thought it unjust "to tax the labor of one class of society to support . . . another"; furthermore, it was improper to tax for "any other legitimate purpose of raising a revenue to pay the debt and expenses of this government."[10] But he wavered on the issue of internal improvements. Although he recognized that his constituents would benefit from new roads and turnpikes that connected them to the marketplace, Polk would support federally financed projects only if his constituents approved them. Jackson was in full agreement. "I am sure the general government has no right to make internal improvements within a state without its consent," he wrote Polk in December 1826.[11] Both men claimed that they represented the will of the people.

Congressman Polk sought the acquisition of federal lands in Tennessee's Western District for use in supporting a common school fund. Throughout his first four years, Polk resurrected the state's 1825 memorial but found little backing. As might be expected, the Adams forces in alliance with land speculators and bankers opposed such proposals on political grounds. Davy Crockett's arrival in Congress in 1827 did not help Polk's cause as the frontiersman focused upon protecting the land titles of his constituents. Polk's legislative record during the Adams presidency not only reflected his views on limited government but also his support for America's working classes.

In foreign affairs, Polk held to the traditions of noninvolvement and mistrust of the British that dated back to the early days of American independence. He objected to U.S. representatives participating in the 1826 Panama Congress called by the Latin American liberator, Simón Bolívar. He contended that such participation would draw the United States into the affairs of Latin America and run the risk of war with Europe. Polk feared the abandonment of George Washington's advice against entangling alliances that threatened "peace with all the world" and permitted U.S. "commerce [to] spread over the ocean, and [to] prosperity at home."[12] Always suspicious of the Eastern elite's ties to Great Britain, Polk erroneously suspected Adams of secretly negotiating with the British for the reopening of West Indian trade, which had been closed by an act of Parliament in 1822. Polk not only thought that the president was serving solely the interests of New England merchants but was also bypassing Congress in the conduct of international affairs.

Polk and his fellow Jacksonians were only one element that revealed the disarray in American politics during Adams's ill-fated administration. The president's call for federal road and canal building, standardization of weights and measures, establishment of a national university, promotion of commerce and manufacturing, and governmental support for the arts and sciences signaled not only the political factionalism but also the emerging sectional conflicts and the increasingly popular democratic politics of the day. Within a year of the inauguration the Adams administration floundered, and thereafter politicians jockeyed for position in the realignment that was under way. Polk may have been oblivious to the developing sectionalism, but he understood the breadth of Congressional opposition to President Adams: "The extraordinary fact now exists for the first time since the days of the elder Adams [President John Adams] that a majority of both branches of Congress are against the Executive Magistrate and opposed to the policies of his administration. . . . No administration can be sustained under such circumstances. The political careers of those now in power must close at the end of this present term."[13]

As Polk and his fellow Jacksonians labored against Adams in Congress, Andrew Jackson's supporters mobilized their forces in preparation for the 1828 presidential election. During the campaign, Jackson masterfully sidestepped any clarification of his position on key issues such as the national bank and tariff. Instead, Old Hickory derided the "corrupt" domination of politics in the Eastern aristocracy and, in its place, promised a more democratic political system with the interests of the people at the center. To this end, Jackson told voters that he intended to reform the government by purging all civil servants who had been appointed solely for political considerations.

Devoid of a discussion of the issues, the 1828 presidential campaign reflected the popular politics of the day as it quickly degenerated into a nasty but entertaining contest. The Democrats organized barbecues, rallies, and parades to whip up enthusiasm and gave out buttons and hats trimmed with hickory leaves. Amid the hoopla, few issues were discussed and both sides engaged in slanderous personal attacks. For example, the National Republicans labeled Jackson an adulterer, bigamist, gambler, cockfighter, brawler, drunkard, and murderer, and his wife, Rachel, was maligned as an immoral and common woman. In turn, the Democrats described Adams as a stingy, undemocratic aristocrat whose administration lacked positive accomplishments. Furthermore, as an intellectual, Adams was a thinker incapable of taking action. Some Democrats even charged Adams with being a pimp!

Jackson swept to victory in November 1828 with 56 percent of the popular vote and a 2-to-1 majority in the electoral college. He captured the South and the West but not the Northeast, a sure sign that sectional politics was on the horizon. Jackson's victory also proved important for Polk, to whom Jackson had taken a liking, particularly after his election to the House of Representatives in 1825; over the next three years, Jackson became very appreciative of Polk's regularly penned letters regarding political affairs in

Washington. As the 1828 campaign drew to a close, Jackson wrote Polk that he did not "doubt . . . the correctness of your conclusions."[14] In the future, Polk would benefit immensely from Jackson's friendship.

The euphoria of Jackson's victory only served to disguise his image as a democratic hero. Jackson was not personally very democratic, nor did the era he symbolize involve any significant redistribution of wealth. He himself owned slaves, defended slavery, and condoned the mob attacks on abolitionists such as Marius Robinson in the mid-1830s. He disliked the Indians and ordered the forcible removal of the Southeast's Indian nations to reservations west of the Mississippi River in a blatant disregard for the treaty rights of the Cherokee Nation and a Supreme Court decision that protected Indian lands in Georgia. In contrast to the rhetoric at the time, the rich got richer. Most farming and urban laboring families did not prosper during the Jacksonian era, which contributed to the decline in the popularity of the Democratic Party and eventually affected Polk's political career.

Despite Jackson's democratic rhetoric, his cabinet nominees, of whom only Van Buren had any independent stature, forecast his desire to dominate the government. Although he often turned for advice to his "kitchen cabinet," an informal group of friends including Van Buren and two western journalists, Amos Kendall and Francis Blair, Jackson made the important decisions himself. This determination was linked to his belief that the executive, the only national officer directly elected by the people, therefore represented all the people and should take charge. More than any previous president, Jackson justified his actions by appeals to the electorate. The centrality of his administration was illustrated by his use of the veto twelve times in eight years, compared to only nine vetoes by all six previous presidents. Jackson's political style symbolized the arrival of American republicanism, and Polk understood the concept that the president had to act decisively.

Sectional politics, a phenomenon that would come to plague Polk's presidency, soon replaced the euphoria of Jackson's victory. The United States was experiencing a period of rapid economic growth, which brought much attention to Jackson's handling of issues affecting commerce and industry, including the construction of the federal road from Buffalo to New Orleans. The proposal died because of the government's failure to determine the route. There was no doubt, even to a "strict constructionist" such as Polk, that the Buffalo-New Orleans road satisfied the constitutional requirement of serving interstate commerce; not so the Maysville Road, which connected that town with Lexington, also in Kentucky. Vice President Van Buren, reflecting Eastern commercial interests, pressured President Jackson to veto the Maysville Road appropriations bill, an action that threatened to erode Jackson's Western support. On the other hand, Polk, a defender of Western settlers, assisted Jackson in writing the veto message delivered to Congress on May 27, 1830, which reflected their strict constructionist interpretation of the Constitution. Clearly, the Constitution permitted the government to support infrastructure projects that benefited the nation as a whole, but the Maysville Road had "no connection with any established system of improvements" and was "exclusively within the limits of a State."

Although Jackson suggested that a constitutional amendment could alter the situation, he argued that it should emanate from the "general intelligence and public spirit of the American people" rather than from the special interests found in Congress, where logrolling tactics among the members resulted in unnecessary expenditures. Therefore, Jackson repeated his plea that Congress should confine itself to distributing any future surplus to the states, which could spend it for improvements if they so wished.[15] Critics wasted little time in chastising Jackson for allegedly making a political decision designed to embarrass his rival, Henry Clay, rather than a reaffirmation of his own strict constructionist interpretation of the Constitution. Neglected was the fact that through his administration, Jackson looked favorably upon those projects that satisfied the constitutional requirement for enhancing interstate commerce. During the eight years of the Jackson presidency, the states received an annual average of $1.3 million from the federal government to spend as each state saw fit on internal improvements.

On the House floor, Polk spearheaded the administration's efforts against the Maysville Road appropriations bill. He understood that anything "is national" when a congressman deems it expedient. In a clear reference to the logrolling practices of the day, Polk noted that "all friends of the system vote for every project, so that they may get their own projects passed."[16] To Polk, corrupt politics at the national level paralleled his experience in the Tennessee legislature. He went on to defend the president's act of courage and criticize his House colleagues for charging Jackson with ignoring congressional wishes. Despite the Maysville veto, the debate over internal improvements continued, and by late 1830 both Jackson and Polk agreed that Congress should not appropriate funds for *any* such projects until the national debt was completely retired. A year later, Polk predicted that the national debt would soon be paid off and that Congress would be able to reduce the general tariff; otherwise, it would "devise ways to squander the money."[17] He continued to make similar statements for the remainder of his political career.

While the issue of internal improvements stirred up sectional emotions, the tariff issue proved to be more explosive. The nation's center of manufacturing, New England and the Middle Atlantic states, favored protective tariffs, but the South had long opposed them because they allegedly made it more expensive for Southerners to purchase manufactured goods either from the North or abroad. In addition, Southerners feared that high tariffs would interfere with trade and curtail the export of cotton and tobacco. Feeling against the 1828 so-called Tariff of Abominations ran particularly high in South Carolina, where many of its citizens saw tariffs as the prime cause of the economic depression that hung over their state (it actually stemmed from the opening of new fertile lands in the West). In addition, some Southerners worried that a federal government permitted to be more activist on economic issues might eventually interfere with slavery, a frightening prospect in states where slaves outnumbered their white masters.

When tariff legislation was introduced into Congress in 1828, South Carolinian John C. Calhoun responded with his theory of nullification. He argued that when federal laws overstepped the limits of constitutional authority, a state had the right to declare that legislation null and void and to refuse its enforcement. The nullification prompted some congressional debate, particularly in 1830, but two years later, when Jackson declared that the Union must be preserved, furor erupted. Calhoun countered that individual liberty and states' rights took precedence over maintenance of the Union.[18] Calhoun and Jackson parted ways as the former resigned the vice presidency.

In 1832, Jackson attempted to steer a middle course on the tariff issue by proposing that Congress approve high duties on goods such as wool, woolens, iron, and hemp and reduce tariffs on other goods to previous rates. Many Southerners felt injured. A special statewide convention in South Carolina adopted a policy of nullification, thereby declaring the 1828 and the proposed 1832 tariffs null and void in the state. The South Carolina legislature voted funds for a volunteer army and threatened secession if the federal government should try to force the state to comply. Jackson was equal to the task. In 1833 he persuaded Congress to approve the Force Bill to enforce collection of the tariff duties. The incident also contributed to the permanent distance between Polk and Calhoun.

Polk and other states' rights representatives, mostly from the Western states, found themselves in a bind. They wanted to support the president on the issue of national authority on the tariff issue but opposed the adverse impact of high tariffs on their largely agricultural states. Polk asserted that high tariffs enabled the manufacturers to sell their goods at high prices and produce a federal surplus that resulted in the expansion of the government's role in internal improvements, both of which he opposed. Yet Calhoun's proposed nullification ruffled Polk's belief in fiscal frugality and commitment to states' rights. Calhoun, in protecting sectional interests, had gone too far.

In recognition of his stand on the tariff and his political skills, the Democratic leadership in the House transferred Polk from the moribund Foreign Affairs Committee to the Ways and Means Committee, where he helped to draft legislation that would roll back tariffs to the 1816 level. Once on the floor, however, the debate between protectionists and antiprotectionists clearly indicated that a compromise was nearly impossible. In the midst of the gridlock, Senator Clay proposed that all tariffs be reduced to a uniform 20 percent level over a ten-year period. Polk understood that he had lost the initiative and caved in. In 1833, Clay's compromise became law. Subsequently, South Carolina repealed its nullification legislation and pronounced the Force Bill void, an action that Jackson adroitly ignored.

Polk's call for lower tariffs was matched by his desire for lower taxes and also reflected his fiscal conservatism. "I would bring the Government back to what it was intended to be—a plain economical Government," he declared.[19] He wanted to "relieve the burdens of the whole community . . . by reducing the taxes" and opposed, as noted earlier, government surpluses beyond those moneys essential for the nation's safety. Polk's fiscal conservatism prompted him to vote against most bills for the relief of individuals and against funds for the U.S. Military Academy at West Point. If Polk's advocacy of a small central government reflected the Western farmers' distrust of the Eastern establishment, his efforts to lower land prices, his insistence that preferences to purchase be given to actual settlers, his call for the extension of the federal court system to the

Western states, and his support of Jackson's policy to remove Indians to reservations west of the Mississippi indicated his expansionist philosophy.

The diversity of sectional and class interests surfaced shortly after Jackson moved into the White House in March 1828. The fate of the Second Bank of the United States emerged as the key political issue of the time. Chartered in 1816 for a twenty-year period and guided since 1823 by the talented Nicholas Biddle, the Philadelphia-based bank and its twenty-nine branches (including one in Nashville) performed many useful financial services for the country and generally played a responsible economic role in an expansionary period. It earned a solid reputation for promoting economic stability and checking inflation. As the nation's largest banking institution, it influenced the amount of paper money in circulation. Businessmen and state bankers needing credit, and prominent politicians such as Henry Clay and Daniel Webster (who were actually on its payroll), all favored the Bank.

Other Americans, including Jackson, distrusted the Bank. Businessmen and speculators in Western lands resented its careful control over state banking and instead wanted cheap, inflated money. So too did some state bankers, especially in New York and Maryland, who were jealous of the Bank's location in Philadelphia. Southern and Western farmers regarded the Bank, which dealt with paper rather than landed property, as fundamentally immoral, while still others thought that it should be abolished on constitutional grounds because that document did not specify the establishment of a national bank.

The Bank issue vaulted to the forefront of national politics in 1832, when Clay and Webster, with Biddle's approval, sought congressional approval to renew the Bank's charter four years ahead of schedule. Congress obliged. Jackson had long opposed the Bank both because of a near financial disaster in his own past and because he and his advisers saw it as a privileged monopoly at the expense of the common man—farmers, craftsmen, and debtors. In other words, the Bank did not serve the interests of the people who comprised Jeffersonian America. Jackson further argued that the Bank actually symbolized the corruption that threatened the republican political order.

Determined to crush the Bank, a furious Jackson vetoed the legislation on July 10, 1832. The president gave Congress a long discourse on "strict construction" and concluded that while Congress may have had the authority to establish a bank, it existed only at the discretion of the executive. And since this executive had no use for the Bank, he had the authority to disband it. Jackson went beyond constitutional niceties and played upon the republican spirit of the day. While admitting that all people were not equal in education and talent, "every man is entitled to equal protection of the law," he asserted. And, he continued, it "is to be regretted that the rich and powerful too often bend the acts of government to their selfish purpose" at the expense of "the humble members of society—the farmers, mechanics, and laborers—who have neither the time nor the means of securing like favors for themselves." Jackson also played upon the isolationist spirit of the day. Pointing out that 25 percent of the Bank's stock was owned by foreigners, he asserted that foreigners potentially could own all of the stock. Not only would Bank profits go abroad, but the United States could also "unfortunately become involved" in a foreign war.[20]

Jackson also made the Bank the centerpiece of his 1832 reelection campaign. Confident that the common man most likely did not understand the rudiments of federal fiscal policy, the Jacksonians skillfully manipulated the voters' fears by linking the Bank to some unidentified commercial conspiracy. In so doing, they helped Jackson to coast to a comfortable victory over Henry Clay in the 1832 presidential election, capturing 55 percent of the popular vote and 219 of the possible 286 electoral votes. Jackson claimed that his margin of victory gave him the mandate to sever the link between the federal government and the Bank, an opinion shared by Polk.

Following the 1832 presidential election, Jackson turned to Polk for assistance in crushing the Second Bank of the United States. The president had Polk assigned to the House Ways and Means Committee which, on Jackson's command, completed an investigation of the Bank. The majority of the committee members, including some Democrats, found no evidence that Biddle had mismanaged the institution. These congressmen understood the need for sound fiscal policy and stable currency in order for the United States to maintain its role in the global economy.

In sharp contrast stood the Polk-authored minority report. It reflected Polk's long-standing opposition to the Bank on constitutional grounds and the belief that it served only the needs of the commercial houses and land speculators. Polk was as determined as Jackson to bring the Bank to its knees, and the minority report accused Biddle of numerous improprieties—in particular, the Bank's inability to cover a sudden withdrawal of government funds in late 1832. The void prompted Biddle to dispatch a special agent to London, where he negotiated a deal with British bankers that enabled the Bank to meet its obligation. To Polk, Biddle's action necessitated a full and thorough investigation of all the Bank's operations. [21]

In the meantime, Jackson ordered the withdrawal of federal funds from the Bank. Jackson removed two secretaries of the treasury, Louis McLane and William Duane, before he found one (Roger B. Taney) who would withdraw the federal funds and deposit them in selected state banks, primarily in the West. With the contraction of the Bank's reserves, Biddle had no choice but to call in outstanding loans, a move that further restricted the amount of currency in circulation. When the nation's leading businessmen called upon Jackson to restore the federal deposits to the Bank, the president used the appeal as evidence that the institution did, indeed, serve only a small elite clientele. By the time the Bank's charter expired in 1836, all federal deposits had been withdrawn, and Jackson's action had adversely affected the national economy.

Throughout the crisis, Polk remained loyal to the president's cause. In two speeches on the House floor on December 30, 1833, and January 2, 1834, Polk defended Jackson against charges of executive tyranny: his decisions to replace recalcitrant cabinet members and withdraw federal deposits from the Bank. Polk also asserted that the Bank rivaled the government in authority and argued that if its charter were renewed for another twenty years, it could become the instrument of corrupt men who would use it for their own purposes. "The question is, in fact," Polk concluded, "whether we shall have a Republic without the Bank, or the Bank without the Republic."[22] At the same time, he understood the need to regulate the federal deposits in state banks, and in June 1834 the House narrowly approved his proposed legislation to do so. The Senate failed to act. At its last meeting of the session, on June 30, it tabled the bill. For the moment there would be no control over the federal funds deposited in state banks.

As the issues of the Jackson administration unfolded, Polk's actions connected him more closely to the president. Early in his career, Polk wavered on the matter of government-financed internal improvements, but during the Jackson years he became an ardent opponent and vociferously defended the president's veto of the Maysville Road Bill. Although Polk's strict constructionist view of the Constitution caused him to favor states' rights, he was reluctant to side with Calhoun on the nullification issue at the expense of his support of the president. When Jackson denounced Calhoun's nullification theory in April 1830, Polk distanced himself from the South Carolinian and his supporters. Most significant, however, was Polk's stance on the issue of the Bank of the United States, which clearly placed him in the Jackson camp and vaulted him into national prominence.

By 1836, while serving as Speaker of the House of Representatives, Polk approached the zenith of his congressional career. He was at the center of Jacksonian Democracy on the House floor, and, with the help of his wife, he ingratiated himself into Washington's social circles. Sarah Polk, as his trusted confidante, joined her husband in the nation's capital in 1830 and immediately began to take an active part in his career. Articulate in political affairs and adept at the social niceties, she moved easily among people of influence in the nation's capital to win supporters for her rigid and inflexible husband. Although childless themselves, the Polks raised the children of James's three brothers, who had died between 1827 and 1831. While James exercised a characteristic stern hand over the children, Sarah lavished them with affection.

In Washington, the Polks lived in a boardinghouse until James assumed his duties as Speaker of the House in late 1835. Their newfound status prompted them to move into more comfortable quarters on Pennsylvania Avenue where they entertained important government figures. In turn, the Polks attended dinners and receptions for dignitaries and diplomatic officials. Despite the increased pace of their social life, the Polks remained committed to the tenets of their religious upbringing. James, who clung to the Calvinist doctrines instilled by his mother, believed that few men could measure up to his own standards of discipline and personal responsibility, and Sarah never wavered from the Presbyterianism of her childhood. As a result, they avoided Washington's more frivolous social activities, such as card games, horse races, and dances. Sunday was reserved for church and reflection.

~

By the mid-1830s, Polk's pleasure in his political success and raised social standing was about to be tested. His fortunes in large part reflected the nation's everchanging political landscape. A new two-party system had emerged in the United States—the Democrats and the Whigs. These parties were formed by a combination of sectional and cultural as well as economic and political factors.

The Democratic Party, rooted in the Jeffersonian tradition, espoused liberty and local rule. The party advocated freedom from legislators of morality and special privilege, and also from excessive government. For the Democrats the best society was one in which all citizens were left free to follow their own interests. Although Martin Van Buren and John C. Calhoun spoke, respectively, for the Northern and Southern wings of the party, Andrew Jackson remained the dominant force that provided a sense of national unity. Beyond these generalizations, the party—asserting that it represented the common man—drew its support from the middle class, small farmers, and pockets of Northeastern urban laborers who were descendants of Scottish, Irish, French, German, and Canadian immigrants and who also were Catholic, frontier Baptists and Methodists, and Free Thinkers. Their religious background emphasized the inevitability of evil in the world. For the most part, Democrats did not participate passionately in the moral crusades of the time— temperance, prison reform, and abolition of slavery.

The Whigs, whose best spokesmen included John Quincy Adams, Henry Clay, and Daniel Webster, represented greater wealth than the Democrats and were strongest in New England and in areas settled by New Englanders across the Upper Midwest. In an appeal to businessmen and manufacturers, Whigs generally endorsed Clay's American System, which favored a national bank, federally supported internal improvements, and tariff protection for industry. Many large planters in the South joined the Whig Party because of its position on bank credit and internal improvements, but Southern laborers and artisans were found in both parties. Whigs appeared determined to remove sin from society. Calling themselves the party of law and order, Whigs argued that Americans did not need more freedom but rather had to learn how to use the freedoms that they already enjoyed. Old-stock New England Congregationalists and Presbyterians were usually Whigs; so too were Quakers and evangelical Protestants, who believed that positive government action could change moral behavior and eradicate sin. Whigs supported a wide variety of reforms and positions such as temperance, antislavery, public education, and strict observance of the Sabbath as well as government action to promote economic development.

The fluidity of national politics became apparent in the 1836 presidential election. Andrew Jackson persuaded the Democratic Party to rally behind his personal choice, Martin Van Buren. In contrast, the Whigs lacked an effective national organization and ideology. Unable to agree on a common platform or a single candidate, they adopted the strategy of running strong regional candidates in the hope of throwing the election into the House of Representatives. In the South the Whigs chose Tennessean Hugh Lawson White, in the East they ran Daniel Webster, and in the West, William Henry Harrison of Indiana. Although Van Buren won with 51 percent of the popular tally and 170 electoral votes (both more than the three Whig candidates combined), the 1836 presidential election results revealed that Jacksonian Democracy was in retreat.

Even before Van Buren took the presidential oath in March 1837, the national economy weakened. By summer a full-fledged depression ensued that lasted until 1843. As the Panic of 1837 accelerated with bank and factory closings, the Democratic Party took a further beating from the public. Rejecting explanations that the depression was a worldwide phenomenon, the voters blamed the Democrats for the economic failure. Jackson's crushing of the Bank of the United States, the only institution capable of curbing speculation and imposing credit controls, received particular attention. The electorate indicated its dissatisfaction in the 1837 congressional elections, when the Democrats retained only a slim majority in the House of Representatives.

The worsening economic crisis stimulated a heightened interest in politics. Party identification became an increasingly important consideration for Americans attracted to the flamboyant new electioneering practices and techniques designed to recruit new voters into the political process, as illustrated in the election of 1840. A decade of intense social change had ended in depression, and no other issue figured so prominently in the daily lives of the people in 1840. Although the Whigs delighted in blaming the Democrats for the depression, the presidential campaign in that year generally avoided a discussion of economic issues in favor of a blatant appeal to the popular prejudices of a mass electorate.

Passing over Henry Clay, the Whigs nominated William Henry Harrison, the aging hero of the Battle of Tippecanoe, fought nearly thirty years earlier. A Virginian, John Tyler, was nominated as vice president in an effort to cement the party's regional divisions. The Democrats had no choice but to renominate Van Buren, who conducted a quiet campaign. The Whigs, divided on national issues, failed to adopt a platform and waged a campaign marked by every form of popularized appeals for votes—barbecues, torchlight parades, songs, and cartoons. Political symbolism was exploited by posing Harrison (who lived in a mansion) in front of a rustic log cabin with a barrel of hard cider, and jugs of cider and coonskin caps were lavishly dispensed to grateful voters. The Whigs further altered conventional images by labeling Van Buren as an aristocratic dandy who drank fancy wines, dined on gold plates, and scented his whiskers with French cologne.

Harrison's sweeping election victory, 234 to 60, did not reflect the narrowness of his triumph. He won the popular count by only 148,315 votes out of the 2.4 million ballots cast. Eighty percent of the eligible voters went to the polls, the highest number in U.S. electoral history to that date. Harrison entered the White House without a mandate. At the time, many political analysts focused upon the sectional and class differences that divided America, but the number of votes cast challenges that assumption and instead reflects the republican spirit of the day.

Within the context of national politics, Polk's fortunes began to change after the issuance of the 1832 House Ways and Means Committee minority report on the Bank of the United States. As the author of the report, Polk became the lightning rod for criticism from the anti-Jackson forces in Congress and in his home state of Tennessee. When Polk returned to the state in 1833 to campaign for reelection, he confronted the angst of the local commercial interests and faced two challengers who considered him vulnerable because of his stand on the Bank. Polk's congressional district had diminished in size as the state population exploded after 1820, and in the process Middle Tennessee became more commercially oriented. Supporters of Bank president Nicholas Biddle entered the political contest by printing thousands of copies of Washington's *National Intelligencer* for distribution in Polk's district. The paper denounced the Bank's detractors, particularly the indignant Polk, who used this attack as an example of the Bank's efforts to control local interests, but it passed over any discussion of the fact that the *Washington Globe* passed out extra copies of its paper praising Polk and the anti-Bank contingent. Polk successfully fended off his critics and was reelected by a wide margin. At the time, local analysts concluded that the election results were determined more by the personalities of the candidates than by the issues.

Polk's actions on behalf of the president made him the undisputed leader of the Jacksonians in the House of Representatives and also whetted his appetite for greater political prominence, but his close identity with the president also made him the focus of the anti-Jackson forces. When Polk returned to Congress in the late fall of 1833, he faced many discontented Democrats who were piqued at Jackson's policies and his confrontational style. Polk fell victim to their anger.

In 1834, Polk sought the House Speakership when the incumbent, Andrew Stevenson, stepped down. Initially, Polk received words of encouragement from several prominent politicians, but between the opening of the Twenty-third Congress on December 3, 1833, and Stevenson's retirement on June 2, 1834, the opposition forces, made up of Whigs and anti-Jackson Democrats, strengthened around the candidacy of another Tennessean, John Bell. The struggle for the Speakership reflected the growing opposition to President Jackson, not only over his controversial internal improvements, tariff, and banking policies but also over the growing sense of an imperial presidency. Polk was too closely identified with the president, and Bell was among the strongest anti-Jackson Democrats. Bell served as House Speaker for only one term, as the opposition coalition, united only in its opposition to Jackson, failed to agree upon policy issues. Polk easily won the Speakership in 1835 and held it until 1839, when he left Congress to seek the Tennessee governorship. The Speakership tested Polk's every political skill. When the Twenty-fourth Congress opened on October 7, 1835, the anti-Polk forces led by Bell, John Quincy Adams, and Sergeant S. Prentiss took every opportunity to question the Speaker on rules of procedure, attack him personally, and identify him with the Jacksonian policies that allegedly were responsible for the country's ills. In surviving the political assault, Polk enhanced his national image, particularly among Democratic Party leaders.

On a broader scale, Polk also had to deal with a divided Democratic Party and Congress at a time when the slavery issue was becoming more volatile. Polk was a slave owner and, like many Southern planters of the time, apologized for the existence of slavery. In his maiden speech before the House of Representatives in 1826 he had pointed out that "when this country became free and independent, this species of population was found amongst us. It had been entailed upon us by our ancestors, and was viewed as a common evil." Although he accepted the premise that slaves were property, Polk admitted that "they were rational; they were human beings."[23]

The apology did not stand in the way of economic gain. In the early 1830s, Polk looked to the cultivation of land that he had previously acquired in Tennessee's Western District as a source of income to supplement his congressional salary. His first cotton plantation venture in Fayette County ended in failure, prompting him to sell the property in 1834. A second venture in northern Mississippi proved more profitable, but at a high cost to the slave labor. Despite Polk's professed determination to treat the slaves well, his concern for profit came first.

The slavery question soon became involved in issues affecting the nation's economic development, particularly in the North and South. Beginning in the late 1820s, Northern commercial interests clamored for increased tariffs to protect fledgling industries from foreign competition. Southern planters feared that high tariffs would affect the slave labor base that made cotton the economic mainstay of the region. The planters argued that U.S. protective tariffs would prompt the British to retaliate by imposing high duties on American cotton and by developing cotton plantations in their far-flung empire.

Such a scenario would not only bring a depression to the South but also create a massive unemployed labor force that would threaten the region's political and social structure. Moreover, Southern planters were increasingly uncomfortable with the rising tide of the antislavery crusade in the North. In response, they defended the "peculiar institution" on economic, political, social, and even moral grounds. Because of his states'-rights, antitariff philosophy, Polk instinctively sided with Calhoun in 1832 when the Nullification Crisis erupted, but he was conspicuously quiet during the debate, remaining confident that President Jackson would "trim the vessel of State so as to escape those dangerous passes, and safely navigate her to a secure haven."[24]

As a Southerner, Polk disliked the abolitionists, but there is no evidence that he took a deep interest in the slavery question, particularly with regard to the extension of slavery into the Western territories. He did believe, however, that the slave issue had to be addressed at the state level. When Northern antislavery petitions arrived on the House floor in 1835, Polk understood the Southerners' consternation at the attacks upon the "peculiar institution." Soon, extremists on both sides of the issue turned the session into a debate over the continued existence of slavery. In order to maintain some semblance of sanity, Polk steered the issue to committee discussion. Before the Twenty-fourth Congress ended its term, the House adopted a "gag rule" resolution that permitted the introduction of antislavery petitions but provided that they immediately be tabled. Polk agreed that the House had the right to refuse such petitions. The House readopted the gag rule at every session until John Quincy Adams managed to have it rescinded eight years later.

As governor of Tennessee in 1840, Polk would advise a British abolitionist society that dealing with the slave issue was the state's responsibility rather than that of a national or international organization. Still, Polk understood that the abolitionist debate was so intense and so divided the nation that "if persevered in, [it] will be attended with terrible consequences to the country, and cannot fail to destroy the Democratic party, if it does not ultimately threaten the Union itself."[25] The abolitionist crusade continued and eventually became enmeshed with Westward expansion.

In 1836, however, the inflammatory issues that contributed to the Democratic Party's factionalism, congressional gridlock, and Polk's fence-sitting were exacerbated when Jackson insisted that Van Buren be the party's presidential nominee. Van Buren never had been popular in the Southwestern frontier states, where he was depicted as a member of the East's effete establishment and a self-serving political operative. To many frontiersmen, their president had not only betrayed them but also raised fears that Van Buren's policies would serve the establishment.

Tennessee politics reflected the larger picture. Governor Hugh Lawson White shared Jackson's popularity in the state, but each man drew support from a different constituency. Jackson remained the idol of the state's small farmers, while White had the backing of the planters, businessmen, professionals, and land speculators. These groups opposed the administration's restrictive policy on internal improvements and insistence on the use of hard currency as impinging upon the state's development and their own economic well-being. Subsequently, these interests unsuccessfully sought White as the Democratic presidential nominee in 1836.

In opposition to the White faction stood Tennessee's older generation of political leaders: Polk, his former mentor Felix Grundy, and former governor and now senator William Carroll. Despite their long friendship with White and the support for his candidacy across Tennessee, these Democrats remained loyal to the party's choice, Martin Van Buren, at the expense of their position in Tennessee. The state had become a microcosm of the nation's differing sectional and economic interests. The controversy revealed that Polk's strength rested with the traditional state leadership and that he was becoming more distant from the new generation of political leaders surfacing in Tennessee. Indeed, when Polk returned to

Tennessee to work on behalf of Van Buren's candidacy, he and a handful of Jackson loyalists could do little more than watch state Democrats jump aboard the Whig bandwagon. The public voted overwhelmingly for White, who outdistanced Van Buren by some 12,000 votes. Nationwide, however, Van Buren defeated the three Whig candidates by a little more than 36,000 popular votes and by 57 votes in the electoral college. Van Buren moved into the White House as the first U.S. president born under the American flag.

After witnessing Van Buren's inauguration, Jackson returned to a tumultuous welcome in Tennessee in the spring of 1837. His protégé, James K. Polk, who accompanied him, appeared as the beneficiary, but the reception concealed the reality of Tennessee politics. The divisiveness that characterized the state's Democrats was exacerbated by the Panic of 1837 and registered in the congressional elections that same year. Running unopposed, Polk survived the purge of Democrats and retained his House seat. Otherwise, the Whigs captured ten of Tennessee's twelve congressional seats and the governor's mansion.

Back in Washington, Polk retained the Speakership by thirteen votes, and in that position served President Van Buren well, as their views on the Constitution and on limited and frugal government coincided. Polk worked tirelessly for Van Buren's legislative program, but the focal point of the administration was the ever-worsening depression. Although many of its causes were beyond the administration's control, Van Buren, as a Jackson disciple, came under vehement attack. Van Buren's solution was to establish a public depository, or "independent subtreasury," for government funds, with no connection to commercial banking. The Whigs delayed legislative approval until 1840, only to have the bill eventually killed by President John Tyler.

As Van Buren's legislative program floundered in Congress, Polk became a target for the opposition's criticism of all that was wrong with America. The invective was so bad that Prentiss wrote an amendment to the customary vote of thanks given to each departing Speaker, charging Polk with conducting partisan politics rather than providing impartial leadership. Fifty-six of Prentiss's colleagues supported the amendment.

Early in the Van Buren administration, Polk had understood his tenuous position in Congress. With the Democratic Party in decline at the national level, he could easily lose the Speakership as a result of the next congressional elections, and he therefore concluded that the best path for a successful political future lay in

Tennessee's Democratic Party. In 1839, Polk agreed to the state party's request that he be its gubernatorial candidate. In accepting the nomination, he reasoned that a governorship would demonstrate his political strength and make him a viable candidate for the Democratic vice presidential nomination in 1840. Polk resigned his congressional seat to seek Tennessee's highest elected office.

Based in Columbia and skillfully managed by Sarah, the 1839 gubernatorial campaign was Polk's first statewide race. In the four months preceding the election, Polk crossed the state in an appeal for votes. Following the initial public debates the confident Whig governor, Newton Cannon, withdrew from the campaign trail, allegedly pressed by state business in Nashville. Polk placed familiar national issues before the voters: the triumphs of Jacksonian Democracy, a history of the Federalist-Whig connections, the republicanism of Martin Van Buren, the iniquities of state and national banks. He devoted little time to Tennessee state affairs. Polk won the election by a narrow margin (2,462 votes), but his vigorous campaign inspired 20,000 more Democrats to vote in this election than in the 1837 gubernatorial contest and to contribute significantly to the party's regaining control of the state legislature and recapturing three congressional seats. Polk's victory impressed the Democratic Party's national leadership as they anticipated the 1840 presidential contest.

If the 1839 electoral victory helped to position Polk for the Democratic vice presidential nomination, the Tennessee governorship did not. His narrow victory did not ensure him the support of the state's various political interests. Furthermore, the state constitution prevented the governor from vetoing legislation and granted power over public policy to the legislature. As a result, Governor Polk's proposals for banking reform and internal improvements were ignored. Conversely, the limitation of political power did not diminish his popularity among the Tennessee Democrats who attached themselves to his resurgent national identity. Almost immediately after his inauguration as governor in October 1839, several state legislative resolutions advocated Polk's vice presidential candidacy for 1840. His gamble appeared to be well taken.

At the national level, the Polk candidacy in 1840 surfaced as a viable alternative to the incumbent vice president, Richard Johnson. Polk's impeccable character stood in sharp contrast to that of Johnson, who had fathered two children by a mulatto mistress and was noted for his heavy drinking. Politically, Polk could balance Van Buren's Northeast connection, and his 1839 statewide election victory gave promise of delivering Tennessee's electoral votes at the party's national convention.

There were several other contenders for Johnson's spot, however, and Polk became part of the maneuvering that prompted the Democratic leadership to delay the selection of a vice president until after the popular vote was cast in November. In the weeks preceding the Democratic convention in Baltimore, Johnson's stock rose among the party operatives, causing Polk to recognize his diminishing chances of gaining the nomination. Three weeks after the convention met in the first week of May 1840, Polk withdrew his candidacy with the explanation that he placed party interests above his personal ambitions. He made an astute decision: not only did Polk preserve his image of party loyalty, but he also distanced himself from the unpopular Van Buren, who was being blamed for the worst depression in the nation's history. Although Polk escaped the Democratic Party's embarrassment that came with losing to Harrison and the Whigs on the national level, the campaign in Tennessee seemed to be for Polk a dark omen for his political future. The Democrats failed to attract the crowds that the Whigs drew to their log cabins, parades, and festivals. Campaigning by such stalwarts as Polk and Jackson failed to dissuade the voters. In the end, Harrison carried Tennessee by some 12,000 votes.

The Whigs' national triumph in 1840 spilled over into the 1841 Tennessee gubernatorial contest in which Polk sought reelection. The Whigs nominated James Jones, a thirty-one-year-old homespun state legislator, to challenge Polk. The governor pursued the same themes as he did in his successful 1839 campaign, but the public would have no part of it. Two issues—banking and Clay's proposal to distribute moneys from the sale of public lands to the states— caught the voters' attention. Polk defended his position of wanting the state banks to resume specie payment and asserted that Clay's distribution proposal was really a device to raise tariffs and consolidate power in Washington. The rambling and extemporaneous Jones supported the Whig call for a national bank and Clay's proposal for the distribution of funds from federal land sales, but Jones refused to debate Polk on details, even on these two key issues. As the candidates canvassed the state, observers noted that the people were more responsive to Jones's entertaining and often comical presentations than to Polk's reasoned arguments. In October 1841, Tennessee voters handed Polk his first electoral defeat after twenty years in politics. Jones captured the governorship by a 3,000-vote margin.

Although discouraged by the loss, Polk did not abandon his political ambitions. He reasoned that the people of Tennessee, like those across the nation, had not lost sight of their Jeffersonian heritage. He confidently expected that they would recognize their error of 1841 and return to support the Democratic Party in 1843 and 1844. Events at the national level reenforced Polk's opinion. President Harrison died of pneumonia one month after taking the oath of office. His successor, Vice President John Tyler, soon became a man without a party, as he vetoed much of the Whigs' national agenda.

In 1843, Polk declared his candidacy for the Tennessee governorship. In the subsequent lengthy campaign during the spring and summer, he traversed the state. Sarah, again stationed in Columbia, acted as his unofficial campaign manager. As before, Polk relied on his debating skills and explanation of the issues, while Governor Jones relied upon his folksy humor. Polk hammered away at the shortcomings of a national bank and the 1842 Whig tariff that increased duties by 20 percent, but Jones would not budge from his flamboyant and unreasonable responses. Throughout the campaign, Polk's confidence soared as party leaders across the state continually reported that he had captured the minds of the voting public. The reports, however, were unrealistic. To many observers, the 1843 campaign was Tennessee's most quiet in recent memory: the voters talked little about either the candidates or the issues and may have grown tired of popular politics. Jones was reelected by 3,833 votes out of the 110,000 cast, a slightly larger margin than two years earlier. The Whigs also gained control of the state legislature, but the Democrats found some solace in winning six of the eleven congressional races.

Polk's immediate call for "a bold rally of our friends throughout the Union . . . to keep their armor on" and fight for the principles of the Democratic Party could not conceal his utter dejection.[26] For Polk, the 1843 gubernatorial defeat lowered his confidence in the people and the Democratic Party. Twice the Tennessee populace had rejected the rationale of his arguments, and the rewards that he expected from his loyalty to the Democratic Party were not delivered. While Polk placed responsibilities elsewhere, he failed to recognize his own shortcomings. His projection of rigidity and high principles did not fit with the forces of free expression ushered in by Jacksonian Democracy.

Contributing to Polk's defeat in Tennessee was the public's loss of interest in serious debate over such issues as centralized banking, the significance of higher tariffs, and the cost of internal improvements. The Tennessee of 1843 differed greatly from that of twenty years earlier when Polk had first entered the political arena. Now, with this second devastating defeat, Polk's political candle seemed to flicker out. He and many Democrats across the nation had anticipated his victory in Tennessee and, with it, the revival of the state party machinery and a restoration of his national prestige. Victory also would have made Polk the front-runner for the Democratic vice presidential nomination in 1844.

~

Polk proved to be more resilient than most observers expected. Despite the election reverses in 1841 and 1843, he retained his political ambitions and decided to act quickly. He understood that in Tennessee, as elsewhere around the nation, a new generation of politicians was anxiously waiting to seize control of the Democratic Party leadership. In anticipation of the 1844 national convention, Polk, like most Democrats at the time, expected Martin Van Buren to be the party's presidential nominee; and, with the need to give sectional balance to the ticket, someone from the South or Southwest would be selected as Van Buren's running mate. Polk, who had harbored vice presidential ambitions since 1839, declined an appointment as secretary of the navy in the Tyler administration because, as he explained to confidant Cave Johnson, it would adversely impact upon his chances of receiving the Democratic vice presidential nomination in 1844. In order to impress Van Buren, Polk urged "the whole party . . . [to] yield to his nomination and make it unanimous."[27]

At the national level avid supporters such as Cave Johnson kept Polk's name before the House of Representatives while the aging and ailing Andrew Jackson, writing in retirement from The Hermitage, reminded Democratic Party leaders that his protégé should be the 1844 vice presidential candidate. In Tennessee, Polk capitalized upon the statewide political base built during three gubernatorial campaigns. At the party's state convention in Nashville, his friends secured a slate of Polk delegates to go to the national convention in Baltimore and ensured passage of a resolution endorsing his vice presidential candidacy. Although the victory demonstrated Polk's control over the state party machine, his national image had not improved since his failed gubernatorial run in 1841.

Democratic Party stalwarts still favored former vice president Richard Johnson.

If Polk faced an uphill struggle in becoming the Democratic vice presidential nominee, Van Buren confronted an equally difficult task in securing the presidential nomination. Soundly beaten in 1840, Van Buren was still blamed by most Americans for the Panic of 1837 and the economic distress that followed. Nor did the Little Magician have the solid support of the South, where opposition to a protective tariff and the antislavery campaign ran deep. These two issues further divided the party—Democrats from the industrial states of Pennsylvania and New York favored the Whig protective tariff program, and several Democrats voted with the Whigs for the lifting of the gag rule on antislavery petitions in the House of Representatives. More than the tariff and antislavery issues, the Democratic Party divided over expansion, particularly the admission of Texas to the Union.

Since gaining their independence in 1836, the Texans had sought admission to the Union, but Presidents Jackson and Van Buren skirted the question, recognizing that it would ignite a battle over the extension of slavery within the United States and perhaps cause a war with Mexico. Polk shared Jackson's hope that Texas would initiate the process, but he was disappointed with Van Buren, who distanced himself from the Texas question. But in 1843, President John Tyler, cast out by the Whig Party, determined to bring Texas into the Union as a means of enhancing his own presidential bid in 1844. He entrusted the notable Southerner, John C. Calhoun, to negotiate an annexation treaty with Texas representatives. Tyler sent the treaty to the Senate in the spring of 1844 on the eve of the Whig and Democratic national conventions.

Before the conventions began in Baltimore, each of the expected candidates, Martin Van Buren and Henry Clay, denounced Tyler's treaty in letters, respectively, to the *Washington Globe* and the *National Intelligencer*.[28] Van Buren's letter caused the greater stir. In an effort to defuse the issue and to recognize Southern interests, Van Buren, who actually opposed annexation, held out hope for the admission of Texas at some future date. The abolitionist crusade continued and eventually became enmeshed with Westward expansion. Van Buren's vague statements did not satisfy the Southern Democrats, who did not favor the immediate admission of Texas to the Union. In retaliation, they disavowed any support for Van Buren. If Southerners could not accept Van Buren, Northerners could not accept Calhoun. His stance on the tariff and his defense of slavery made him anathema to most Northerners. Some party stalwarts viewed the quagmire as an opportunity to replace the old guard with new leadership.

As the Democratic maneuvering continued, the Whigs held their convention. In April they nominated Clay by acclamation and selected Theodore Frelinghuysen of New Jersey as his running mate. The party platform contained only four resolutions, including lofty eulogies for both candidates and the reaffirmation of traditional Whig principles regarding currency, the tariff, and the distribution of moneys from the sale of public lands:

> RESOLVED: That these principles may be summed as compris-
> ing: A well regulated currency; a tariff for revenues to defray the
> necessary expenses of the government and discriminating with
> special reference to the protection of the domestic labor of the
> country; the distribution of the proceeds from the sale of public
> lands; a single term for the presidency; a reform of the executive
> usurpations; and generally such an administration of the affairs
> of the country as shall impart to every branch of the public ser-
> vice the greatest practical efficiency, controlled by a well-
> regulated and wise economy.[29]

The only astonishing clause in the document pledged the party to the single-term presidency. On the assumption that the Democrats would do the same, the Whigs avoided any statement on territorial expansion. This love feast contrasted sharply with the upcoming tumultuous Democratic convention.

Neither Clay's nomination nor the emptiness of the Whig platform calmed the infighting among the Democrats. In the midst of these stirrings, Andrew Jackson advised Van Buren to step aside in favor of Polk, who, as a Southwesterner and pro-Texas annexationist, stood the best chance of uniting the party. Still, the evidence indicates that until two weeks before the convention opened, Polk publicly and privately remained committed to Van Buren's nomination, believing it the best route for him to gain the second spot on the ticket. Polk's attitude changed on May 13, 1844, when he called on Jackson at The Hermitage. During the meeting, which marked the beginning of Polk's quest for the nomination, Jackson explained to Polk that Van Buren's statement in the *National Intelligencer* on Texas expansion was unacceptable to Southerners and Southwesterners. For the Democrats to recapture the White House, Jackson asserted, the party needed to unite behind a pro-

Texas expansionist, and Polk "would be the most available man." Polk seized the opportunity and immediately instructed Cave Johnson and the chairman of the Tennessee delegation, Gideon Pillow, to actively work the convention floor for his nomination. If they would "undertake this [opportunity] with energy and prosecute it with vigor," then the nomination would be secured.[30]

Although the emergence of Polk as a serious contender for the presidential nomination enlivened the convention, his victory was hardly assured. Van Buren remained the party favorite as the 1844 convention opened on May 27. The anti-Van Buren factions could not focus upon another single candidate, and many Democratic leaders were beholden to him for certain considerations during his presidency. Ironically, the rules of nomination that Jackson used to strengthen Van Buren's candidacy for the vice presidency in 1832 proved to be the New Yorker's undoing in 1844. Twelve years earlier, the party had approved Jackson's proposal requiring support from two-thirds of the convention delegates to guarantee the nomination of the party's presidential and vice presidential candidates. The Democrats held fast to this rule thereafter. At the 1844 Baltimore convention, two-thirds required 177 of the 266 delegates. Fearing the potential impact of the two-thirds rule, the Van Buren forces hoped to persuade the convention to accept a simple majority stipulation. They failed largely because of the efforts of Mississippi delegate Robert Walker, who led a group of expansionists. Continued use of the two-thirds rule gave clear indication that Van Buren could not survive beyond the first ballot. He fell twenty-six votes short of the necessary two-thirds, and his hope for the party's nomination died.

Van Buren's defeat, however, did not ensure another man's victory. Walker and his followers favored Michigan's Senator Lewis Cass, but his call for the immediate admission of Texas as a slave state on the assumption that it would free Northern states from black migration doomed the senator's chances. After the first ballot, Cass received more votes than Van Buren but never enough to secure his nomination. By the seventh ballot a stalemate was obvious and a "new man" was needed, whereupon Pillow, George Bancroft, and Benjamin Butler worked to end the impasse. They suggested Polk and New York's Senator Silas Wright as the presidential nominees. Unbeknown to many delegates, however, Wright had already sent a letter to the convention refusing the presidential nomination should the Van Buren effort fail. Once that refusal became known on the convention floor, the delegates swung toward Polk.

Bancroft, the head of the Massachusetts delegation, put Polk's name before the convention and noted that he had certain advantages. Polk's stand in favor of Texas annexation made him acceptable to the expansionist wing of the party, and he remained on good terms with the New Yorkers because he played no part in sabotaging Van Buren's candidacy. And with Andrew Jackson's blessing, Polk satisfied the old-timers who saw him as a vehicle to restore the party's past grandeur. As Jackson had stated before the convention, Polk was "the most available man." On the ninth ballot, Polk generated enough votes to secure the nomination; finally, he became the unanimous choice. The party sought to mollify the Van Burenites by offering the vice presidential nomination to Wright, but he refused because he was convinced that the convention delegates had robbed Van Buren of the nomination. Walker, flexing his newfound political muscle, put forward Pennsylvania's Senator George M. Dallas. Although critics noted that Dallas was a distant relative of Walker's by marriage, he supported the annexation of Texas, and his connection to Pennsylvania's business community reduced the fear that Polk might pursue a further lowering of the protective tariff.

Almost as an afterthought the Democratic convention ended its labors by endorsing the platform that Walker had proposed to the Resolutions Committee the night before. For the most part the resolutions simply repeated the 1840 party platform by reciting the Democrats' historic commitment to "strict construction" of the Constitution and opposition to a national bank, an excessive tariff, a federal system of internal improvements, federal assumption of state debts, and federal interference in state affairs. One new resolution proved to have momentous consequences. The Democrats asserted "that our title to the whole of the territory of Oregon is clear and unquestionable; that no portion of the same ought to be ceded to England or any other power; and that the reoccupation of Oregon and the re-annexation of Texas, at the earliest practicable period are great American measures, which this convention recommends to the cordial support of the Democracy of the Union."[31] The strong statements on Texas and Oregon apparently were adopted almost accidentally, without any unusual demand. In fact, it is questionable whether the whole set of resolutions received any serious consideration from the Resolutions Committee, much less from the sparse rump session of delegates that finally approved it.

While the choice of Polk and Dallas, combined with the party platform, gave the appearance of sectional balance and Democratic unity, Polk clearly understood the party divisions when he accepted the presidential nomination with the promise to serve only one term. The America of 1844 was poised to go in new directions. The Jacksonian period was drawing to a close, and the issues that had united it no longer existed.

~

With the nominating conventions over, attention again focused upon Congress where, in an effort to defuse the Texas issue before the presidential campaign got under way, the Whigs and Van Buren forces joined together to defeat President Tyler's proposed Texas treaty in June 1844. Their joint action, however, failed to sway Tyler. He immediately announced that he would resubmit the Texas treaty to the next Congress in the form of a joint resolution, which required only a simple majority rather than the two-thirds majority needed for Senate ratification. Tyler also remained a presidential candidate until August 1844, when he realized that his only contribution to the campaign was to split the expansionist vote. He withdrew, leaving Clay and Polk to debate the expansionist issue.

The Whig platform had scrupulously avoided the Texas question, but, as the campaign developed, Clay became aware of its importance, particularly to his Southern brethren. In early July 1844 he softened his rigid stand. His newfound profession in favor of Texas annexation was qualified by the caveat that it be achieved without going to war with Mexico. Subsequently, throughout the campaign, Clay issued inconsistent statements on expansion. While he may have satisfied the Southern wing of the Whig Party, his inclination to support Texas annexation horrified many Northerners. The more that Clay equivocated on the issue, the more that it damaged his campaign. If Clay's position on Texas enhanced the party's strength in the South, it was offset by the negative reaction in the Northern states where some traditional Whig voters bolted to the Liberty Party.[32]

For his part, throughout the campaign, Polk remained at his home in Columbia, directing overall strategy and corresponding with state Democratic Party leaders throughout the country. During the campaign he faced two major obstacles—John Tyler, and the tariff. First, with Jackson's assistance, Polk persuaded Tyler to withdraw his candidacy in August. And second, regarding the tariff, Polk explained his position in a letter to Pennsylvania manufacturer John Kane on June 9, 1844. In that letter, which subsequently appeared in several newspapers, Polk declared his opposition to protectionism in principle while pledging to support a tariff sufficient only to meet the needs of the federal government.[33] Designed to quiet the fears of the business community, his initiative was not a bold policy statement but one designed to straddle the fence. Polk issued no other policy statements during the campaign.

The campaign also was free of the mudslinging that had characterized recent presidential contests. The worst Whig charge was that Polk's grandfather, Ezekiel Polk, had been a British loyalist during the American Revolution. Polk denied the allegation, and the issue had no apparent impact on the election. In the end, Polk carried fifteen states, winning majorities in all of them except New York and Michigan, where he secured pluralities. Clay carried eleven states. The narrowness of Polk's victory became obvious when the ballots were counted. Polk won by 38,180 popular votes, 1,337,243 to 1,299,063, which translated into a 51-to-49 percent margin. Liberty Party candidate James Birney captured 62,300 votes, less than 1 percent of the total cast.

In the North, Polk carried the states of New York, New Hampshire, and Pennsylvania, the latter by only 6,000 votes of the 330,000 cast. Much to their delight, the Whigs carried Tennessee, including the Jackson and Polk precincts. The minuscule 62,300 votes that Birney received do not obscure their importance. In New York, for example, Birney spoiled Clay's hopes for victory. There, Birney garnered nearly 16,000 votes, enough to ensure the Democrats victory because Polk only drew 5,000 more votes than Clay. New York's 36 electoral votes, the largest number of any state in the Union, were crucial to the national outcome, where Polk had won 170 electoral votes compared to Clay's 105. Had Clay carried New York, he, not Polk, would have become the eleventh president. Furthermore, Polk did not win either a majority or a plurality of the popular vote in South Carolina, where the legislature, not the people, chose the presidential electors.

Although many observers argued that the Texas question was the paramount issue of the campaign, the *Democratic Review* noted that the election was not about the Texas question but was rather a contest over the issues, such as the tariff and the national bank, that divided the two parties as never before. Equally important in the Northeast was the rising tide of Nativism that prompted Catholics and immigrant groups to vote against the Whigs and the elite class that they represented. In this scenario, Van Buren's candidacy was doomed to failure and the Democratic Party chieftains were wise in their selection of Polk. At the time, the Democrats were the majority party and represented, as noted earlier, "the common man"—laborers, farmers, foreign-born, and planters. Indeed, many observers, including the foreign press, interpreted Polk's victory as one of an "adventurous democracy" over the "respectable classes." Or, as one New York stockbroker put it, "Nothing can withstand the Democracy of this Country," as set in motion by Andrew Jackson.[34]

The editor of the *New York Express* argued that the diversity of America's social and economic groups was so great that Polk's victory could not be attributed to any single issue. In his editorial, "Who Elected James K. Polk ?" he assigned credit:

> "I," says the free trade man of South Carolina, "I did it; hurrah for free trade!" "No," says the Annexationist from Mississippi, Alabama and Louisiana, "It was I that did it; I went for the enlargement of the territory of slavery." "Not so fast," respond the Annexationists of the North, "It was we who did it—we who went for getting rid of slavery by taking Texas and thus enlarging the bounds of freedom." "No, no," declare the tariff men of Pennsylvania, "we did it, and did it by shouting for the tariff of 1842." . . . "Don't boast too much," say the Tyler men, "we did it; the post-office and custom house did it; we did it by giving you public offices and public money"; and these are not all who say they did it. The friends of Silas Wright and Mr. Van Buren in New York declare that it was their work. The Irish say they did it—the Germans that they did it; and the Abolitionists of the locofoco creed exult by proclaiming, "We did it."[35]

Whatever the analysis of the 1844 presidential election, clearly Polk did not receive a public mandate.

In contrast to the presidential election, the Congress that accompanied Polk to Washington in March 1845 provided the Democrats with a comfortable margin. In the House they held a 142-to-79 advantage over the Whigs, and in the Senate they held a 34-to-22 majority. But that, too, was deceptive. The same issues that divided the party—the tariff, national bank, internal improvements, abolition—were reflected by the fact that Democrats entirely represented only eight states in the House. Their control of the Senate was more complete, with thirteen states.

~

As a strong-willed person, Polk wanted to be his own president, but he understood the narrowness of his victory and the party factionalism that surrounded him. He had been the first dark-horse candidate and a virtual unknown throughout the country. The Van Burenites remained angry; sectional representatives did not trust this Jacksonian, and the newer and younger Democrats sought another champion. Correspondence from party members across the nation and consultations with Andrew Jackson reaffirmed Polk's tenuous position, and his pledge to serve only one term exacerbated the situation because it ignited the desires of many likely successors. Furthermore, the giants of his own party—Jackson, Van Buren, and Calhoun—were old, embittered, and recalcitrant. And the Whig leadership—Adams, Clay, and Webster—had greater followings than the president-elect. Despite the fact that he came to the office with no clear title, even in his own party, Polk insisted that he be its controlling force. Steeped in the Jacksonian tradition, Polk was determined to be the responsible agent of government. "In any event I intend to be *myself* President of the U.S.," he wrote to his friend Cave Johnson in December 1844.[36]

In selecting his cabinet, Polk realized the necessity of balancing the party's divergent interests with his own determination to assert his independence and personal responsibility for the conduct of every action in the executive branch. For the most prestigious post, secretary of state, Polk chose Pennsylvania's Senator James Buchanan. Considered a rising star in the party, the urbane and polished Buchanan promised to strengthen the president's hand in this key industrial state, but he also brought political baggage. Not only might Buchanan rival Vice President George Dallas for the president's attention, but he also coveted the presidency itself and did nothing more than promise to consult with Polk if he sought the party's 1848 nomination. Anxious to mend fences with the Van Buren faction, Polk offered cabinet posts to Silas Wright and Benjamin Butler, two key advisers to the former president. Embittered over the results of the 1844 Democratic convention, each man refused the appointment. When William Marcy accepted the offer to be secretary of war, Polk thought that he had bridged the gap, but the selection did not please Van Buren because the two men had parted ways over Marcy's pro-Texas annexationist stance. Under tremendous pressure to satisfy Southern interests, Polk selected the same Robert J. Walker who had exerted great influence at the 1844 party convention to be secretary of the treasury. Walker's selection only further infuriated the angry Van Burenites, but Polk was heavily indebted to the Mississippi senator.

The remaining three cabinet appointees proved to be less controversial: George Bancroft, who had placed Polk's name in nomination at the 1844 convention, became secretary of the navy; Cave Johnson, Polk's most trusted confidant, was appointed postmaster general; and John M. Mason, a Polk classmate at the University of North Carolina, became attorney general. The appointments did not resolve the Democratic Party's disharmony, but it is doubtful whether other selections would have accomplished that goal. The Van Burenites were deeply annoyed by the appointments of Marcy and Walker, and the simmering Buchanan-Dallas feud threatened to erupt into political confrontation. This group of Jacksonians did not gain the confidence of the new and younger Democrats.

Polk brought many Jacksonian traits to his administration. Like his mentor, Polk maintained that as the only federal officeholder elected by a national constituency, he was the people's true representative, and that as a vigorous chief executive he was the most effective safeguard against legislative abuse. He held department heads accountable and took time to inquire about administrative detail, often working closely with the staff members. Over time, Polk came to know the operations of each department. True to his past record, he demanded government frugality and insisted that the secretaries restrict patronage to a bare minimum. In the end, Polk made a significant contribution to the power and duty of the presidency, believing that the people would hold him responsible.

His management style reflected the rigidity of his past. As a stern taskmaster, Polk demanded that his six cabinet members serve in Washington on a full-time basis. He came to rely on their collective and individual wisdom, as virtually every major policy decision was made during the twice-weekly cabinet meetings. Polk would not offer his own opinion on a topic until every member had had a chance to speak. The cabinet often debated issues until a consensus was reached, but Polk would ignore the decision if he disagreed with it.

As president, Polk remained as much a loner as he had been before. He preferred the solitude of his own office, where he read government reports and wrote policy papers and directives to his subordinates. He appeared consumed by the affairs of state. He maintained a rigid schedule for visiting congressmen and for conducting cabinet meetings, interrupted only by a political crisis.

Although he enjoyed the powers and prestige of the office of the president, Polk viewed himself as a humble servant of the people, who, unlike the majority of Washington's politicos, was working on behalf of the nation's interests. Combining his personal traits with a generation of battles in the political arena made Polk a skillful politician in the eyes of his supporters and a devious schemer in the eyes of his detractors.

The presidency did not change Polk's long-held habits. His puritanical background did not permit him to enjoy frivolity, even including entertainment by White House performers. Uncomfortable with the ceremonial events required of the presidency, he relied on Sarah to deal with visiting politicians, foreign dignitaries, and the general public, and she earned high praise from Washington's elite for so doing. Polk appeared content to stroll and occasionally ride horseback on the White House grounds. He demonstrated little desire to learn about the world beyond his rural Tennessee by confining his leisure reading to the Scriptures.

~

Polk came to the White House convinced that he represented all of the people of the United States and that his role was a more important one than Congress's in the legislative process. Therefore, Polk concluded that he, not Congress, should shape the pattern of the legislative program. He felt obliged to introduce legislation that benefited the entire nation and to veto congressional actions that favored only singular or sectional interests. In his Inaugural Address, Polk promised to oppose "any policy which shall tend to favor monopolies or the peculiar interests of sections or classes [that] operate to the prejudice of their fellow citizens."[37] At the same time, Polk clearly understood that Congress possessed sufficient power to block the chief executive's proposals or override presidential vetoes, a risk he was willing to take.

As could be expected, congressmen on both sides of the aisle did not share Polk's view of authority over the legislative program. In the factionalized Twenty-ninth Congress, dissident Democrats and disgruntled Whigs argued that Polk lacked leadership skills and that he interfered too much in the affairs of Congress. Further, many congressmen charged that, given the narrowness of the popular vote, they had carried Polk to Washington, not the other way around. Polk could not expect to run roughshod over them.

The Senate, where committee chairmen wielded exceptional power, more than in the House, exhibited the most hostility to the president.

The conflict between Polk and Congress played out in his domestic program. As reflected in his Inaugural Address, Polk remained a "strict constructionist" and maintained that the federal government did not have the authority to intervene in the nation's economic affairs or in the practices of the individual states. Surely, he told his audience on March 4, 1845, "the Government of the United States is one of delegated and limited powers," and he intended to abstain from the "exercise of doubtful or unauthorized implied powers" that would result in a conflict with the states. By the same token, however, Polk cautioned the states that in the "maintenance of their rights they do not overstep the limits of powers reserved to them."[38] Within these parameters, Polk remained committed to the promises of Jacksonian Democracy—to the programs that promised to generate conflict with Congress.

The origins of these issues dated to the years immediately after the end of the War of 1812, when President James Madison called for a protective tariff to secure the infant U.S. industries, the establishment of the Second Bank of the United States, and the construction of a federally subsidized network of roads and canals to speed economic development and enhance national security. Subsequently described by Henry Clay as the American System, these ideas were consistently opposed by Polk on the grounds that they served the interests of particular groups or geographic sections of the country and that they were an unnecessary and unconstitutional intrusion of the federal government into the states' internal affairs. By 1832 a compromise, engineered by Clay and supported by John C. Calhoun, provided for a reduction in tariffs over a ten-year period. There matters stood until Congress approved new tariff legislation in 1842. Although the rates differed little from those established a decade earlier, the tariff touched off another public debate that awaited Polk in 1845.

Polk's congressional record established him as an opponent of protective tariffs. Like other Jeffersonians and Jacksonians before him, we know that Polk supported tariffs sufficient only to fund government obligations, as he explained in his Inaugural Address in March 1845 and in his first Annual Message to Congress in December 1845. Moreover, the federal government had no "right to tax one section of the country, or one class of citizens, or one occupation, for the mere profit of another," and to protect manufacturers and industrialists at the expense of the working and agrarian classes was unjust.[39] He urged the repeal of the 1842 tariff as well as a downward revision of rates, and invited Congress to initiate the appropriate legislation. In sum, the president embraced only a nonprotective tariff that yielded revenues sufficient for government operations.

In response to the president's proposals, Treasury Secretary Walker initiated an exhaustive study of the tariff system and its impact upon the national economy. Finally, in February 1846 the House Ways and Means Committee developed a tariff package that Walker helped to craft and two months later submitted it to the full House for consideration. As originally designed, the proposed legislation established a sliding scale of tariffs with the highest placed on luxury goods and the lowest on various consumer items. For nearly three months the House debated the issue, with low tariff advocates bringing British wares to the floor that would be available to the American consumer with lower tariffs. Not to be outdone, the protectionists sponsored a fair of American manufactures that needed to be made secure from foreign competition. Polk, as he noted in his diary, was unimpressed with the fair, viewing it as overt pressure by the American capitalists who "swarmed this city for weeks . . . [and] spared no effort within their power to sway and control Congress."[40] Democratic opposition to the proposed Walker Tariff came from Pennsylvania and New York, where industrialists feared the uncontested British presence in the marketplace, and from disgruntled Midwesterners annoyed by Polk's compromise on the Oregon question (discussed in chapter 3). Others awaited Britain's repeal of its protective Corn Laws, which came in June 1846 and opened the British market to American grains.

Finally, on July 3, 1846, the House of Representatives approved the Walker Tariff with its many protectionist features. The vote followed party lines: 85 percent of the Democrats supported the bill, while 98 percent of the Whigs opposed it. The same party and sectional divisions characterized the Senate debate and caused Polk to meet with hesitant senators or dispatch cabinet members to Capitol Hill to do the same. Polk persuaded Illinois's Democratic senator James Semple to stay in Washington and vote for the Walker Tariff, and the president and others worked diligently to keep Tennessee Whig Spencer Jarnagin in the fold. The administration's pressure upon North Carolinian William Haywood, a longtime

Democrat and Polk supporter, was so intense that he resigned rather than vote on the measure.

When the Senate finally approved the Walker Tariff by one vote on July 29, the count also was along party lines: 80 percent of the Democrats approved the measure, while 96 percent of the Whigs voted against it. In the end, the Walker Tariff did not abandon American manufacturers to foreign competition because the tariff reductions were not sufficient to open the floodgates to European-made goods. Ironically, on the European continent, railroad construction opened up additional markets for American manufactures and agricultural products. Increased demand and the potato famine in Ireland enabled the American farmer to fare well in the international market during the Polk administration. Although the Walker Tariff did not reflect all that the president wanted, he appreciated the victory, albeit it was one that further revealed the sectional factions plaguing the nation.

In comparison to the tariff debate, the one over a national bank was muted. At the beginning of his administration, Polk asserted that the country did not need "national banks or other extraneous institutions planted around Government" because the nation's history revealed "how unnecessary they are . . . [and] how impotent for good and how powerful for mischief" they could be.[41]

The role of the federal government in banking dated to the Federalist era, when the first Bank of the United States was established in 1791 and rechartered in 1816. While it provided for sound fiscal policy and contributed to stability in international commerce, critics saw the bank as benefiting only the commercial class at the expense of the workers and farmers. Despite its success, President Jackson destroyed the Bank, as noted earlier, by ordering the withdrawal of government funds and their placement in state banks, or "pet banks," across the country. In response to the depression that began in 1837, President Martin Van Buren successfully pushed legislation through Congress in late 1840 that provided for the withdrawal of federal funds from the "pet banks" and their deposit in the Treasury. Ironically, in 1841 the Whig-controlled Congress rescinded the legislation, effectively leaving the federal funds in Jackson's "pet banks." Subsequently, President Tyler vetoed two bills providing for a new national bank.

Polk, who helped to engineer Jackson's breaking of the Second Bank of the United States in 1836 and subsequently supported Van Buren's call for an independent Treasury, came to the presidency determined to completely separate the government from the nation's private banking system. In his 1845 Annual Message to Congress, Polk argued that the Constitution limited the deposit of federal moneys solely into the Treasury, not into some other institution such as a national or state bank, because the federal funds would be used for private purposes. He went on to attack both the former Bank of the United States and the various state "pet banks" that profited from the use of government funds for doing just that. Instead, Polk called for the "establishment of a constitutional treasury . . . with all Executive discretion or control over it . . . removed, except such as may be necessary in directing its disbursement in pursuance of appropriations made by law."[42] In effect, Polk repeated Van Buren's proposal for an independent Treasury. Polk envisioned the construction of fireproof vaults into which federal moneys would be deposited until they were needed for payment of bills.

The administration's proposed legislation for an independent Treasury worked its way slowly through Congress without, surprisingly, much fanfare. When it appeared on the House floor in late March the debate, as did the subsequent vote, followed party lines, but the Whig opposition was not intense. On April 2, 1846, the Independent Treasury Bill was approved by the House, 122 to 66, with no Whigs voting for it and no Democrats voting against it. In the Senate, Finance Committee chairman Dixon H. Lewis (D., Ala.) appeared in no hurry to discuss the proposed legislation or bring it to the Senate floor for action. Despite pressure from the administration he did not report it out of committee until June 8, but nearly another two months passed before the full Senate voted upon it. The debates about the independent Treasury were subdued compared to those during the Van Buren administration, and Polk himself did not seem very excited about the measure. The war with Mexico (discussed in chapter 5) preoccupied both the legislators and the president. Finally, on July 31, two days after approving the Walker Tariff, by a 28-to-25 vote the Senate approved the Independent Treasury Bill. As in the House, the vote was strictly along party lines.

Polk's strict constructionist views conflicted with the political atmosphere of the 1840s regarding federal financing of roads, canals, and other means of internal transportation. He also argued that the congressional use of surpluses produced by the tariff was a plunder of the Treasury to serve special interest groups. For these reasons he had supported Jackson's infamous Maysville veto in 1830 and further argued that such projects were the rightful responsibility of the individual states. Westward expansion in the 1840s took farmers farther from the East's urban markets and exits to the sea, prompting their call for improvements in the interstate transportation system. Even Southerners came to support internal improvements in the 1840s, despite their perennial call for a smaller federal government. Representatives of these two sectors convened at Memphis in 1845 to discuss a Mississippi River development project. Thus, it was Congress, not the president, that pushed for internal improvements from 1844 to 1848.

The executive and legislative branches clashed over internal improvements in the summer of 1846 after Congress approved a $1.4-million "harbors and rivers" bill that appealed to several Western and Southern states. Western Democrats in both houses of Congress parted with the president and joined with the Whigs to support the measure in July. Polk quickly vetoed the legislation, repeating the traditional Jacksonian argument that the federal government did not have authority to fund state infrastructure. He pointed out that twenty of the proposed projects included harbors and rivers that no foreign vessel had ever visited, or from which U.S. goods found their way into the international marketplace. To support such projects with expenditures "of the public money . . . benefiting but a few at the expense of the common Treasury" was unconstitutional, according to Polk. He added that implementation of the measure would set an unhealthy precedent for the government to fund all such future projects. [43]

Although Congress failed to override the president's veto before adjourning in August, it was not deterred from trying again. Just prior to its adjournment in March 1847, Congress, again along party lines, approved a $500,000 rivers and harbors bill to which the president promptly applied the "pocket veto." Polk used the time to prepare a lengthy, well-researched, and reasoned message that he finally presented to Congress on December 15. He firmly reiterated his previous position.[44] Congress again threatened to approve an internal improvements bill, but Polk's advance warning that he would again veto it deterred further legislative efforts for the remainder of his administration. Polk would leave office claiming the intertwined acceptance of his strict constructionist interpretation of the Constitution and his legislative program. The 1842 tariff had been revised, an independent Treasury established, and lavish expenditures on internal improvements rejected.

~

James K. Polk came to the presidency with the principled scruples that had guided him since childhood and made him a very private person. Yet, as a veteran of the political wars that reflected the changing U.S. landscape of his time, Polk continued to express confidence in the will of the American people. Together—that is, his rigidity and his confidence in the people—contributed to his belief that only a strong executive could serve the nation. This belief was reenforced by his congressional experiences during the Jackson administration, and his confidence in the people reflected the ideals of Jeffersonian Democracy.

"The largest portion of our people are agriculturists. Others are employed in manufactures, commerce, navigation and the mechanic arts . . . and their joint labors constitute the national or home industry," Polk noted when taking office in 1845,[45] and as the people's representative he needed to protect them from the nation's special interest groups. Polk's "strict constructionism" became the vehicle for so doing. The national government need not interfere in the people's affairs, Polk argued, because the most effective government was at the state and local levels. Thus, in the domestic arena, Polk's policies on banking, the tariff, and internal improvements served the masses, not special interest groups.

While Polk's record clearly established his position on domestic policy, the same record paints a picture of his foreign policy, although it is less vivid. In part, this can be attributed to the primacy of domestic affairs during the generation that preceded the Polk presidency. Still, like many of his generation, Polk distrusted the British at every turn, anticipating that their every move had sinister intentions. And like most people of his time, Polk argued that the United States should avoid foreign entanglements because they promised only to drain the country of its prosperity and to limit its freedom of action—but he was not averse to pursuing markets for American goods and products.

As to territorial expansion, Polk favored the protection of Americans in the distant territories, particularly the rights of the small farmers. Polk also came to the presidency favoring the incorporation of Texas into the Union, but he thought that entry should be initiated by the Texans; otherwise, the United States might risk the wrath of national sectionalism as well as a war with Mexico. Thus, in his Inaugural Address on March 4, 1845, Polk easily claimed that Oregon and Texas belonged to the United States.[46] He made no mention of California. That topic would come later.

Notes

1. James D. Richardson, comp., *A Compilation of the Messages and Papers of the Presidents*, 20 vols. (New York: Bureau of National Literature, 1917), 5:2227.

2. Quoted in Thomas G. Paterson, ed., *Major Problems in American Foreign Policy: Documents and Essays*, 2 vols. (Lexington: D. C. Heath and Company, 1978), 1:185.

3. The U.S. perception of Latin America's backwardness during this time is described in T. Ray Shurbutt, ed., *United States-Latin American Relations, 1800–1850* (Tuscaloosa: University of Alabama Press, 1991).

4. Quoted in Charles G. Sellers, *James K. Polk: Jacksonian, 1795–1843* (Princeton: Princeton University Press, 1957), 83.

5. Ibid., 86.

6. Ibid., 97.

7. Herbert A. Weaver, ed., *Correspondence of James K. Polk*, 6 vols. (Nashville: Vanderbilt University Press, 1969), 1:39.

8. Thomas H. Benton, ed., *Abridgment of the Debates of Congress from 1789 to 1856*, 16 vols. (New York: D. Appleton and Company, 1857–1861), 9:11–14

9. Richardson, *Messages and Papers*, 2:863–65.

10. Quoted in Sellers, *James K. Polk: Jacksonian*, 119.

11. *Correspondence of James K. Polk*, 1:64.

12. Ibid., 42.

13. Ibid., 101.

14. Ibid., 200.

15. Richardson, *Messages and Papers*, 3:1044–56.

16. Quoted in Sellers, *James K. Polk: Jacksonian*, 154.

17. Ibid., 156

18. Calhoun explains his view of states' rights in Ross M. Lence, ed., *Union and Liberty: The Political Philosophy of John C. Calhoun* (Indianapolis: Liberty Fund, Inc., 1992), 369–402.

19. *Register of Debates in Congress*, 14 vols. (Washington, DC: Gales and Seaton, 1824–1837), 7:92.

20. Richardson, *Messages and Papers*, 3:1139–54.

21. Eugene I. McCormac, *James K. Polk: A Political Biography* (New York: Russell and Russell, 1965), 33.

22. *Register of Debates*, 10:32.

23. Benton, *Abridgment of Debates*, 9:16–17.

24. Quoted in Sellers, *James K. Polk: Jacksonian*, 146.

25. Quoted in McCormac, *Political Biography*, 619.

26. Quoted in Sellers, *James K. Polk: Jacksonian*, 448.

27. "Documents—Letters of James K. Polk to Cave Johnson, 1833–1848," *Tennessee Historical Magazine* (March 1915), 1:234–36, hereafter referred to as "Polk-Johnson Letters."

28. Justin H. Smith, *The Annexation of Texas* (New York: AMS Press, 1971), 240–44.

29. Arthur M. Schlesinger, Jr., ed., *History of American Presidential Elections, 1789–1968* (New York: Chelsea House, 1971), 1:811.

30. "Polk-Johnson Letters," 239–41.

31. Schlesinger, *Presidential Elections*, 1:800–801.

32. The Liberty Party, founded in 1840, again nominated James L. Birney for the presidency. The party's only platform plank was its opposition to the extension of slavery; otherwise, Birney, a former Democrat, favored Democratic views on the issues. The Democrats even nominated him for the Senate in his home state of Michigan. Subsequently, he professed to prefer Polk over Clay.

33. McCormac, *Political Biography*, 261

34. Charles G. Sellers, *James K. Polk: Continentalist, 1843–1846* (Princeton: Princeton University Press, 1966), 158.

35. Ibid., 159–60.

36. "Polk-Johnson Letters," 251.

37. Richardson, *Messages and Papers*, 5:2227.

38. Ibid., 2224.

39. Ibid., 2228–29, 2254–55.

40. Milo Milton Quaife, ed., *The Diary of James K. Polk, During His Presidency, 1845 to 1849*, 4 vols. (Chicago: A. C. McClurg and Company, 1910), 2:55.

41. Richardson, *Messages and Papers*, 5:2227.

42. Ibid., 2257–58.

43. Ibid., 6:2311–14.

44. Ibid., 2460–76.

45. Ibid., 5:2229.

46. Ibid., 2229–31.

2

The Path to Texas Annexation

> The Republic of Texas has made known her desire
> to come into our Union, to form a part of our Con-
> federacy and enjoy with us the blessings of liberty
> secured and guaranteed by our Constitution. . . . I
> regard the question of annexation as belonging ex-
> clusively to the United States and Texas. . . . Foreign
> powers should therefore look on the annexation of
> Texas to the United States not as the conquest of a
> nation seeking to extend her dominions by arms and
> violence, but as the peaceful acquisition of a terri-
> tory once her own, by adding another member to
> our confederation, with the consent of that mem-
> ber, thereby diminishing the chances of war and
> opening to them new and ever-increasing markets
> for their products.
> —James K. Polk, Inaugural Address, 1845[1]

In the seventy years preceding the presidency of
James K. Polk, three themes emerged as guiding
principles in U.S. foreign policy, and each is represented
in his Inaugural Address. The first was to secure the nation from European intrigues, either by noninvolvement
in continental affairs or by keeping Europe from
America's shores and its periphery. These concepts were
expressed by three presidents: in George Washington's
call for the avoidance of "entangling alliances," in Thomas Jefferson's recommendation to shun "permanent alliances," and in James Monroe's proclamation that the
Western Hemisphere was off limits to European colonization.[2] John Quincy Adams was more direct when he
noted that the fundamental objective of the nation's foreign policy was to protect the independence and security
of the United States and those New World territories on

its immediate periphery.[3] And when Andrew Jackson entered the White House in 1829, he had not forgotten that the British were his nemesis at New Orleans and in Florida nearly a generation earlier. In the eyes of most Americans, Great Britain was the most sinister of the continental powers.

The second characteristic of U.S. foreign policy since independence revolved around the broad concept of economics. American merchants anticipated that the world's ports were theirs to exploit. Thus, despite the travails of Europe, they wanted the freedom to trade with belligerent nations and their outposts in the Caribbean during the French Revolution and the Napoleonic Wars. When the right to do so was not respected, President James Madison determined that it was cause for war against Great Britain in 1812.[4] These same merchants clandestinely traded with Spain's Caribbean colonies beginning in the late 1780s, and as the Latin Americans struggled for their independence in the second decade of the nineteenth century, U.S. agents traversed the Southern Hemisphere to report on the economic opportunities that awaited the United States. Kentucky's Congressman Henry Clay anticipated bountiful markets throughout South America. American merchants were overjoyed in 1830 when President Jackson renegotiated the opening of the British West Indies to U.S. ships. But expansive trade with Latin America did not develop in the nineteenth century largely because the British reaped the benefits from the aid they had given to the rebellious Spanish colonials.

Territorial expansion satisfied both the security and economic needs of the new nation. Jefferson's Louisiana Purchase in 1803, for example, not only secured the U.S. frontier from potential European threats and guaranteed the free use of the port of New Orleans, but it also served as a safety valve for the needs of American farmers. In the North, "War Hawk" congressmen from the western districts of New York and Pennsylvania and states newly admitted to the Union, such as Ohio, sought the acquisition of Canada in the War of 1812 to secure the frontier from the British-supported Indian menace as well as to meet the land needs of the expanding agricultural sector. As cotton became a primary U.S. export by the 1820s, the hunger for additional land suitable for the plantation economy whetted the appetite for further territorial expansion.

Two years after coming to America from England in 1774, Tom Paine penned a pamphlet entitled *Common Sense*. The sun was about to set upon monarchical Europe and rise upon republican America, he wrote; the latter would serve as the model for the rest of the world to emulate. In making this observation, Paine set the tone for the third pillar of U.S. foreign policy. In 1789 the turbulence of French politics prompted him to note that not only were the Americans prosperous in comparison to the people of monarchical Europe, but "the principle of [their] government, which is that of the equal Rights of Man, is making rapid progress in the world."[5] Subsequently, the American mood reflected the path of the French Revolution from its initial demand for democracy to the dictatorship of Napoleon Bonaparte. The euphoria turned to disappointment.

The same can be said for Latin America. As the Latin Americans achieved their independence and their leaders authored constitutions based on that of the United States, President Monroe was happy in 1823 to point to the differences between monarchical Europe and the democratic Western Hemisphere. Henry Clay went further, envisioning the unity of the hemispheric nations as "a sort of counterpoise to the Holy Alliance . . . to operate by the force of example and moral influence."[6] The North Americans soon became disillusioned as oligarchical and conservative governments quickly appeared in the capitals south of the Rio Grande.[7] To others, the American democratic model was to extend beyond the hemisphere. Secretary of State John Quincy Adams, for example, stated that the United States had become "a beacon on the summit of the mountain, to which all the inhabitants of the Earth may turn their eyes for a genial and saving light."[8] Sixteen years later, in March 1837, Adams's political adversary, Andrew Jackson, uttered similar words in his Farewell Address: Providence had chosen the Americans "as the guardians of freedom to preserve it for the benefit of the human race."[9]

James K. Polk's life spanned the early nineteenth century as these principles of U.S. foreign policy took root. He shared his contemporaries' distrust of the British, and his congressional record clearly established him as a defender of the frontiersmen's economic interests. Polk's advocacy of a small central government and his description of the nation as one dominated by small farmers, entrepreneurs, and artisans reflected the democratic and republican spirit of the day.

The country's democratization, its more egalitarian society, and its economic growth and technological advances gave rise to a confidence in the 1830s and 1840s that had not been previously measured on a national scale. The self-confidence came at a time when Americans were in the mood for continental expansion. Unlike previous expansionists who envisioned a series of separate republics

across the continent, the current group anticipated the incorporation of these territories into the United States. The Europeans, journalist John O'Sullivan wrote in the summer of 1845, acted "in the
spirit of hostile interference against us, for the avowed object of
thwarting our policy and hampering our power, limiting our greatness and checking the fulfillment of our manifest destiny to overspread the continent allotted by Providence for the free
development of our yearly multiplying millions."[10]

Manifest Destiny became the rallying cry of expansionists, as
it reflected the nation's political and economic democracy at that
time. For some expansionists, Manifest Destiny meant the inclusion of Mexico, Central America, and possibly Cuba, but in practice it meant the incorporation into the Union of the like-minded
Texans and Americans residing in Oregon and California. Elsewhere
in the article, O'Sullivan identified the British and the French as
the foreign threats to U.S. security in the West. That pragmatic concern along sectional and economic interests proved to be more important in the fulfillment of the nation's Manifest Destiny than the
idealistic vision that the term represented.

Polk's Inaugural Address in March 1845 reflected the character
of a strong-willed person and his determination to embark on an
expansionist policy. The path to Texas annexation was an arduous
one that transcended the period of Polk's political career. His Inaugural Address identified many of the obstacles cast in its way and
also addressed the pillars that best described the tenets of U.S. foreign policy. Polk spoke highly of Texans whose political institutions and cultural fabric were American and asserted that, as an
independent nation, Texas's pursuit of annexation was not the business of Mexico, Britain, or France, each of whom tried to thwart it.
What Polk did not say was equally important. He made no reference to the sectional crisis that divided his nation and hindered the
incorporation of Texas into the Union.

~

When the United States purchased Louisiana from France in
1803, the western boundary of the newly acquired territory was
not clearly defined. At the time, the governments in Madrid and
Washington laid claim to much of what is contemporary Texas, including the communities of San Antonio, Goliad, and Nagadoches.
In 1819 the border dispute was apparently settled with the Trans-
Continental Treaty (or the Adams-Onís Treaty), which set the Sabine

River as the western boundary of the Louisiana Territory. However, more attention was given to the treaty stipulations that provided for the U.S. acquisition of Florida and the Spanish claims to Oregon.[11]

Clarifying the Texas boundary meant little to American merchants who conducted a lucrative trade with San Antonio beginning in 1804 and to the few Americans who intrigued for Texas during the Mexican war for independence from Spain after 1810, largely in hopes of obtaining land grants and political offices. Following Mexican independence, U.S. settlers continued to stream into Mexico, whose restrictive policies did not deter them. For example, the Mexican government gave American entrepreneur Moses Austin a generous land grant near present-day San Antonio. Encouraged by his son Stephen F. Austin, some 300 American families settled between the Brazos and Colorado rivers by 1824, a number that swelled to 15,000 six years later. By 1836 an estimated 30,000 Anglo-Americans (as the Mexicans referred to the U.S. immigrants) as well as 5,000 slaves had migrated into the Texas territory across an open frontier, free of Mexican inspection or regulation. Texas also became a refuge for restless and violent men from the towns along the Mississippi River and Gulf Coast. According to Moses Austin's contract, these new arrivals had to swear allegiance and pay taxes to the Mexican government, convert to Roman Catholicism, and pay ten cents per acre for their land on easy credit terms. But the Americans showed little interest in adopting any part of the Mexican culture, particularly renouncing allegiance to the United States and converting to Roman Catholicism, and viewed the nonwhite Mexicans as inferior. They also resented the presence of Mexican government officials and military personnel stationed throughout Texas.

Events further west proved to be of equal significance. As early as 1812, New England merchants envisioned profitable trading links with the Mexican states of Chihuahua and Zacatecas through Santa Fe in the present-day state of New Mexico. By 1821 a permanent trading route was established between St. Louis, Missouri, and Santa Fe, where American merchants received a warm welcome from both the local officials and the general populace. By 1828 an estimated $150,000 worth of merchandise arrived in Santa Fe to supply the consumer-starved citizens and provide the local government with badly needed tax revenues. In addition, several hundred Americans settled in Santa Fe and Taos, and a few moved on to California. While Mexican officials in New Mexico looked

Santa Fe, New Mexico, about 1846

favorably upon these developments, authorities in Mexico City fretted that such contacts might eventually weaken their hold over all of the Northern provinces.

The Americans were not the only ones to arrive in Mexico during the 1820s. Independent Mexico had inherited a bankrupt treasury and broken economy from the departing Spaniards; and, in rejecting every vestige of Spanish colonialism, the new Mexican government was unable to impose its tax and tariff laws. British bankers willingly filled the void, and by 1827 the Mexican government was $27 million in debt to them. British mining companies also went to Mexico in anticipation of quick profits from the gold and silver mines. As these investors overextended themselves and the mining ventures proved unprofitable, the British government increased its concern with Mexican affairs.

Throughout the 1820s, life and property in Mexico were insecure. In urban and rural areas alike any political disturbance brought death and destruction to foreigners and their property. Along federal highways, government troops could not control marauding bandits. And at all government levels, officials imposed "forced loans" upon foreigners. By the decade's end the American and British citizens residing in Mexico had numerous grievances against the Mexican government and begged their home governments to settle their claims.

At the time when Polk's congressional career commenced, the U.S. government began its quest to acquire the Texas territory. In 1825, four years after Mexico won its independence from Spain, President John Quincy Adams authorized the first U.S. minister to

Mexico City, Joel Poinsett, to offer $1 million for the territory and to point out to the Mexican authorities that such a cession would place their capital more nearly in the center of the country![12] In response, the Mexicans suggested that the Americans withdraw all their claims and that U.S. citizens relocate to the east bank of the Mississippi River. From the start, the American and Mexican claims for the Texas territory were far apart.

By the time that Andrew Jackson took the presidential oath in March 1829, two competing nationalisms had emerged in the United States and Mexico. The Jacksonian period ushered in several years of self-confidence in the American way of life and a marked disregard for anything not American. At the same time, the Mexicans had become increasingly defensive about the foreign intrusions, particularly American, into their Northern territories and feared that the consequences of bankruptcy would bring foreign intervention into their country.

~

Jackson came to the presidency with a long-standing belief that Texas belonged to the United States and that the sale of the territory to the United States was required. He maintained that Texas had been part of the Louisiana Purchase in 1803 and that John Quincy Adams had erroneously relinquished the U.S. claim in the 1819 Trans-Continental Treaty. The new president reasoned that because Mexico could not govern its distant territory, it should relinquish Texas to the United States in order to avoid war. Polk shared Jackson's opinions regarding Texas.

Thinking that he could persuade the Mexicans to surrender Texas, Jackson dispatched Anthony Butler to Mexico City in 1829 with instructions to seek the "retrocession of Texas." Butler proved to be the wrong man for the assignment. His arrogance and the Mexican perception that he represented the proslavery forces in east Texas doomed his mission from the start. Undaunted, Butler persisted and even suggested to President Jackson that he consider bribing the appropriate Mexican officials. Butler's maneuverings resulted in new instructions in 1835 that included a virtual blank check to complete a new transcontinental treaty to encompass not only Texas but also land west to the Pacific Ocean that included San Francisco Bay.[13] The latter proffer so infuriated the Mexicans that they demanded Butler's recall. Just as Adams before him, Jackson failed to comprehend that Mexican nationalism prohibited the sale of Texas or any other territory, just as American nationalism would prevent the sale of any U.S. territory to a foreign government.

The increasingly strained relations between Mexico City and Washington became entwined in Mexican politics. Mexico's independence from Spain in 1821 caused an internal debate over the structure of the republic's government. Centralists advocated a continuance of the Spanish practice whereby authority rested with the national government at Mexico City. In contrast, the federalists sought to place the greatest amount of political power in the republic's twenty-nine states, and those states most distant from Mexico City sought the greatest degree of autonomy. The controversy reached a high-water mark in December 1834 when revolutionist general Antonio López de Santa Anna seized power, dismissed the congress, and established a centralized dictatorship that resulted in the replacement of elected state officials with his own appointees. Such a move threatened the free-spirited Texans.

As Polk's congressional career blossomed in the early 1830s, Americans continued to pour into Texas. Some brought their slaves with them despite Mexican laws in 1829 and 1830 that outlawed slavery and banned further immigration. Like their predecessors, the new arrivals refused to abide by Mexican laws or to pay local taxes. Moreover, the majority were Protestants who refused to convert to Catholicism. Initially, most Texans believed that greater local autonomy would solve their problems and therefore supported the Mexican federalists. Because Santa Anna refused all proposals for decentralization, Texan sentiment for separation from Mexico increased. By 1834 this faction found a powerful spokesman in Sam Houston, the former governor of Tennessee and a close friend of President Jackson. To stem the tide of immigration and Texan sentiment for separation, Santa Anna appealed to the U.S. government to control the exodus and to enforce its neutrality laws. His pleas fell on deaf ears. Secretary of State Martin Van Buren asserted that U.S. citizens were free to go wherever they chose, that securing the boundary was a Mexican problem, and that American neutrality laws did not prevent its citizens from serving in a foreign army.[14]

Tensions reached new heights in 1835 when representatives of several Texas communities met in San Antonio and committed themselves to resist Mexico's centralist authority. By the end of the year, fighting broke out between the Texans and Santa Anna's forces near San Antonio. Santa Anna understood his need to crush the Texan revolt; otherwise, his indecision would encourage the Mexican federalists elsewhere.

On March 6, 1836, at San Antonio, Santa Anna's forces over-whelmed the Texans at the Alamo, and two weeks later he ordered the brutal execution of three hundred troops entrapped at Goliad. By the end of March, with only the remnants of his ragtag army, Houston plotted a strategic retreat that resulted in the overexten-sion of Santa Anna's supply lines. Finally, at San Jacinto on April 21, Houston's troops routed the Mexicans and captured Santa Anna. Under duress, the beleaguered revolutionist signed two contradic-tory peace treaties on May 14 that provided for an end to the fight-ing, the return of his troops to Mexico, and preparations for a peace commission. The treaties also stipulated that the Texas boundary was not to extend beyond the Rio Grande. When Santa Anna was finally freed and repatriated, he denounced the treaties as illegal and free of any obligations for Mexico.

Mexican newspapers and government officials blamed the United States, and particularly the Jackson administration, for in-triguing on behalf of Texan independence and for encouraging the revolt. In October the Mexican minister to Washington, Manuel de Gorostiza, left for home, infuriated by the pro-Texas sentiments expressed across the United States and the supposed unauthorized entry that preceding May into east Texas by General Edmund S. Gaines, who would ostensibly protect Americans fleeing from Santa Anna's advancing army. Given the magnitude of contrary evidence, Jackson's professions of U.S. neutrality did not alter Mexican opin-ion. The Texas independence movement encouraged anti-Americanism in Mexico that lasted far into the future.

The Texans wasted little effort in their quest for annexation to the United States. Immediately after the declaration of indepen-dence on March 19, 1836, two commissioners were dispatched to Washington, and in early April a third was appointed. In late April, after his victory at San Jacinto, Houston sent his own representa-tives to Washington. Finally, after the establishment of a constitu-tional government in July, William H. Wharton was appointed minister, but he did not arrive in Washington until December. All six Texans sought annexation, but with several conditions: 1) the confirmation of Texas laws; 2) the assumption of the Texas debts by the U.S. government; 3) the recognition of slavery's legal status in Texas; and 4) the liberal appropriation of land for educational purposes. Secretary of State John Forsyth talked with the commis-sioners informally on several occasions, and Jackson met with Wharton on December 20. Neither the secretary nor the president promised immediate annexation.

Despite the national enthusiasm for the Texans' independence crusade and Jackson's professed visions of a continental America, the annexation of the Lone Star Republic, as independent Texas was known, proved to be no easy task. Jackson needed Senate approval for any treaty, and funding from the House of Representatives to implement the agreement. In the Senate the Whigs and Northern Democrats opposed any treaty; and in the House, Speaker James K. Polk, whose image had been battered on the Bank of the United States and tariff issues, could not guarantee funding.

Jackson also confronted the slavery issue. The Texas constitution legalized slavery, which pleased those Southerners who envisioned that the territory would be divided into several slave states. These states would balance the free states that were expected to be carved out of the Northwest Territory. This issue promised a ferocious congressional debate that Jackson wanted to avoid. Thanks to Polk's leadership, a gag rule was effected on the slavery issue in the House of Representatives.

International concerns also influenced Jackson's decision. He considered the consequences of a complete diplomatic break with Mexico after the departure of Minister de Gorostiza from Washington. Jackson also feared that any swift action on Texas would bring international criticism of future U.S. expansion. Apparently, Jackson was sensitive to charges of imperialism. He was particularly concerned with Great Britain, with whom relations were already strained over issues regarding Canada and the West Indies.

Furthermore, the results of a fact-finding mission to Texas by Henry M. Morfit also impacted upon the president's decision to avoid the Texas question. Morfit reported on the Texans' fervent desire for annexation, the Mexican government's inability to retake the territory through military action, and the growing European interest in the region. Still, Morfit cautioned the president against acting quickly because the American settlements across Texas were widely dispersed and conflicting interests among them did not suggest a harmonious state government.[15] In a letter to Jackson, Houston appealed to his old friend to save Texas from self-destruction. In Washington the Texas emissaries warned that the Lone Star Republic would seek alliances with the Europeans if the Americans postponed annexation. Jackson was not moved to act by either Houston's appeal or the emissaries' threats. Morfit's report proved more persuasive.

Finally, Jackson was also eyeing the 1836 presidential election. The 1832 Nullification Crisis had revealed sectional fissures within the Democratic Party, which thereafter intensified because of the growing abolitionist crusade. To annex Texas in this election year would guarantee a further rift in the Democratic Party and a boost for the newly established Whig Party. Furthermore, Jackson's protégé and Democratic nominee, Martin Van Buren, was in no hurry either to extend recognition or to annex Texas.

Jackson clearly understood the issues dividing the nation in 1836 as well as the fact that involvement with the Texas question only served to deepen those divisions. He also understood that he would need congressional approval to prosecute a war with Mexico should one be precipitated by the annexation of Texas, but he had no guarantee of such support. To save Van Buren from confronting the crisis at the outset of his administration, Jackson sidestepped the issue in his State of the Union message on December 5, 1836. While acknowledging the "desire of the Texans to become part of our system," he declared that the United States "should neither anticipate events nor attempt to control them."[16] On December 21 the president cautioned that "a premature recognition . . . if not looked upon as justifiable cause for war, is always liable to be regarded as proof of an unfriendly spirit" further straining relations with Mexico. Therefore, Jackson accepted the preamble to a previous House resolution that proclaimed that "the expediency of recognizing the independence of Texas should be left to the decision of Congress," which, he thought, the divided body could not make. Instead, Jackson suggested that action be delayed until Mexico, or a European power, first extended recognition or until Texas could adequately sustain itself.[17] He abandoned his vision for empire and, instead, was willing to let the course of events dictate U.S. decisions about Texas.

Jackson's hesitancy did not discourage the Texas agents from lobbying both the public and Congress for diplomatic recognition, if not annexation. Although Jackson privately admitted to Minister Wharton that the time had come for recognition, he would do nothing until Congress acted first. It did, and in so doing returned the Texas question to the president's desk. On February 28, 1837, the House approved the funds necessary for formal recognition and directed the president to send a diplomat to Texas. Polk voted with the majority, and the Senate concurred the next day. As Congress dallied until the end of February, Jackson was alarmed at reports from Mexico City and London that Britain would support Mexican antislavery efforts in Texas. He fumed at the thought of a foreign power intervening in a state's right, a position that Polk had staked out while governor of Tennessee. In addition, U.S. security would be threatened by a British military presence in Mexico or the Gulf of Mexico. In extending recognition to Texas on March 3, the last day of his presidency, Jackson clearly indicated that he was concurring with the advice of the Senate to do so.[18] Subsequently, Great Britain, France, Holland, and Belgium did the same. Mexico never extended recognition but instead made belligerent statements about retaking its lost province. The impact of the tumultuous events in Texas, the potential danger of Mexican nationalism, the controversy over the extension of slavery, and the presence of European powers on the U.S. periphery were not lost on Congressman Polk. He understood and accepted President Jackson's course of action.

~

In early 1837 new presidents took office in Washington and Mexico City. Both men were confronted with serious domestic crises that pushed Texas into the background of national interests. In Washington, Martin Van Buren confronted not only the same obstacles that Jackson had faced regarding Texas annexation but also an ever-deepening economic depression. As a result, the American public lost interest in Texas, and stories about the Lone Star Republic disappeared from the newspapers for weeks at a time. In this political atmosphere, Van Buren received two Texas diplomats, Minister Wharton and special agent Memucan Hunt, in June, but not until October did the president dispatch to Texas Minister Alcée La Branche, although he had been appointed in March by the Jackson administration. For the most part, Van Buren left foreign policy issues to Secretary of State Forsyth. For the same reasons that Jackson had hesitated over annexation, neither Van Buren nor Forsyth cast a covetous eye toward Texas. At best, they appeared willing to accept Texas as a buffer on the U.S. southern border. Although Van Buren did reestablish diplomatic relations with Mexico, suspended since 1836, he remained frustrated over the administration's ability to settle decades-old claims of Americans against the Mexican government.[19] After securing his party's nomination for reelection in 1840, Van Buren was not anxious to have Texas become an election-year issue.

In April 1837, General Anastasio Bustamante took the presidential oath of office in Mexico City. Like Van Buren, he confronted a domestic crisis, but it threatened to be a more violent one. The centralist-federalist controversy continued to simmer and was aggravated by the maneuverings of politicians and generals in the distant states of the Californias, Chiapas, Yucatán and present-day New Mexico. These outbreaks prevented Bustamante from pursuing a coherent foreign policy, including the mounting of a campaign to retake Texas. Not even the French blockade of Veracruz and Fort San Juan de Ulúa in the so-called Pastry War incited Mexican nationalism.

While domestic events forced Presidents Van Buren and Bustamante to focus their attention at home, actions taken by the Texas government continually reminded them of the unresolved problem. By mid-1838 the Texans lost patience with Washington's hesitancy to move forward with annexation and in October formally withdrew their offer to join the Union. For the next six years, Texas pursued an independent course that strained U.S.-Mexican relations.

That relationship was further strained after 1839 by the activities of Texas President Mirabeau B. Lamar. He attempted to persuade Mexico to recognize the Lone Star Republic's independence, even offering $5 million. Subsequently, Lamar accused the Mexicans of stirring up the Indians as part of a larger plot to recapture the territory. He ignored Mexico City's wrath when he sought U.S. assistance to prevent the destruction of American properties along the Rio Grande by Mexican belligerents, and he further irritated the Mexican government when he stationed Texas's three-ship navy in the Gulf of Mexico. (He later leased the ships to the rebellious Yucatán state in 1841.) Lamar's most damaging adventure came that same year when he attempted to take over Santa Fe, but his anticipation of a glorious victory turned into an ignominious defeat. Finally, Lamar antagonized the United States by dispatching emissaries to London and Paris in search of recognition and commercial treaties. These missions stirred up anti-British sentiments in Washington.

In the interim, a solid commercial connection between Texas and the United States had developed. New Orleans became an entrepôt for Texas trade, which reached a value of $2 million by 1840. Moreover, soon after the Republic of Texas was born, its agents came to the United States peddling bonds and land scrip. Many prominent Americans invested, including Samuel Swartwout, Thomas W. Gilmer, and Duff Green. Nicholas Biddle, the president of the Bank of the United States, cooperated with Texas loan commissioner James Hamilton in advancing cash for bonds. Robert J. Walker, the politically influential U.S. senator from Mississippi, was also an active speculator in Western lands. While Biddle and Walker advocated annexation of Texas, the latter had visions of an empire stretching to the Pacific.

Despite the European intrigues in Texas and the growing commerce between American and Texan merchants, official Washington remained noncommittal. By the end of the decade, however, several policymakers understood that the longer Texas remained independent, the greater the chances were for trouble with Europe and Mexico. These Americans believed that it had become too dangerous to turn down the annexation of Texas. National security was at stake.

During the same six-year period, Polk returned to Tennessee, where he served as governor of the state from 1839 to 1841. In his campaigns for the governorship and while holding that office, he focused upon domestic and statewide issues, not expansion. While out of politics from 1841 to 1844, Polk anticipated his return to the national scene as the Democratic Party's vice presidential candidate. His political maneuvering, however, did not include dealing with foreign affairs. Given his public isolation and his penchant for not reading the popular literature, there is no evidence that he understood the drift of events in Texas or their implications for U.S.-Mexican relations on the eve of the Democratic Party's national convention in 1844.

~

The 1840 presidential election was devoid of issues. Aware of the sectionalist debate generated by Texas, Martin Van Buren avoided any discussion of it. The Whig candidates, William Henry Harrison and John Tyler, were content to focus on personalities in their frolicking "Hard Cider" campaign. Harrison's victory over Van Buren seemed to have few implications for U.S. relations with Mexico.

By 1842, while Polk was pondering his political future, "Texas fever" struck the United States and soon engulfed the White House. Vice President Tyler, who replaced Harrison as president following the latter's unexpected death only a month after taking office, soon found himself isolated from the Whig Party for refusing to support its domestic agenda. In need of an issue to improve his political stature, President Tyler, an avowed expansionist, took up the Texas cause but with the caution that the slavery question might prevent annexation.

Tyler's personal interest coincided with a growing national consciousness about Texas and a concomitant disdain for the Mexicans. When the new U.S. minister, Waddy Thompson, arrived in Mexico City in 1842 to win the release of the Texan troops imprisoned there, he took a verbal lashing from the Mexican foreign minister over border incidents along the Rio Grande. The internment of Texans in Mexico and the news of Thompson's rebuke prompted a nationalistic response in the U.S. press. At the same time new conflicts between the Texans and the Mexicans aroused American emotions.

In September 1841, Santa Anna had returned to the presidency and ruled with an iron fist until 1844. Throughout his administration the centralist-federalist controversy continued to plague Mexican political stability and the states on the periphery. Although Santa Anna grudgingly granted independent status to Yucatán, which had strong economic links to Texas, he refused to do so elsewhere. He had long fretted over the loss of territory to the Americans and now determined to reincorporate Texas into the nation. In early January 1842 his administration issued a proclamation demanding that the Texans accept the rightful authority of the Mexican government. Governor Sam Houston promptly rejected Santa Anna's edict. Fighting ensued, and in late spring 1842 at Mier, Houston's army was overwhelmed. Houston used the incident to undertake a public relations campaign in the United States in hopes of convincing the Americans to secure Texas from Mexican threats. Although Houston's effort failed to dissuade Secretary of State Daniel Webster from his neutral stance on Texas-Mexican relations, which persisted until his resignation in May 1843, it did generate newspaper headlines across the United States and rekindled public interest in the Southwest.

A more assertive British policy also contributed to America's reawakening to the significance of Texas. In August 1842 the British chargé d'affaires in Galveston, Charles Elliot, devised an elaborate plan by which his government would extend recognition to Texas, persuade Mexico to do the same, and mediate outstanding differences between them. At the same time, London banks were to extend credit to Texas to provide for commercial expansion and funds for Texan owners to free their slaves. The plan intended to check U.S. continental expansion, reduce Britain's dependence on Southern cotton, and provide a market for British manufactures. In return, Texas would abolish slavery in return for British loans and security guarantees against Mexico. The project failed because Santa

Santa Anna, the "wily *caudillo*," general, and president

Anna understood that recognition of Texas served to encourage other peripheral Mexican states to assert their independence.

Despite the failure of the British plan, it provoked American reaction. The prospect of a British presence on the Southwestern frontier was unacceptable. Many Americans viewed the British intrigue in Texas as a threat not only to U.S. expansion but also to national security. The *Washington Madisonian* declared: "If Great Britain . . . entertains a design . . . to interfere in any manner with the slaves of the Southern States, but a few weeks we fancy . . . will suffice to rouse the whole American people to arms like one vast nest of hornets. The great Western States . . . would pour their noble sons down the Mississippi Valley by the millions."[20]

President Tyler, already interested in Texas annexation, seized the moment. Rejected by both Whigs and Democrats, he viewed the Texas question as an opportunity to assert his executive leadership. He took the perceived British threat to U.S. security to be a real one. Tyler's thoughts were shared by Abel P. Upshur, who replaced Webster as secretary of state in May 1843. As a Southerner, Upshur also feared that a British presence in Texas threatened the expansion of slavery westward. To thwart the British effort, Upshur moved quickly. First, he declared that the preservation of the Union depended upon the annexation of Texas. Next, he instructed the American special agent in Galveston, William S. Murphy, to dissuade Sam Houston from joining with the British.

At the same time, Upshur assured the Texas emissaries in Washington that the Tyler administration was making every effort to persuade the Senate to approve annexation. The secretary also assured them that the United States would defend Texas territory against a Mexican invasion. Upshur's actions encouraged Houston, who promptly dispatched J. P. Henderson to Washington to assist Minister Isaac Van Zandt in concluding an alliance with the United States should the Senate refuse to annex Texas. The Tyler administration, however, underestimated Whig resistance in the Senate, where John Quincy Adams, Clay, and Webster worked against Texas annexation out of concern that it would result in the Southern domination of the House and provoke sectional conflict.

Tyler's Texas policy moved in a new direction on February 28, 1844, when Secretary Upshur, aboard the USS *Princeton* on the Potomac, was killed by the accidental explosion of a gun. His replacement, South Carolina's John C. Calhoun, who anticipated eventual U.S. expansion into the Southwest, proved to be more energetic than Upshur in working for Texas annexation. Calhoun had been an outspoken advocate of annexation since 1836, when he supported recognition of the Lone Star Republic and promised a welcoming hand if it sought U.S. statehood. Calhoun also articulated the prevailing Southern view that an independent Texas, supported by foreign powers opposed to slavery, threatened the Union. During Upshur's brief tenure as secretary of state, Calhoun launched a public relations campaign across the South to educate its people of the potential danger caused by a British presence in Texas.

Twelve days after taking office on April 1, Calhoun concluded Upshur's work with a treaty that provided for Texas annexation and that included a proviso that during "the pendency of the treaty," U.S. military and naval forces would meet any emergency in Texas. Calhoun wasted no time in advising Mexican Minister John N. Almonte that his government had no choice but to accept the new reality. With equal haste, President Tyler implemented the treaty's military provisions. He dispatched troops to the Sabine River and three naval ships to the Gulf of Mexico. The proposed treaty, Calhoun's advice to Almonte, and the positioning of U.S. forces near Texas further inflamed Mexican nationalism.

Secretary Calhoun also met with British minister Richard Pakenham, apparently in the hope of getting British approval of the American actions. Pakenham, anything but receptive, asserted that his government would continue its diplomatic and economic policies toward Texas and Mexico. More significant, however, was his indication that the British would not interfere with slavery in either Texas or the United States despite their moral opposition to the "peculiar institution."

Calhoun missed Pakenham's point. Instead, the infuriated Calhoun issued a long response in defense of slavery. Using the inaccurate 1840 census, he argued that the slaves in the South received better care, in terms of their welfare and health, than the free blacks in the North. He asserted that neither Britain nor any other power had the right to interfere in U.S. domestic matters and revealed that protection of slavery was, in fact, the motivating factor behind the Texas annexation treaty.[21] The British foreign minister, Lord Aberdeen, tried to cool the crisis by reemphasizing his government's intention of not interfering with slavery in the Western Hemisphere, particularly in the United States, but to no avail. Calhoun continued to question British intentions in Texas. On the home front, his defense of slavery provided the abolitionists with arguments to use against annexation.

In this emotionally charged atmosphere, Tyler submitted the Texas treaty to the Senate on April 22, 1844. Attempting to appeal to every interest group, he warned of dire consequences if Texas were not annexed to the Union, arguing that an independent Texas would block further U.S. westward expansion. If Texas became a republic devoid of slavery, it would also become an asylum for runaways. In contrast, if Texas became a new slave republic, Tyler explained that it would exert a powerful attraction that might pull the Southern slave states out of the Union into a new confederation that would stretch from the Gulf of Mexico to California's Pacific shores. But if Texas came into the Union, it offered a market for both Northeastern manufactures and Midwestern agriculture. Admission also provided security from foreign interlopers, not only for the South but also for the nation as a whole. And as before, extending the territory of the United States also extended the confederative form of government.[22] For all the emotion surrounding the Texas issue, Tyler presented a reasoned argument. However, the Senate did not take immediate action, choosing to await the outcome of the national party conventions scheduled for May.

On April 27, five days after Tyler's submission of the treaty to the Senate, the major Washington newspapers printed letters from the anticipated Whig and Democratic presidential nominees, Henry Clay and Martin Van Buren.[23] Both men decried annexation as inexpedient, particularly in the face of Mexican opposition, but each one suggested that Texas might be admitted at some future date. Clay's brief letter represented his erroneous belief that the Southerners were not ardent expansionists and therefore he only needed to reassure the party's Northern wing. The more pragmatic Van Buren understood the need to restrain the Democratic Party's expansionists, especially the Southerners, without alienating them.

During May each party held its national convention in Baltimore. The Whigs nominated Henry Clay and Thomas Frelinghuysen as their presidential and vice presidential candidates. Their party's platform avoided the expansion issue in general and Texas in particular. In contrast, the tumultuous Democratic convention finally settled upon James K. Polk and George M. Dallas. Its platform clearly called for the "reannexation" of Texas and the "reoccupation" of Oregon. Within the Democratic Party, divisiveness over expansion reflected broader public sentiment.

While extremists in South Carolina demanded that the Union be disbanded unless Texas was brought into the Union as a slave state, the St. Louis *Old School Democrat* explained that "in order to balance the sections in Congress and protect an important Southern interest recognized by the Constitution," Texas should be annexed. Northern abolitionists decried these arguments, asserting that slavery did not follow the flag. The Vermont legislature best summed up their argument in late 1843 with a resolution that annexation of Texas would be "unconstitutional, and dangerous to the stability of the Union itself." [24] Moderates called for greater statesmanship and a reasonable solution but failed to propose one.

Muted in comparison to these arguments were those voices that spoke of annexation as an extension of republican America. Walt Whitman, one of the nation's foremost writers, declared that expansion would "make the continent indissoluble" and provide for a politically cohesive "American race." Memucan Hunt, a Texas diplomat in Washington, argued that annexation was "coupled with the paramount security of Republican institutions in the United States." Congressman Ezra Dean did not see annexation as preserving the republic but rather extending to Texans "America's blessing of civil, political and religious liberty."[25] Despite such pronouncements, the idealists did not have much of an audience.

The same gamut of emotions and logic characterized the Senate debate throughout May and into June. Much of the opposition was along party lines, but the sectional implications were equally apparent. Former president Andrew Jackson, near death at The Hermitage, wrote letters to the senators advocating annexation as being in the national interest. Southerners found reasons to support the cause. For example, Mississippi's Robert J. Walker argued that failure to ratify the treaty only invited war from Mexico and Great Britain. South Carolina's George McDuffie bluntly asserted that when "slavery in the United States was threatened, that the Southerners had a constitutional right to demand protection, and that it was the constitutional duty of the federal government to extend it." Missouri's Senator Thomas Hart Benton, himself an expansionist, challenged Walker when he asserted that to ratify the Texas treaty meant to incorporate all the land that it claimed to the Pacific Coast; and, he emphasized, "this means war." [26]

The Whigs' dislike of Tyler and their loyalty to Clay also were part of the equation. Finally, on June 8, 1844, the Senate rejected Tyler's treaty by a 35-to-16 vote, which reflected a tormented nation. Senators from most Northern states voted against the treaty, while two Northern and four Southern delegations voted for it. Secretary of State Calhoun was so distraught that he considered resigning from the cabinet, but he stayed on because of Tyler's ongoing determination to secure the Texas annexation by any constitutional means possible. The embittered Calhoun reassured Van Zandt that the United States remained committed to defending Texas against a Mexican attack.

By midsummer 1844 the Texas issue became intwined in the presidential election. Although Whig candidate Henry Clay equivocated about annexation, it is difficult to determine what support he may have gained or lost because of his softened position. In New

York and Connecticut, for example, where the abolitionists had a strong following, voters may have moved away from Clay to either Polk or the Liberty Party's candidate, James Birney. In these commercial states the bank and tariff issues may have been the motivating factor for any shifts in ballots, prompting voters to follow party lines, yet Clay did well in some of the Midwestern states where the expansionist sentiment of the national legislators favored annexation. Clay also had to deal with a small party base and cling to the hope that issues other than expansion would contribute to his victory.

The Democratic Party was equally divided. The pro-Texas faction split into three groups. The first followed Calhoun and were mostly Southerners who whipped up enthusiasm for Texas and were determined not to be robbed of this potential gain for slavery. "Texas or Disunion," more than one "fire-eater" shouted. This group wanted protection for the South's social and economic structures. The second group, while not friends of Calhoun, wanted to wrest control of the party from its elders but also recognized that the annexation of Texas would give the South a dominant place within the party. Some of its members, such as Robert J. Walker, were linked to the profits expected from Texas land scrip. The third group included Polk, who favored annexation but not the Southern domination of the party; he argued that the states, not the federal government, should determine the slave issue. Despite the party's internal differences, it presented itself to the public as unified on the Texas question.

Although Polk's razor-thin victory could not be attributed to any single issue, he interpreted the results as a referendum for annexation. Polk saw himself as the spokesman for Manifest Destiny, the main campaign issue that separated him from Clay. Polk would go to Washington determined to carry out continental expansion.

While most Americans focused upon the presidential campaign throughout the summer and fall of 1844, the discredited Tyler remained determined to restore his honor by bringing Texas into the Union. The November election results gave him his opportunity. Like Polk, Tyler interpreted the election as a mandate for expansion. "A controlling majority of the people and a large majority of the States have declared in favor of immediate annexation," Tyler told Congress in his last annual report to the legislature on December 3.[27] Already isolated from the Whigs, Tyler now sought to deny the Jacksonian Democrats the opportunity to acquire Texas. Knowing that he could not obtain the necessary two-thirds Senate vote

for a treaty ratification, Tyler turned to the concept of a joint resolution, which required only a simple majority vote in both houses
of Congress. The joint resolution had not been used in previous
acquisitions of a foreign territory.

Tyler acted immediately after Congress convened in December
1844. In proposing that Congress approve a joint resolution supporting the annexation of Texas, Tyler abandoned his strict constructionist view of the Constitution. The president now argued
that the Constitution granted to Congress the right to admit new
states into the Union, but that it was not limited to any specific
means. He also asserted that the potential British presence on the
Southwestern border was of greater national interest than the extension of slavery. The Whigs disagreed. Along with those who
opposed the expansion of slavery, the Whigs charged that such a
resolution would make the Constitution a "dead letter." The opposition also claimed that Tyler sought only the extension of slavery,
which, if accomplished, threatened the very existence of the Union
itself. Other concerns focused upon the vagueness of the Texas
boundaries, the assumption of the Texas debt, and the right of Texas
to immediate statehood.[28]

Again, the nation and Congress debated the annexation of
Texas. The arguments of the preceding spring and early summer
were repeated. Finally, on January 25, 1848, by a narrow vote of
120 to 98, the House approved the annexation resolution. The vote
revealed the sectional divisions over bringing Texas into the Union.
Eight Whigs and 53 free state Democrats voted with 59 Democrats
from the slave states to approve the measure, while 80 out of 133
Northerners voted against it. The House resolution also included
several controversial stipulations. While Texas would be admitted
as a state, its debt and public lands remained its own. Additional
states could be carved from its territory, but slavery was prohibited in any of those new states if they extended north of the Missouri Compromise line.

The political wrangling was not over. The boundary, debt, constitutional, and slavery issues were rehashed in the Senate. More
important, however, were the actions of Senator Benton. Motivated
by a strong dislike of Calhoun and the belief that annexation would
lead to war with Mexico, Benton wanted negotiations to precede
any annexation. He also preferred that incoming President Polk
have the honor of adding Texas to the Union. Knowing that Benton
and his allies could delay any action on a resolution, Senator Walker
devised a compromise that provided for acceptance of the House

resolution but with Benton's proposed negotiation amendment included. The Senate approved the Walker proposal by a 27-to-15 vote before a packed gallery on the evening of February 27. Three Whigs joined the Democrats to approve the measure, and senators from thirteen free states joined fourteen colleagues from the slave states. On the next day the House approved the Senate version, and on March 1, 1845, President Tyler signed the joint resolution to the joy of expansionists and the dismay of their opponents.

The terms of the joint resolution were more favorable to Texas than those of the original annexation treaty. According to the former, Texas was to be admitted as a state without going through the territorial period. With the consent of the Texans, up to four new states could be carved out of its territory, but those north of the Missouri Compromise line of 36° 30' were to be admitted as free states. The status of slavery in any states carved out of the territory south of that line was to be determined by the local residents. In addition, Texas was to assume its own debt but retain its public lands. The Texas boundaries remained undefined. Ominously, Senator Benton warned that, because of annexation, "a state of war was established . . . and it was only a matter of time before hostilities were to begin."[29]

Most members of Congress thought that Polk, as incoming president, would determine the implementation of the resolution, but Tyler and Calhoun acted first. They agreed that Andrew Jackson Donelson, the former ward and secretary of President Jackson, should be appointed as chargé d'affaires to Texas because he would be able to influence Sam Houston and Texas's President Anson Jones into accepting annexation as quickly as possible. When Donelson arrived in Texas in April, he found that international maneuvering and Texas politics had complicated the process.

~

Polk was not an innocent bystander during the closing days of the debates on the Texas annexation resolution, but the extent of his influence remains uncertain. Before coming to Washington, Polk told his friend Senator William Haywood that he accepted Tyler's decision to seek annexation through a joint resolution and that he saw no reason to scuttle the plan. After all, Polk later recalled, "I had been elected as the known advocate of the annexation of Texas and was very anxious that some measure with that object should pass Congress."[30] Immediately after his arrival in Washington in mid-February 1845, Polk met with a number of influential congress-men. He claimed that time prevented his study of the proposals in any detail and therefore urged that either the House resolution or the Benton plan be adopted, but not the hybrid. In contrast, Benton recollected that it was well understood at the time that Tyler agreed to turn the matter over to President-elect Polk, who offered prein-augural assurances of accepting the Benton plan. There also is evi-dence that Polk played a role in working out the details of the Walker compromise and that he exerted pressure upon Walker to introduce it on the Senate floor.

Letters written during the 1848 presidential campaign by Ohio's Senator Benjamin Tappan and Francis P. Blair confirmed Benton's assertion that Polk preferred the Benton plan. In response, Polk charged that the letters were designed to aid the Free Soil Party's candidacy of Martin Van Buren. Polk also pointed out that at no time prior to the summer of 1848 did either Tappan or Blair ex-press his opposition to annexation.[31]

Polk and Calhoun conferred on February 16 but apparently only exchanged pleasantries. There is no indication that they discussed the Texas question. Polk had no intention of reappointing Calhoun to the cabinet, from where it would appear that he had a major role in planning the new administration's national agenda and making slavery its centerpiece. Instead, Polk was willing to offer Calhoun the post of minister to Great Britain, but the South Carolinian de-clined it.

Whatever his role in the congressional maneuvering over the annexation resolution, Polk got what he wanted by letting Tyler make the decision and save himself from the wrath of the antiexpansionists. Clearly, Polk favored bringing Texas into the Union. A year earlier, in an April 1844 letter to a group of Ohioans, Polk had declared without hesitation that "I am in favor of the *im-mediate reannexation* of Texas to the territory and government of the United States"; further, according the 1803 treaty with France, "Texas once constituted a part of . . . the United States," and John Quincy Adams "had unwisely ceded it to Spain in the Treaty of 1819." He added that it should be firm administration policy "not to permit Great Britain or any other foreign power to plant a colony or hold domain" over any portion of Texas.[32] Thus, it was easy for Polk to support the 1844 Democratic Party platform, which called for the "re-annexation of Texas,"[33] and Tyler's course of action, which brought Texas into the Union.

Upon his inauguration, Polk took charge of the Texas matter. He could have countermanded the instructions given to Donelson but deliberately did not do so. Instead, on March 7 he instructed Donelson "not to take any definite action until after you receive" instructions which "will probably be altered."[34] At the time, Polk was awaiting Senate confirmation of his cabinet appointees, each of whom indicated their agreement with the Tyler decision and Polk's instructions to Donelson that the Texans accept the terms of annexation unconditionally. Following the confirmations, Polk met with the members of his cabinet on March 10, at which time Texas annexation was irrevocably decided, thus leaving the president free to implement the congressional resolution.[35]

Not fully trusting Donelson, Polk sent special agents Archibald Yell and Charles Wickliffe to Texas to assist him in whipping up popular support for immediate annexation. A fourth man, young and aggressive Commodore Robert F. Stockton, was dispatched with his ships to Galveston, largely in response to reports of the British-French efforts in the Texas-Mexico dispute. Everyone, including Minister de Gorostiza in Washington, understood that Polk did not intend to reverse the congressional resolution or Tyler's decision to implement it. At the end of March, de Gorostiza requested his passport from the State Department and went home.

Polk's determination did not mean automatic annexation of Texas. The British government made one final effort at mediation, which prompted the government at Washington de Brazos to demur in its decision to join the Union. In January 1845, Lord Aberdeen, with French support, launched an effort to mediate Texas's independence from Mexico along with a guarantee of its boundaries. He promptly dispatched these instructions to Chargé Elliot in Texas, but the French foreign minister, François Guizot, waited two weeks, during which time he learned of Santa Anna's overthrow one month earlier. Given the volatility of Mexican politics and the ongoing emotional American debate over the proposed joint resolution, Guizot did not want to strain French relations with Washington by participating in the British plan. Thus, he instructed the French chargé in Texas, Alphonse de Saligny, to conduct only private and informal talks with the Texans. The British did not know of this change in the French plans.

Elliot and Saligny received their instructions in late March, when they learned of Tyler's signing of the joint resolution on annexation. They also anticipated Donelson's arrival, most likely with

concrete proposals to influence Texan public opinion toward annexation. The European diplomats conferred with President Jones
and his staff on March 27 and persuaded them not to convene the
congress for ninety days, while Elliot traveled to Mexico City with
a proposal for Texas independence. The proposal, worked out by
Jones, Elliot, and Saligny, provided for recognition by Mexico but
with Texan promises to reject any future annexation to the United
States, to reject an alliance with any other power, and to negotiate
or arbitrate its boundaries and financial disputes. The proposal
guaranteed Texas independence, checked U.S. expansion into the
Southwest, and addressed Mexican pride by promising the arbitration of outstanding issues with Texas.

The threat of a British presence again ignited American fears.
The *New Orleans Courier* opined that the vast majority of Texans
were "roused to the highest pitch" by Jones's willingness "to throw
the republic into the arms of England."[36] Timing was of the essence.
En route to Galveston, Elliot and Saligny encountered Donelson,
and, after a brief but meaningless discussion, each man went on
his own way. Donelson hurried to Washington de Brazos, Elliot
proceeded to Mexico City, and Saligny went to Washington, ostensibly to confer with the French minister but actually to deflect attention from Elliot's mission.

In Mexico City, President José Joaquín Herrera, who deposed
Santa Anna in December 1844, had inherited a divided and bankrupt nation. The centralist-federalist controversy remained at the
forefront of national politics, and the government barely had funds
sufficient to carry on its daily operations, much less prosecute a
distant war. After a three-week wait, Elliot finally met with Foreign Minister Luis G. Cuevas, who, under relentless pressure from
the British, French, and Spanish ministers, accepted the plan with
the proviso that it be guaranteed by Britain and France. In reality,
the Herrera government could not influence the outcome of the
Texas question, even though it recognized that Mexican nationalism strongly militated against the loss of Texas. The distraught
Cuevas considered resigning his post, but the intervention of the
foreign diplomats prevented him from doing so. Unfortunately, for
the Mexican government, the show of European unity soon disappeared and was not repeated before the outbreak of the Mexican-
American War. Elliot returned to Texas in a triumphant mood on
June 4, 1845, but it was too late for Lord Aberdeen's grand plan to
be accepted by the Texans.

In Texas, Donelson, Yell, and Wickliffe quickly learned the details of Elliot's mission and set out to counter its potential impact. When Donelson failed to convert President Jones to support annexation, he turned to Texas's secretary of state, Ebenezer Allen, who shared Donelson's opinion about a probable Mexican invasion if Texas embraced annexation. Donelson apparently persuaded Allen to request U.S. military protection in the event of such an invasion. Polk and Buchanan then wasted no time. Buchanan informed Donelson on May 23, 1845, that as soon as Texas accepted the U.S. annexation proposal, Polk would "then conceive it to be both his right and his duty to employ the army in defending that State against the attacks of any foreign power."[37] About the same time, Zachary Taylor's forces, then stationed in Louisiana, were transferred to the Texas border and held in readiness. This transfer was not enough to satisfy the anxious Donelson, who feared that the British would encourage some Mexican military action near the Rio Grande. Polk agreed. In early June he ordered Taylor to move his troops into Texas and deployed additional naval forces to the Gulf of Mexico.

Austin, Texas, 1840

The Texas leadership capitalized upon Polk's eagerness. Although cautious and circumspect in the past about their Southern boundary, the Texans now claimed it to be the Rio Grande. The obliging Polk accepted the claim and pledged that it would be upheld and that an invading army would not be permitted to occupy a foot of soil east of the river.

While Donelson conferred with the Texas political leaders, Yell, Wickliffe, and Stockton attended meetings in various Texas communities to drum up support for annexation. In their zeal, these men made extravagant promises of federal monies for internal improvements and assurances of federal patronage; in private, they allegedly promised Jones large appropriations for Texas after annexation so that the new state could buy up Indian land and acquire Santa Fe from Mexico. In public, the three emissaries accused Jones of selling out the interests of the Texan people. Stockton supposedly went beyond his instructions or even, as some observers suspect, had a secret set of orders. He relished the role of alerting Texans to the imminent danger of a possible Mexican invasion and purportedly spoke to President Jones and General Sidney Sherman of the Texas militia about recruiting an expeditionary force to seize the port of Matamoros and to secure the Rio Grande boundary.

Influenced by the rising clamor for annexation, Jones called for a special legislative session to consider both the U.S. and Mexican offers, to be followed by a general convention to determine the future of Texas. He promised to carry out the popular will, whatever it might be. Chargé Elliot understood his predicament when he arrived in Galveston from Mexico City on June 4. He interpreted the American actions and Jones's call for a convention as pretenses for a Mexican declaration of war against Texas. And when Jones publicly proclaimed that Elliot's brokered deal ended the Texas conflict with Mexico, the Texans accused the British of political intrigue in their internal affairs. Elliot, realizing that his influence in Texas was over, departed for the United States and then Britain.

Jones also understood that his call for a special convention might invite a Mexican war declaration. Anxious to benefit from Polk's earlier pledge, he informed Donelson that U.S. troops could pass through Texas to its western frontier. Acting on his own, Donelson replied that the troops along the Sabine River and the naval warships already in the Gulf of Mexico were prepared to help. About the same time, unconfirmed reports indicated that the Polk administration appeared willing to provoke a Mexican attack as a pretext for going to war. While the reports could never be substantiated, they strengthened the hands of Texan annexationists.

If Polk would not intrigue on behalf of annexation, he was certainly willing to defend Texas against a Mexican attack. On June 15, the day before the Texas senate acted on annexation, Polk wrote Donelson that at the moment when Texas became part of the Union, "all questions of Constitutional power to defend & protect her by driving an invading Mexican Army out of her Territory will be at an end and our land and naval forces will be under orders to do so."[38]

On June 16 the Texas senate unanimously passed two joint resolutions: one accepting the U.S. proposal for annexation and approving the special convention, and the other rejecting the proposed treaty with Mexico. On July 4 the special convention, composed primarily of American-born Texans, accepted the U.S. terms of annexation and subsequently completed a state constitution. In October the various Texas communities accepted this constitution by voice vote. When a formal bill for annexation appeared before Congress, both houses promptly passed it by large majorities. In February 1846, President Jones delivered his valedictory address and turned over his powers to the new state government. To no one's surprise, one of the two new senators from Texas was Sam Houston.

Despite the renewed fear of British interference that the Elliot mission had aroused in the United States, opponents of annexation mounted a final struggle during the summer and fall of 1845. Horace Greeley's *New York Tribune* and a few other newspapers continued their editorials against annexation. Charles Francis Adams, son of John Quincy, joined several other New Englanders to form the Massachusetts State Texas Committee as a splinter party against annexation to propagandize and to prepare petitions for Congress. Their effort gained little public support. For the most part the nation seemed resigned to annexation. The *Philadelphia North American* reflected this view in an editorial on November 12, 1845:

> It is now plain that the American people have, all along, desired the acquisition of Texas. Nature seems to have included it in our borders; it was believed to have been disintegrated from our territory, and to regain it was to give the nation its own; besides the monopoly of an article, so necessary to the world, is the most certain source of national wealth, and the monopoly of cotton could only be secured by annexing Texas. It was peopled by our brethren, and its gravestones were marked with the names of those cradled with us.[39]

The editorial alluded to all the reasons for Westward expansion, except one. It affirmed the U.S. legal right to Texas, explained that the Southerners sought it for the extension of slavery, and that by having already populated the area the nation was extending its republic and democratic society. The *North American* editorial failed to mention national security, but the *New York Courier and Inquirer* did so on August 1, 1845: "The interference of the Governments of England and France has not only reconciled nearly the whole country to annexation, but even to the manner of accomplishing it." [40]

When the Mexican government learned of the Texas special convention in late June, it came to grips with its oft-promised threat of war if Texas were annexed by the United States. With nineteen thousand troops within marching distance of the border, the government was tempted by overconfidence to declare war, but the British and Spanish ministers, Charles Bankhead and Salvador Bermúdez de Castro, persuaded President Herrera otherwise. The ministers pointed out that many of the troops were unreliable; that Yucatán, Chihuahua, Zacatecas, and other centers of federalism on the periphery were awaiting any opportunity to revolt; and that an American squadron in the Pacific would use the war as an excuse to take California. After a great show of military preparations and much debate, the Mexican government contented itself with securing authorization from the congress to contract a war loan.

In London, Lord Aberdeen understood that Elliot's draft treaty had little chance, given the state of public opinion in Texas and Mexico's weakness. At the same time he confronted an aggressive American policy in Oregon. Unable to influence the course of events in North America, Lord Aberdeen lost interest in mediation and therefore reluctantly accepted the U.S. annexation of Texas. In Paris, Guizot also distanced himself from the Mexican problem. The summer of 1845 was indeed an unhappy one for Mexico. The United States had seized one of its provinces and appeared ready to launch an invasion of its country, while prospects for European aid vanished.

~

The events since 1836 that led to the annexation of Texas during the first year of the Polk presidency revealed a divided nation, with the various proponents of annexation using political, economic, and security reasons to justify their positions. Little was said about extending the American republic. Indeed, since the time of Texas independence in 1836 the sectional controversy over such issues such as slavery and the tariff prompted Presidents Andrew Jackson and Martin Van Buren to avoid the Texas question. The admission of a new state, potentially slaveholding and agricultural, raised political fears among the Northeast's abolitionists and commercial interests, while Southerners increasingly demanded that

Texas be admitted as a slave state. This sectionalism played out in national politics and contributed to the political isolation of President John Tyler. An analysis of the congressional and presidential elections since 1840 does not establish a mandate for expansionism. Congressional voting patterns on the 1845 joint resolution that opened the door to annexation also support this view. Only the strong will and determination of Tyler and Polk bridged the gap of national divisiveness.

After achieving independence in 1836, the Texans feared that Mexico might reclaim its lost territory. Apparently rejected by the Americans, the Texans sought support elsewhere and found a sympathetic ear in London and Paris. Initially, the British and French governments saw benefits in an independent Texas: it would thwart further U.S. expansion westward, provide another source of raw cotton for their textile industry, and broaden the market for their manufactures. In time, however, the British and the French lost interest in their Texas adventure, but, before doing so, their endeavor fueled U.S. nationalism and the desire to annex Texas for security reasons. Polk benefited from the brief European intrigue.

Polk's policy also benefited from events in Mexico. Since its independence in 1821 the state of the country's politics and finances steadily deteriorated. The centralist-federalist crisis weakened the political center, contributed to the rise of *caudillos* such as Santa Anna, and drained the national treasury. By the early 1840s most Mexican politicians understood that the loss of Texas could contribute to the breakup of the nation; other states on the periphery might declare their independence. In 1845, given the absence of the capability to fight a war, the emptiness of the treasury, and the absence of European support, President Herrera had no choice but to capitulate on the loss of Texas. His decision served to increase Mexican antipathy toward the United States and heighten the national consciousness to resist any further U.S. transgressions into Mexican territory. Shortly, the Mexicans and the Americans would clash again, but it would be more than a war of words. In the meantime, the Americans cast a covetous eye toward the Pacific Coast.

Notes

1. Richardson, *Messages and Papers*, 5:2229–30.
2. Richardson, *Messages and Papers*: for Washington, 1:205–16; for Jefferson, 1:309–12; and for Monroe, 2:786–89.

3. Charles Francis Adams, ed., *Memoirs of John Quincy Adams*, 12 vols. (Philadelphia: J. B. Lippincott, 1874–1877), 6:197–98.

4. Richardson, *Messages and Papers*, 2:484–90.

5. Quoted in M. D. Conway, ed., *Writings of Thomas Paine*, 4 vols. (New York: AMS Press, 1967), 2:367.

6. Monroe quoted in Richardson, *Messages and Papers*, 2:786–89; Clay quoted in Arthur P. Whitaker, *The United States and the Independence of Latin America* (Baltimore: Johns Hopkins University Press, 1941), 345.

7. Shurbutt, *United States-Latin American Relations*.

8. Quoted in Bradford Perkins, *The Creation of a Republican Empire, 1776–1865* (New York: Cambridge University Press, 1993), 50.

9. Richardson, *Messages and Papers*, 4:1527.

10. John O'Sullivan, "Annexation," *United States Magazine and Democratic Review* 17 (July/August 1845): 5–10, quote on page 5. In the article, O'Sullivan identified England and France as the foreign threats to the United States.

11. Charles I. Bevans, comp., *Treaties and Other International Agreements of the United States, 1776–1949*, 12 vols. (Washington, DC: Government Printing Office, 1968–1974). For the Louisiana Purchase Treaty see 7:812–17; for the Trans-Continental Treaty see 11:528–31.

12. William R. Manning, ed., *Diplomatic Correspondence of the United States Concerning Latin American Independence*, 3 vols. (New York: Oxford University Press, 1925–26), 1:229–33.

13. Historians have argued over the degree of Jackson's role in Butler's scheming. The argument is summarized in John M. Belohlavek, *"Let the Eagle Soar": The Foreign Policy of Andrew Jackson* (Lincoln: University of Nebraska Press, 1985), 228–29.

14. John Niven, *Martin Van Buren: The Romantic Age of American Politics* (New York: Oxford University Press, 1983), 444–47.

15. George L. Rives, *The United States and Mexico, 1821–1848* (New York: Scribner's, 1913), 2:386–96.

16. Richardson, *Messages and Papers*, 4:1456.

17. Ibid., 1485–86.

18. Ibid., 1500–1501.

19. Ibid., 1595, 1702, and 1750.

20. Quoted in Smith, *Annexation of Texas*, 115.

21. William R. Manning, ed., *Diplomatic Correspondence of the United States: Inter-American Affairs, 1831–1860*, 12 vols. (Washington, DC: Carnegie Endowment for International Peace, 1936), 7:18–22. Hereafter referred to as Manning, *Diplomatic Correspondence, IAA*.

22. Richardson, *Messages and Papers*, 4:2160–66.

23. Smith, *Annexation of Texas*, 240–44.

24. Ibid., 135.

25. Albert K. Weinberg, *Manifest Destiny: A Study of Nationalist Expansionism in American History* (Chicago: Quadrangle Books, 1963), 121 and 125.

26. Smith, *Annexation of Texas*, 263 and 265–66.

27. Richardson, *Messages and Papers*, 5:2197.

28. Ibid., 2193–2205.

29. Thomas Hart Benton, *Thirty Years View*, 2 vols. (New York: D. Appleton and Company, 1854–1856), 2:638.

30. Quaife, *Diary*, 4:41. Polk recorded this statement on July 31, 1848.

31. Benton, *Thirty Years*, 2:636–37.

32. John S. Jenkins, *The Life of James Knox Polk* (Hudson, NY: P. S. Wynkoop, 1850), 120–21.

33. The term re-annexation was used by those who argued, like Polk, that Texas belonged to the United States as a result of the 1803 Louisiana Purchase Treaty, and that John Quincy Adams abandoned that claim in the 1819 Trans-Continental Treaty.

34. St. George L. Sioussat, ed., "Polk-Donelson Letters," *Tennessee Historical Magazine* 3 (April 1918): 357.

35. John Bassett Moore, *The Works of James Buchanan: Comprising His Speeches, State Papers, and Private Correspondence*, 12 vols. (Philadelphia: J. B. Lippincott, 1908–1911), 6:118–20.

36. Quoted in Smith, *Annexation of Texas*, 453.

37. Quoted in McCormac, *Political Biography*, 358–59.

38. "Polk-Donelson Letters," 359.

39. Quoted in Smith, *Annexation of Texas*, 465–66.

40. Ibid., 466.

3

A Compromise on Oregon?

> [It is] my duty to assert and maintain by all consti-
> tutional means the right of the United States to that
> portion of our territory which lies beyond the Rocky
> Mountains. Our title to the country of Oregon is
> "clear and unquestionable," and already our people
> are preparing to perfect that title by occupying it
> with their wives and children. . . . To us belongs the
> duty of protecting them adequately wherever they
> may be upon our soil. The benefits of our republi-
> can institutions should be extended over them in
> the distant regions which they have selected for their
> homes.
> —James K. Polk, Inaugural Address, 1845[1]

In announcing his Oregon policy in March 1845, President Polk reflected popular opinion. At the time of his
assertion, however, few responsible people argued that
the United States had clear title to all of the Oregon Territory, north to 54° 40'. Rather, the claim to legal title justified the challenge to the British presence. Likewise, Polk's
need to extend the benefits of republicanism to the pioneers settling in Oregon expressed the notion of Manifest Destiny, by which American institutions would be
implanted on the continent from the Atlantic to the
Pacific.

Rhetoric aside, practical concerns drove the Americans westward. Representatives from the Old Northwest
envisioned Oregon as a place for small farmers, just as
Southerners viewed Texas as an attractive area for the
expansion of slavery. Given less public attention at the
time was the Northeast's commercial interest in the ports
stretching from the Oregon Territory in the North to San

Diego in southern California. As time passed, these sectional interests became intertwined to present an image of a unified demand for expansion, but they simultaneously revealed the sectionalism that divided the nation.

~

As in Texas, the groundwork for the U.S. claim to Oregon predated Polk's presidency. Until the mid-1820s the Americans, British, Russians, and Spaniards staked claims to the Oregon country, after which the dispute settled into an American-British rivalry. The American claim dated to 1792, when Captain Robert Gray discovered the "river of colored water" and renamed it the Columbia after the vessel he commanded. In 1804, President Thomas Jefferson dispatched Meriwether Lewis and William Clark to explore the huge Louisiana Territory and the extent of the U.S. frontier. They made their way to the mouth of the Columbia River, and American traders followed soon thereafter. The most notable was John Jacob Astor who, in 1811, established a fur-trading center bearing his name on the southern side of the Columbia.

British exploration of the Pacific Northwest had dated to Sir Francis Drake's voyage in 1579 and Captain James Cook's in 1778. The British claim to Nootka Sound, a small inlet on the western coast of Vancouver Island, conflicted with that of the Spaniards until the Convention of 1790, by which Spain surrendered this colonial outpost. Spain then abandoned its claim to all Oregon in the 1819 Trans-Continental Treaty with the United States.[2] In the years between 1790 and 1819, British traders established a string of fur trading posts along the Fraser and Columbia rivers. Between them was a vast no-man's-land destined to become the focal point of U.S.-British disputes.

In the late eighteenth and early nineteenth centuries Russian traders established posts along the coast of the Pacific Northwest from Alaska to Spanish California, where they competed with American fur traders who reached north to Alaska. Between 1821 and 1824 a war of words ensued between the U.S. and Russian governments regarding the protection of their nationals along this coastal region. Following the collapse of the Russian-American Company in 1824, the Russians granted U.S. and British citizens nearly unrestricted access to the Northwest Coast and waters up to 54° 40'. Thereafter, the Russian presence disappeared. At the time when Polk was embarking on his national political career, the Pacific Northwest, between the 42d parallel and 54° 40', was settling into an American-British problem.

The legal basis for the U.S. claim to Oregon rested in Article 1 in the Treaty of Ghent, which officially ended the War of 1812; it recognized the U.S. possessions south of the Columbia River.[3] Henceforth, the United States based its negotiating position on the assumption that the territory north of the Columbia was open to compromise. Washington expressed a willingness to limit its territorial claims to the 49th parallel, but a compromise with London was not forthcoming. Instead, an 1818 agreement provided for the joint occupation of the region between the Columbia and the 49th

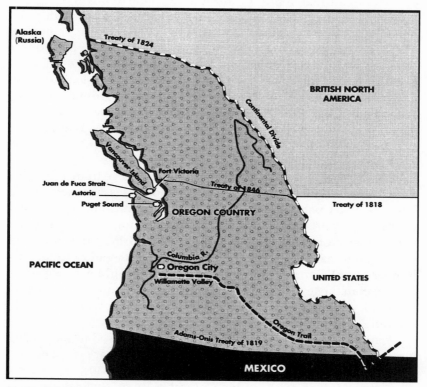

Northwest boundary dispute

parallel. The agreement was extended indefinitely in 1827 with the proviso that it could be abrogated with twelve months' notice. Albert Gallatin, the U.S. diplomatic representative in London at the time, predicted with remarkable accuracy that the Oregon question would not be settled until American pioneers firmly established themselves in the territory. These pioneers, however, were slow in coming.

As Polk began to make his way in Washington, U.S. commercial interests ventured into the Pacific Northwest. First came the search for sea otter pelts, followed by the lucrative fur-trading business; and then, in the mid-1830s, the pursuit of whales for oil. The ships' needs for repair, provisions, and fresh vegetables led them to the Oregon and California coasts and to Hawaii. The search for adequate ports along the Northwest Coast directed U.S. interests north of the Columbia River because of the huge sandbar that choked its mouth. American policymakers became aware of this problem in an 1826 report by Boston merchant William Sturgis to President John Quincy Adams. The Sturgis report persuaded the president to insist upon settlement at the 49th parallel. Thereafter a number of authoritative reports, such as those by Robert Greenbow, Thomas J. Farnham, Charles Wilkes, and Eugene Duflot de Mofras, confirmed Sturgis's findings. These experts looked north to the tranquil waters of the Juan de Fuca Strait, Admiralty Inlet, Puget Sound, and Hood's Canal. As a result of these surveys, U.S. possession of the coastal frontier to the 49th parallel was implanted in the American psyche.

Like Astor, many of the Northeast's merchants looked to the Pacific coastline as the starting place for a lucrative trade with East Asia. President John Tyler deliberately chose Massachusetts Whig lawyer Caleb Cushing to negotiate a treaty with China in 1842 that opened five ports, including Canton and Shanghai, to American merchants. From Hawaii, U.S. consul Peter Brinsmade informed Washington that the Pacific Northwest's forests would provide the lumber essential for coastal shipyards, which would have a greater impact than those of Maine had had upon the Atlantic Coast. These economic interests in the Pacific Northwest helped to define U.S. diplomacy regarding the Oregon Territory.

While U.S. commercial activity slowly increased in the Pacific Northwest, only a few American missionaries, trappers, and adventurers made their way to Oregon by the late 1830s, and almost all of them settled south of the Columbia River. By 1840 the outpost in the Willamette Valley included just sixty families of missionaries, trappers, and Canadians employed by the British Hudson's Bay Company, and they were wholly dependent upon the company for their supplies.

Until the mid-1830s most Americans, including Polk, directed their attention to the popular issues of Jacksonian Democracy: internal improvements, the national bank, and the tariff. That focus changed with the Panic of 1837, which ushered in a period of insecurity east of the Mississippi River that made the land beyond the Rockies an attraction for the less fortunate. A number of travelers' accounts whetted the American appetite for more information about the Northwest. Washington Irving's *Astoria, or Anecdotes of an Enterprise beyond the Rocky Mountains* (1836), Zenas Leonard's *Narratives* (1838), C. A. Murray's *Travels in North America* (1838), and Farnham's *Travels in the Great Western Prairies* (1839) extolled the virtues of Oregon, particularly the Willamette Valley, with its rich soil for agriculture and its abundance of timber for the construction of houses and ships. Newspaper articles described boundless grasslands, fertile valleys, and fish-choked rivers. In the short run, Oregon would be a self-sustaining territory, after which the China trade beckoned. Significantly, these writers noted that the settlements did not infringe upon the claims of the Hudson's Bay Company north of the Columbia River.

Beginning in 1838, as Polk contemplated his political future, expansionist congressmen commenced a barrage of memorials addressing the Oregon Territory. Among the most zealous was Senator Lewis Linn (D., Mo.), who called for the abrogation of the 1827 agreement with Great Britain, U.S. military occupation of the Columbia River, and the safeguarding of free land for American settlers. In the House of Representatives, Caleb Cushing promoted the commercial advantages of Oregon and demanded that the United States "attain its 'natural boundary' on the Pacific Ocean and give American merchants access to the enormous Asian markets."[4] American bravado knew no bounds.

Increased awareness of Oregon's bountiful potential brought with it an acknowledgment of the British presence in the Pacific Northwest, as embodied in the Hudson's Bay Company with its principal outpost at Fort Vancouver, located on the north side of the Columbia. By the end of the 1830s the company had strengthened its hold over the entire Columbia River Valley northward into present-day Canada. And like their American counterparts, British merchants increasingly looked north of the Columbia for secure ports to defend the interests of the Hudson's Bay Company and to serve the trade anticipated with East Asia.

In contrast to the U.S. fixation on the 49th parallel, the British looked to pushing the Americans farther south. George Simpson, a longtime Hudson's Bay official who became the governor-in-chief of American operations in 1839, was determined that the British government would never abandon its claim to the Columbia. To solidify that position, Simpson insisted that British diplomats persuade their American peers to accept England's title to all territory south of the river to the 42d parallel, the northern boundary of present-day California.

The British presence in the Pacific Northwest was first detailed in the 1837 report to President Andrew Jackson by Navy purser William Slacum, who asserted that the British exercised nearly full control of Oregon as far south as the 40th parallel and within this domain had armed the Indians to deter American pioneers. He described the Hudson's Bay Company as having a monopoly over essential supplies for American settlers in the area. Finally, because both Puget Sound and the mouth of the Columbia were important to U.S. interests, Slacum argued that the United States should possess Oregon to at least the 49th parallel.[5]

By 1841, as Polk's political career went into decline in Tennessee, the American presence in Oregon began to markedly increase. Governor Simpson understood the dimensions of the dispute. He believed that the United States would never consent to any agreement that did not include the Juan de Fuca Strait, Puget Sound, and the adjacent coastal areas. Despite the small number of American settlers in the Oregon Territory and their dependence upon the British company, Simpson also understood that these pioneers came with the preconceived notion that the British, not they, were the intruders with no legal right to be in Oregon. Simpson correctly feared that it would only be a short time before the government in Washington came to the pioneers' defense. For the moment, however, the British position was secure because the Hudson's Bay Company dominated the disputed Oregon Territory.

Any negotiated settlement would have to take into account U.S. public opinion. In the generation after 1820, statesmen in London came to believe that Americans' arrogance and dislike of the British would interfere with any reasonable resolution. London newspapers commented upon the 1820 visit to the United States by the Frenchman Alexis de Tocqueville, when he took note of the venomous attitude held by Americans toward the mother country. The British press wrote that English bondholders were berated as imperialists for the estimated $150 million invested in the construction of canals, roads, and railroads throughout the United States in the 1830s. At the same time the Americans missed no opportunity to ridicule the shortcomings of British society: political corruption, the exploitation wages paid to women and children, and class distinctions.[6]

Likewise, the British criticized the Americans. Besides the appetite for territorial expansion, they were irritated by the absence of a copyright law, which left the works of British authors unprotected in the United States. British travelers were scandalized by the drunkenness, dueling, fisticuffs, cattle rustling, lynching, and slave beating observed in American society. Detailed stories made their way into the British press. London's *Morning Chronicle* wondered whether any American could be "judged by European standards of moderation, decency and honor."[7] In sum, the British found the Americans to be a cruel and ungodly lot, incapable of self-rule.

~

Against a backdrop of dubious and conflicting claims to the same territory, hardened by years of frustrating diplomacy and complicated by mutual visions of the future and distrust of one another, the Americans and British would play out the Oregon question after 1842, when it appeared as a sudden and almost overwhelming issue. At stake was an empire in the Northwest that spanned fertile farmland, dense timber forests, a valuable though declining fur trade, and an opportunity for commercial expansion to East Asia. As Washington and London probed for a diplomatic solution, Polk retreated from public life in Tennessee.

In addition to Oregon and Texas, other issues strained American-British relations at the beginning of the 1840s and prompted Prime Minister Lord Palmerston to dispatch Lord Ashburton to the United States to seek a negotiated settlement with Secretary of State Daniel Webster. The resulting 1842 treaty that bears their names settled the smoldering Maine-Canadian boundary dispute, curtailed the African slave trade, and compromised the *Creole* affair.[8] In November 1841 the *Creole* was sailing from Hampton Roads, Virginia, to New Orleans with a cargo of slaves, who overpowered the ship's crew, killing one white passenger. The slaves found refuge in the British Bahamas, where British authorities refused to return the ex-slaves, except the murderers, to U.S. authorities. The Webster-Ashburton Treaty provided that the governors of British colonies would henceforth not interfere with American vessels that were driven to their ports by accident or violence. The treaty, however, was not well received in either country, where criticism focused mainly upon the Maine-Canadian border agreement. Nationalists on each side of the Atlantic abhorred any territorial adjustments. Their reaction to the Webster-Ashburton Treaty served notice as to what to expect when the Oregon issue was addressed.

During the negotiations, Ashburton, working without specific instructions, offered proposals on Oregon, but they did not include a division of the territory at the 49th parallel to the Pacific Ocean or the surrender of the Columbia River. As could be expected, Webster rejected the British proposal. He countered with a "Tripartite Plan" whereby the United States would accept the Columbia River as Oregon's southern boundary in return for British recognition of U.S. control of San Francisco. Without consulting London, Ashburton immediately rejected the suggestion. One cannot blame Ashburton alone for the failure to settle the Oregon dispute in 1842. Webster, who was not an advocate of expansion, also bears responsibility; he refused to read the preparatory papers. In addition, neither diplomat comprehended the growing U.S. nationalism about Oregon. Instead, they focused their attention on Mexico, which they correctly judged would reject ceding San Francisco to the Americans.

Although Ashburton had blundered in his outright rejection of Webster's proposal, Foreign Secretary Lord Aberdeen saw it as an opportunity to settle the Oregon issue. In October 1842 he informed the Americans of his desire to resolve the problem by using Webster's proposal as the basis for further negotiations. Webster's positive response caused Aberdeen to conclude that a compromise appeared in sight, but his optimism defied the reality of American politics.

With communications between Washington and London delayed by distance (a transatlantic voyage then took about four weeks), Webster's proposal arrived in London about the time when President Tyler was delivering his State of the Union address to Congress on December 6, 1842. The president signaled only his desire to talk about the Oregon Territory, not to negotiate it. In fact, he ignored Aberdeen's proposal and urged the British to settle the boundary dispute while asserting that Oregon already belonged to the United States.[9] Tyler then abandoned the possibility of sending Webster to London to conclude a settlement of the Oregon question.

Throughout 1843 and until the inauguration of President Polk in March 1845, diplomacy continued to sputter. In London, Aberdeen appeared oblivious to the growing American presence in Oregon and to the rising tide of nationalism that was demanding possession of the territory. He contended that the settlement of Oregon would come from Europeans, not Americans. Throughout 1843 he continued to express his hope for a negotiated settlement to the new U.S. minister in London, Edward Everett. For his part, Everett suggested a compromise that included extending the 49th parallel to the Pacific Coast but leaving Vancouver Island in British hands, and providing for Britain's special rights on the Columbia River.

Encouraged by the U.S. inclinations to resolve the dispute, and pressured by the Palmerstonian Whigs and some livid sentiment calling for the removal of the Americans from Oregon by force, if necessary, Aberdeen concluded that a compromise was essential—but only if it preserved British honor. In December 1843, therefore, Aberdeen replaced the unpopular minister in Washington, Henry Fox, with Richard Pakenham, an Anglo-Irish diplomat then on assignment in Mexico City.

Pakenham arrived in Washington in early 1844 with clear directives to hold the Americans to previous offers that relinquished their claims above the 49th parallel, in return for British concessions on Vancouver Island; on the mainland south of the 49th parallel; or the use of all ports on the Juan de Fuca Strait below the 49th parallel. If these proposals failed, Pakenham was to offer either arbitration or an extension of the joint occupation agreement. He soon received another directive: to divide the Oregon Territory at the 49th parallel with joint use of the Columbia River and the British retention of all of Vancouver Island. Pakenham did not view the last one as negotiable. Alone in Washington, and given the time and distance from London, he had the authority to determine the significance and sincerity of any U.S. proposal.

Based upon the optimism expressed by Everett in London, Pakenham came to Washington confident that the Oregon question could be brought to a satisfactory conclusion. Once in Washington, however, he quickly realized otherwise. During 1843, "Oregon fever" had gripped the nation. Encouraged by the promise of free land, settlers headed for Oregon, doubling their number in the Willamette Valley in 1843 and again in 1844. By the end of that year, some five thousand Americans resided in Oregon, as compared to only seven hundred British subjects. By late 1844 sizable agricultural villages appeared. Oregon City, for example, boasted of its one hundred houses, two gristmills, a sawmill, three tailor shops, two cabinetmakers, a tannery, two blacksmiths, a brickyard,

An Oregon community, 1840s

two taverns, a doctor, and a printing press. The Oregonians set up their own provisional government, supported by local taxes. As the American community grew, it became less dependent upon the Hudson's Bay Company.

Across the continent, in Washington, some observers in Congress saw the Great Migration as a prelude to annexation and the rightful extension of American ideals. Representative William Sawyer (D., Ohio), for example, believed that by bringing Oregon into the Union, the United States would "hand down to posterity, pure and unadulterated, that freedom we received from the fathers of the Revolution." Senator William Allen thought that permitting continued British interference in Oregon would be a "dangerous threat to the liberties of the people of America."[10]

While the government in London may have been lulled into complacency by its belief that the Hudson's Bay Company dominated the region, company officials on the scene knew otherwise. In October 1843 the company reported to London that it would only be a few years before the Americans overran the entire Oregon Territory. The growing American presence prompted Governor Simpson to approve the relocation of the Hudson's Bay Company's headquarters to Vancouver Island.

Throughout 1843 the Great Migration stimulated congressional debate over the Oregon Territory—a debate that revealed a nation divided over its future course of action. The presence of Americans in Oregon caused their relatives and friends in the Old Northwest to challenge the British claim to the entire territory. Among the most vociferous was Missouri's Senator Linn, who continued his call for the construction of armed forts to protect the Oregon Trail. Moreover, he proposed that every white adult male settling in Oregon receive 640 acres of land and that U.S. laws be applied from the 42d parallel to 54°40'. While Linn's swaggering was nothing new, Missouri's Senator Thomas Hart Benton and several other Democratic congressmen, such as John C. McClerand (Ill.) and Andrew Kennedy (Ind.), claimed that border security, territorial limits, commercial interests, and the nation's political influence and power were being challenged by the British in the Pacific Northwest. The Midwestern congressmen pointed out that the Oregon settlers refused to be intimidated by the British and thus their patriotism needed to be defended.

Eastern Whigs anticipated the commerce offered by access to the Pacific Ocean. For example, Pennsylvanian Charles J. Ingersoll asserted that the control of Oregon, coupled with the existing Atlantic trade, would centralize world commerce in the United States.[11] Subsequently, the Ultras, as the Midwestern expansionist Democrats were known, recognized that the possession of Oregon would provide for America's preeminence in Asian trade.

Despite these clamorings, a bipartisan policy could not be forged. The acquisition of Oregon presumed more votes for the Democratic Party, while the Whigs' acceptance of ports on the Juan de Fuca Strait and Puget Sound sufficiently met their needs. Therefore, the Whigs, opposing the jingoism that taunted the British, feared that the acquisition of Oregon not only would further diminish their political base but also endanger their commercial connection with Great Britain. Moreover, the Democrats and Whigs also differed on the significance of diplomacy. Western Democrats, knowing that negotiations meant that all of the territory could not be obtained, opposed a diplomatic solution. In contrast, the Whigs, who viewed Oregon as of secondary importance to the national interest, favored a diplomatic compromise.

While the Democrats and Whigs argued over the limits of expansion and the merits of diplomacy, Southerners stood opposed to the acquisition of any additional Northern territory, particularly by force. For example, South Carolina's George McDuffie described Oregon as a great desert not worth arguing over. With his eyes focused on Texas, McDuffie's colleague, John C. Calhoun, advised Americans to temper their emotions. Like Albert Gallatin and

Governor Simpson, Calhoun suggested that American migration into Oregon would solve the problem peacefully. He had no desire to challenge the British over Oregon at the expense of protecting Southern cotton interests.

Outside the halls of Congress public meetings in Midwestern states, such as those in Illinois and Ohio, called for the U.S. government to resist British encroachments in the Pacific Northwest. In July 1843 over one hundred Democrats gathered in Cincinnati to demand that the United States secure the Oregon Territory up to 54° 40' by force, if necessary. Their battle cry reflected the growing Oregon fever and the alleged British intention to encircle the globe with a series of military outposts so that "no other nation might be allowed to interfere with Oregon consistently with our safety."[12]

Despite the rhetoric, there existed some sentiment for settling the Oregon issue. In Washington, Secretary of State Webster continued to tinker with his Tripartite Plan until his departure from office in May 1843. Afterward, President Tyler dispatched Marylander Duff Green on a special mission to London. If the British lowered their tariffs on agricultural goods, Green told Lord Aberdeen, the Tyler administration would consider a compromise on Oregon. The offer was unacceptable to the British Whigs and other Conservatives. In October 1843 the new secretary of state, Abel P. Upshur, instructed Everett to informally offer the 49th parallel as a compromise or any other terms that might bring progress to the stalemated discussions. In comparison to the expansionist rhetoric, these gestures appeared muted.

With American emotions at a high pitch, President Tyler delivered his Annual Message to Congress in December 1843. Placing responsibility on the British for the lack of progress on the Oregon question, he clearly indicated that in any negotiations the United States would not sacrifice its honor or interests, which now included all of the Oregon Territory to 54° 40'. In addition, Tyler also asked Congress to appropriate funds for the construction of military posts along the Oregon routes. The president confidently told the nation that "under the influence of our free system of government, new republics are destined to spring up at no distant day on the shores of the Pacific similar in policy and in feeling to those existing on this side of the Rocky Mountains, and giving a wider and more extensive spread to the principles of civil and religious liberty."[13]

Tyler's speech was significant for several reasons. It reflected not only the republican spirit of Manifest Destiny and the congressional and popular bombast of 1843 but also the righteousness of the American way of life. The president also repeated the oft-noted observation that the presence of U.S. pioneers in the territory would determine its fate. Regarding diplomatic discussions, his demand for 54° 40' meant little, given the fact that on three previous occasions the U.S. government had indicated its willingness to compromise at the 49th parallel. More important was the fact that Tyler's speech ignited the voices for all Oregon and repeated nationalistic jingoism. Unfortunately, Lord Aberdeen failed to understand Tyler's determination. He viewed Tyler's speech as a kind of publicity statement.

Negotiations took another turn on February 28, 1844, when Secretary of State Upshur lost his life in an accident on board the USS *Princeton*. Upshur, an expansionist who expressed a willingness to compromise on the Oregon question, was replaced by Calhoun, who had little interest in the Pacific Northwest. Calhoun's appointment also signaled the linkage of the Oregon question to U.S. designs on Texas. Tyler, Calhoun, and many of their Southern colleagues were convinced that the British sought to block the annexation of Texas, preferring instead to create an independent republic that would abolish slavery and ensure the British commercial position. From that vantage point, Calhoun interpreted Pakenham's mission as nothing more than an attempt to divert attention from Texas. Given the political and emotional atmosphere in 1844, Pakenham understood that he could do little more to achieve his mission's objective.

In the midst of the Great Migration into Oregon, the ongoing debate over Texas annexation, and the political posturing in Washington, the Whig and Democratic parties held their national conventions in Baltimore in May 1844. The Whigs and their nominee, Henry Clay, ignored the nation's expansionist mood, but the Democrats did not. Once the Democrats nominated James K. Polk, the expansionists imposed their views upon the party platform, which called for the "re-annexation of Texas" and the "re-occupation of Oregon." Party leaders assumed that the Texas plank placated the slaveholding Southerners who had long held designs on Texas, and that the Oregon statement satisfied the land-hungry Midwesterners and Northerners who desired ports on the Pacific Coast.

In reality, the Northerners' preference for Pacific ports could come without annexing Oregon, but they would not oppose U.S. jurisdiction over the territory. Most Southerners accepted a quid pro quo—Oregon for Texas—but they were not willing to provoke the British over the former. Midwesterners were determined to incorporate every inch of the Oregon Territory into the Union. The differences in sectional opinion were momentarily overshadowed by a cooperative expansionist spirit that gave credence to the nation's Manifest Destiny to extend and protect American democracy across the continent.

Despite the expansionist mood, President Tyler could not persuade Congress to approve the Texas annexation bill in the late spring and early summer of 1844, nor would the reluctant Calhoun make a sincere effort to negotiate a settlement to the Oregon question with Minister Pakenham. Moreover, Oregon was not a burning expansionist issue in the 1844 presidential campaign. Greater concern was given to Texas, and speakers often added Oregon as an afterthought. Not even in the Old Northwest did the Oregon issue grab front-page headlines. Whatever influence the Oregon issue had in the Northwestern states, Polk could have lost them all and still won the election. In the final days of the campaign he issued a long list of party priorities, but Oregon was not among them. The Whigs also avoided any discussion of the Oregon issue and maintained that once Texas was annexed, interest in Oregon would fade away. Even as Clay began to hedge on Texas, he continued to ignore Oregon during the presidential campaign. Subsequent newspaper analyses of the election attributed Polk's victory not to Oregon but to his stand on Texas, free trade, the national bank, and the federal assumption of state debts.

Polk's victory in November 1844 disheartened Pakenham, who took seriously the boisterous campaign assertions such as those of Robert J. Walker, who charged that Britain intended to plant its flag on U.S. territory in Oregon. Pakenham found little solace in Tyler's final Annual Message to Congress in December, in which he repeated the calls for continued emigration and extension of U.S. law into the Territory and for the construction of military posts along the Oregon Trail.[14] The lame-duck Congress followed the lame-duck president. Championed by Midwestern Democrats, legislation was introduced in both houses for the construction of forts along the Oregon Trail, the establishment of a territorial government for the entire region, and the distribution of land to Oregon-bound Americans.

Pakenham now worried that the United States might seize the Oregon Territory. He correctly judged that the House would pass the legislation but that the Senate would not. The House approved the measure in early February 1845 by a 140-to-59 vote, with the inclusion of an amendment to serve notice to Britain of the intention to abrogate the 1827 agreement. The Senate closed its session without taking action on the proposed Oregon bill despite the efforts of Western senators.

On the other side of the Atlantic, in London, Edward Everett held out the hope that his government would accept Aberdeen's latest arbitration proposal. If the arbiter ruled in favor of the American claim, the United States would receive all of Oregon to 54° 40'; and if not, he would recommend a compromise line of demarcation based upon the claims of both nations. But the British willingness to settle the question on terms favorable to the Americans changed in February when the House passed its version of an Oregon bill. Aberdeen now warned Everett that Britain was willing to defend its Oregon claims with force; and if the Senate passed similar legislation, he would direct the flagship of the Pacific Fleet to Oregon. That threat was not carried out, but tensions heightened in anticipation of the Polk presidency. The British understood that Polk, as the champion of Manifest Destiny, would enter the White House with his sights set on all of Oregon. This perception was best stated by Ohio's Senator Allen in his rallying cry, "Fifty-four Forty or Fight!" He asserted that if the new president could have his way, there would be "no red lines on the map of Oregon."[15] Allen stated that there would be no dividing lines—all of Oregon would be U.S. territory. In the time between Polk's Inaugural Address in March and his State of the Union message to Congress in December, the Oregon question developed into a national issue.

~

The rain-soaked crowd cheered Polk during his lengthy Inaugural Address on March 4, 1845, in which he claimed that the U.S. title to the Oregon Territory was "clear and unquestionable," but he did not specify the northern boundary. Although the president did not mention 54° 40' in his speech, most Americans believed it to be Oregon's northern boundary.

Polk arrived at the White House with his mentor's (Andrew Jackson's) anti-British attitude that was inherent in American-British relations dating to the Revolutionary War. Polk also accepted Jackson's advice to stay the course over Oregon. "To prevent a war with England," Old Hickory had told Polk to pursue "a bold and undaunted" course because, in the end, "England with all her boast dare not go to war."[16] The new president also measured policy decisions against the former Palmerston administration, not the more conciliatory Peel government, in London. As a Jacksonian, Polk's suspicions of commercial interests contributed to his rejection of suggestions that came from U.S. and British commercial circles, through Navy Secretary George Bancroft, that Aberdeen wished to reach a compromise solution.

The new president's bold inaugural statements did not overly concern Pakenham, who came away from the ceremony convinced that Polk had left the door open for further discussions. He also had other reasons for optimism, including the Senate's recent rejection of the proposed abrogation of the 1827 joint occupation agreement. Pakenham left his first meeting with the new secretary of state, James Buchanan, with the impression that a new approach to the Oregon problem would be forthcoming and most likely would lead to a compromise. Pakenham was further encouraged when Senator William Archer (D., Ohio) told him that Polk favored arbitration over war with Britain. Given these signals, Pakenham suggested to Buchanan that an American proposal to extend the 49th parallel to the Juan de Fuca Strait and around Vancouver Island would result in a British move toward compromise.

In London, Pakenham's superiors did not share his optimism. Prime Minister Robert Peel and Foreign Secretary Lord Aberdeen focused on Polk's harsh words and the attitudes of Secretary Buchanan and Postmaster General Robert J. Walker. In addition to their anti-British sentiments and opposition to arbitration, each man supported the claim in Oregon to 54° 40'. Given this evidence, Aberdeen expected the United States to abrogate the 1827 agreement; indeed, if no settlement were reached in a year, war might soon follow. Aberdeen was so incensed that he favored terminating negotiations if the Americans refused to submit the Oregon question to arbitration. With British patience coming to an end, Louis McLane, Everett's successor, noted that Britain could not compromise its national honor. In anticipation of a possible conflict, Aberdeen quietly solicited military information from the Colonial Office and proposed the deployment of a covert reconnaissance unit to the Oregon Territory from Canada.

In early 1844, Aberdeen and Peel took their case to the British public. They asserted that the British, not the American, claims to Oregon were "clear and unquestionable" and that the government was prepared to defend them. Peel publicly predicted a break in diplomatic relations with Washington. The British press picked up the charge by hurling insults and threats at the overbearing, aggressive Americans, describing them as arrogant in words and feeble in deeds. The London *Times* bluntly stated that nothing short of war would wrest Oregon from Britain. U.S. Minister Everett feared that Peel's posturing left little room for compromise, and as a result the press and the politicians backed him into a corner. For all their stammering the British failed to notice that Polk had carefully respected the sanctity of treaties and that, in proposing to extend legal protection to American settlers in Oregon, he was only following the example of the British government itself toward the Hudson's Bay Company.

Beyond the emotion that characterized British relations with the United States, the Peel administration considered the nation's wider interests. On the domestic scene, Peel anticipated the Whigs' wrath if he compromised on Oregon, just as Ashburton did with Webster in 1842 over Maine. Peel also had to contend with the British advocates of free trade who looked favorably upon the U.S. Democratic Party's desire to reduce tariffs. Privately, Peel and Aberdeen agreed that a compromise on Oregon was worth the benefits of improved commercial relations over the Whigs' wrath. In addition, the British-French relationship was fragile at the time. Although France had no specific interest in Oregon, London policymakers anticipated a stiffening attitude in Paris were they to take aggressive measures toward the Americans. Given these considerations, Peel and Aberdeen faced a balancing act.

These same factors prompted Aberdeen, in April 1845, to send two sets of instructions to Pakenham, thinking that they would open the door to a compromise. Officially, he authorized Pakenham to offer the United States free access to all ports south of the 49th parallel, but, if this offer was rejected, arbitration remained London's only recourse to settle the dispute. In an accompanying private letter, however, Aberdeen softened his stance by stating that he would not reject a U.S. proposal to partition Oregon at the 49th parallel. Britain would be left all of Vancouver Island and access to the Juan de Fuca Strait.

Aberdeen's proposal failed to impress Everett, nor did the U.S. minister accept Aberdeen's explanation that British saber-rattling differed little from the bellicose words coming from America. When reports of British jingoism reached Washington, along with the announcement that British ships would be sent to the Oregon coast, much of the U.S. press demanded the defense of American honor. Significantly, the Eastern and Southern press were more moderate in their protestations than that in the Midwest, which declared that the British actions were a cause for war. The difference in editorial opinion demonstrated the extent of sectional commitment to the Pacific Northwest.

Amid the heightened tensions on both sides of the Atlantic came an unexpected turning point in May 1845, when Pakenham bluntly asked Buchanan if the United States were willing to go to war over the disputed territory or settle the question through arbitration. Buchanan took the question as a signal for the United States to put forth a proposal and for the new administration to assign its own minister to London. After Calhoun rejected the post, Polk selected Louis McLane, former secretary of state and minister to London (1829–1831)—a choice pleasing to the British, but not to the Democratic Party, because of his pro-British attitude and his identification with U.S. commercial interests. Western Democrats were particularly displeased with McLane's opposition to their demand for 54° 40' and for the fact that he currently served as president of the Baltimore and Ohio Railroad, which carried goods for the maritime trade with Britain. The Ultras' belief that McLane's appointment indicated Polk's willingness to compromise on the Oregon issue may have been misplaced, but McLane himself favored a settlement short of war.

With McLane's appointment, the Polk administration implemented simultaneous discussions on both sides of the Atlantic. When McLane arrived in London, Buchanan approached Pakenham in Washington. The plan, however, was hampered by time and distance: the usual month's sailing time across the Atlantic mitigated against the give-and-take that Pakenham had anticipated two months earlier. McLane's instructions indicated Polk's willingness to compromise. Although he again rejected arbitration, Polk offered an extension of the 49th parallel from the Rocky Mountains to the Pacific Ocean, along with Britain's use of free ports on the soduthern end of Vancouver Island. McLane also was empowered to offer all of Vancouver Island, but under no circumstances was he to grant Britain any concessions on the mainland south of the 49th parallel. This position was based on the fact that the United States had already offered three times to divide Oregon at the 49th parallel and had agreed to the free navigation of the Columbia River. The president advised McLane that most Americans preferred war with the British to dishonor.[17] Although Polk may have misjudged public opinion at the time, his decision shifted responsibility to the British. If they failed to accept a compromise, then the president would be free to pursue the all-Oregon crusade in the name of national honor.

In July, shortly after McLane departed for London, Secretary Buchanan, as planned, met with Pakenham. He again justified the U.S. claims to all of Oregon but added, in a cavalier manner, that only out of deference to the offers made by previous administrations was Polk now willing to compromise.[18] Unlike McLane's instructions, Buchanan made no mention of Vancouver Island, a bargaining chip that he intended to hold for later use. Now, Polk's grand design quickly unraveled. Pakenham, provoked by Buchanan's attitude, rejected the proposal out of hand. He not only denied U.S. claims to Oregon but also was further aggravated by Buchanan's failure to make any reference to the Columbia River. Frustrated by the inability to make any progress during the past year and one-half, Pakenham urged Aberdeen to take a more aggressive stance in order to force Polk into a conciliatory response.

Buchanan also became cautious, as he linked Oregon to Texas. He reasoned that by denying Britain an outlet to the Pacific, the London government would be pushed into a Mexican alliance in order to check U.S. expansion in the Southwest. Polk dismissed Buchanan's suggestion. To the president, Oregon and Texas were entirely separate issues. Polk maintained that the British were insincere in their previous overtures about an Oregon compromise and that his opinion was confirmed by Pakenham's refusal to refer the current U.S. offer to London. At a cabinet meeting on August 26, the indignant Polk had his way: the offer was withdrawn. Only at Buchanan's insistence did Polk agree to receive any future British proposals, but the president did not commit to their consideration. "The only way to treat John Bull was to look him straight in the eye," Polk later recalled; "I considered a bold & firm course on our part [to be] the pacific one."[19]

Buchanan relayed the president's indignation to Pakenham at their next meeting, on August 30, and chided the minister for not having referred Polk's offer to the Foreign Office.[20] Pakenham appeared shocked at Polk's tough stand. Granted, the American offer was less than what Aberdeen wanted, but Pakenham had failed to make a counteroffer. Subsequently, Pakenham understood that he had missed an opportunity for a quick settlement, and in September and October he attempted to repair the damage in private meetings with Buchanan. Polk refused these unofficial inquiries, instead demanding a response directly from the Foreign Office. Unable to nudge the Americans toward negotiations, Pakenham asked for his own recall on October 28. Aberdeen refused the request.

Pakenham was not solely responsible for the stalled negotiations. Polk also must share blame for the impasse. His abrupt action failed to give Aberdeen an opportunity to explain and excuse his minister's mistake, and even to delay a response sent the wrong message. "A postponement," Polk argued, "would carry the idea to Great Britain, as well as to our own people, of hesitancy and indecision on our part . . . which would be an erroneous inference."[21] However, he may have welcomed the impasse. Knowing that he had to have Senate approval for any Oregon settlement, the president could not make concessions unacceptable to that body. Polk needed to know what was acceptable to it.

Throughout the autumn of 1845, interest in and demand for Oregon increased. More and more Americans looked to Oregon as their land of opportunity and the fulfillment of the nation's Manifest Destiny. The press, including New York's *Morning News* and *Democratic Review* and *Herald*, Boston's *Bay State Democrat*, and Washington's *United States Journal*, reflected the administration's view that Oregon rightfully belonged to the United States. Typical was the latter's proclamation that "Young America stands in strength . . . [with] its right foot upon the Northern verge of Oregon, and its left upon the Atlantic crag, and waving the stars and stripes in the face of the once proud Mistress of the Ocean."[22]

Meanwhile, in Oregon, where Americans outnumbered the British by five to one, relations between them became more tense as American farmers began to settle on land claimed by the Hudson's Bay Company. Britain's local political administrator, John McLoughlin, reported that the inflammatory rhetoric coming from Washington prompted the Americans to become even more arrogant, and he speculated that they might go so far as to establish an independent state. War clouds thickened in the late spring of 1845 when U.S. Army Colonel Stephen Kearny marched toward Santa Fe, New Mexico. Many observers, including Pakenham, were convinced that Kearny was sent in advance of an attack on Oregon. The dispatch of the USS *Congress* to the Oregon coast in August only inflamed the rhetoric and enhanced the image of eminent military incursion.

Equally significant was the fact that no one lost sight of Oregon's maritime value. For example, representatives from New York and Massachusetts described its ports as the gateway to Pacific trade. Agrarian congressmen came to understand the maritime importance of Oregon and envisioned it as a route to East Asia for the grains and other produce coming out of the Mississippi Valley. What they opposed, however, was the implied willingness to compromise at the 49th parallel. The Ultras would not relent. They reminded their listeners that the loss of Vancouver Island and the lands north of the 49th parallel would deprive the shipping industry of timber and other supplies essential to build and maintain its vessels.

In the final months of 1845, Polk confronted expansionists who demanded Oregon because it provided additional land and new ports and were convinced that the United States had clear title to the entire territory. The expansionists appealed to a higher order. John O'Sullivan wrote in the *New York Morning News* that "our manifest destiny [is] to overspread and to possess the whole of the continent which Providence has given us for the development of the great experiment of liberty and federate self-government."[23] On the floor of Congress, Robert Winthrop (Whig, Mass.), Edward D. Baker (Whig, Ill.), Frederick P. Stanton (D., Tenn.), and John Quincy Adams (Whig, Mass.) affirmed O'Sullivan's assertion that God had chosen the United States to extend democracy across the continent, not a monarchical England with its limited economic interests in the Northwest. And there was to be no compromise on the Oregon boundary. Cullen Sawtelle (D., Me.), for example, demanded that the government not barter away any more of its territory, as Daniel Webster had done with Maine three years earlier. When Calhoun arrived in Washington in December 1845, he found it dangerous to even whisper the words "forty-nine."

In Britain, where the mood was more subdued, McLane became frustrated when he learned about the U.S. surging nationalism because it hindered his diplomatic efforts. And when Buchanan failed to explain Polk's real intentions, McLane was furious. In defense of Buchanan, however, he knew only that Polk was determined to submit an acceptable British offer to the Senate for its consideration. But what would Polk consider a reasonable offer, which the Senate would accept?

At a meeting in Aberdeen's home in late September 1845, McLane found the foreign secretary disheartened by Pakenham's failure to refer Polk's July proposal to London. Although it was inconsistent with British policy, Aberdeen explained that it could have served as the basis for a settlement. Aberdeen understood that Pakenham's action placed Polk in a position to terminate all efforts toward a solution of the Oregon problem, but since the problem rested in Washington, he told McLane that a solution must be found there. What Aberdeen failed to say was equally important: his instructions to Pakenham had provided an opening for rejection.

McLane's report of the meeting and suggestion that the United States take the initiative was dismissed by Polk. "We had made a proposition which had been rejected," he told his cabinet on October 21, adding that he "was satisfied with the state of the negotiations as it stood."[24]

A month later, after considering the evidence before him, Aberdeen concluded that Oregon was not worth a conflict because, other than the Hudson's Bay Company, there were few British interests in the region. Texas, already lost to the Americans, had greater commercial and political value. Aberdeen predicted that the Western expansionists would be tempered by the repeal of England's Corn Laws, which would open British grain markets to American farmers. To the British exporting community, a favorable commercial treaty with the United States was more important than territory in the Pacific Northwest. Although confident that a solution could be found, Aberdeen sent conflicting signals. He inflamed the situation by securing Parliament's approval for an increase in military expenditures for Canada, including fortification of the Great Lakes, but ironically, he also initiated a press campaign in England to educate the public about the benefits to be gained from a favorable U.S. trade treaty.

~

As the winter of 1845 approached, neither Polk nor Aberdeen made any effort to rekindle negotiations for fear of inciting nationalistic responses. While the governments in Washington and London continued their posturing, the seeds of compromise were being sown from the first week of November 1845 through the first week of January 1846. Several moderating factors now influenced Polk. In opposition to the Ultras stood those who understood the significance of William Sturgis's 1844 report that described the shortcomings of the Columbia River for navigation and asserted that U.S. maritime interests could be best served by controlling the Juan de Fuca Strait and its numerous branches. Sturgis also downplayed the agricultural value of Oregon and saw nothing wrong with letting the British have Vancouver Island and the use of the Juan de Fuca Strait.[25]

The Sturgis report did not calm the fears of the Northeastern commercial sector. M. T. Ward of Boston's Baring Brothers asked Polk "if it would be safe to enter into commercial arrangements . . . if there was a probability of war" with Great Britain, but the president did not answer the question.[26] Outside Congress, the Northeastern press continued to extol the virtues of the Pacific Coast but observed that the best ports lay south of the 49th parallel, therefore making it unnecessary to demand a treaty north of that line. The need for Pacific ports also alerted Americans to California, particularly the ports at San Francisco and San Diego. The British press understood this new U.S. emphasis on California and wondered whether a compromise on Oregon was at hand.

With time, Polk's uncompromising position faced several challenges. He confronted a split in the Democratic Party. With the Texas annexation complete, Southern Democrats wrote off all of Oregon. Although many Southerners understood the potential of East Asia's markets, it was not enough to persuade them to do anything other than support a compromise on the Oregon question. In addition, Southern Democrats such as George McDuffie (S.C.) and Jefferson Davis (Miss.) continued to express doubts about the economic value of the territory and questioned the U.S. right to absorb the Native Americans residing there.

Polk also heard from influential Northern Democrats, among them Secretary Buchanan, who linked Oregon, Britain, and Mexico together. The editorials calling for all of Oregon in expansionist papers such as *Morning News and Democratic Review* and the *Niles Register* so influenced Polk that he failed to recognize the Senate's willingness to accept a compromise at the 49th parallel. Buchanan did not believe that the American people would support a war for territory above the 49th parallel; nor did Congress, because it was willing to accept a compromise with Britain on the Oregon question.

Senator Benton shared Buchanan's opinion. During a private meeting with the president, Benton explained that any claim to territory north of the 49th parallel could not be justified by the historical record. He maintained that the U.S. right to territory up to the 49th parallel dated to the 1713 Treaty of Utrecht and had been confirmed in various diplomatic acts since then.[27] Polk dismissed the advice of both men, arguing that the United States had every legal right to 54°40' and claiming that the congressmen with whom he spoke supported expansion. He went on to describe Buchanan as being "too timid and too fearful of war over the Oregon question by yielding and making greater concessions" than the president was willing to extend.[28]

While others found reason for compromise, Polk did not. Since the rejection of his July proposals, he remained steadfast. His determination was apparent on October 21, when he informed the cabinet that in his forthcoming Annual Message he "intended to maintain all our rights . . . take a bold and strong ground, and reaffirm Mr. Monroe's ground against permitting any European power to plant or establish any new colony on the North American continent."[29] Polk was true to his word. In his State of the Union address to Congress on December 2, the president boldly defended the administration's position on Oregon. He painstakingly reiterated the legality of U.S. claims to the whole of Oregon, and he called upon Congress to extend government protection to U.S. citizens in the territory, to provide generous land grants to the Oregon pioneers, and to serve Britain with the required one-year's notice to abrogate the 1827 joint occupation agreement. In a burst of chauvinism, Polk evoked Monroe's 1823 noncolonization principle, the first such public statement in twenty-one years. Rejecting the British application of its laws to the Oregon Territory and its right to use the Columbia River, he went on

> to reiterate and reaffirm the principle avowed by Mr. Monroe . . . due alike to our safety and our interests that the efficient protection of our laws should be extended over our whole territorial limits, and that it should be distinctly announced to the world as our settled policy that no future European colony or dominion shall with our consent be planted or established on any part of the North American continent.[30]

As measured by the newspapers of the day, the public favored Polk's aggressive statement, but his critics asserted that he only intended to stir up emotions to support his policy of brinkmanship because, to that point, he had taken no measures to prepare the nation for war with Britain. If unprepared for war, the critics asked, how could Polk support his demands and force a British retreat? The president pointed to the previous offers to compromise at the 49th parallel and the British rejection of such proposals. He also shifted responsibility to the divided Congress by challenging it to appropriate funds for the protection of U.S. citizens in the Oregon Territory and to define the terms of abrogating the 1827 agreement. In the political climate of the day, however, it was unrealistic to expect quick congressional action. The Oregon question and the quest for ports on the Pacific Coast became entangled in the coils of the abolitionist movement, the confusion of personal ambitions, partisan loyalties, and ideological convictions.

Polk was encouraged by the signals of support given by influential senators immediately after Congress received the December 2 message. Michigan's Lewis Cass called at the White House to express "his entire concurrence," and Virginia's William S. Archer expressed his gratification "especially [with] that part of it relating to Oregon."[31] Through Secretary Bancroft, Polk learned that Congressman John Quincy Adams was determined "to support my administration on the Oregon question."[32] Adams, long committed to trade with China, anticipated the commercial advantages for Northeastern merchants who could access Pacific Coast ports. On Christmas Eve, Senator Allen informed the president that the Senate would not consider arbitration and most likely would not accept a compromise at the 49th parallel, should the British recommend one. Allen also urged the president, in advance, to submit any British proposal to the Senate for its consideration.[33] This recommendation fit with Polk's strategy and allowed him to know what the Senate response would be to any settlement offer.

Two days after Christmas, Polk's cabinet agreed to this procedure, and at the same time agreed to reject suggestions of arbitration.[34] Only a firm British offer would suffice. When Pakenham met with Buchanan on December 27, he indicated that the British would be glad to be rid of the Oregon question "on almost any terms," but still recommended arbitration as the means to do so. For the third time, Buchanan rejected that approach.[35] These events so bolstered Polk's confidence that, at the end of December, he refused to sanction Buchanan's instructions to McLane that suggested a possible compromise.

Outside the administration, however, several individuals indicated a willingness to compromise. For example, Senator Archer, the ranking Whig on the Foreign Relations Committee, and William W. Corcoran, a prominent Washington banker, advised Pakenham that a British proposal that included the extension of the 49th parallel to the Pacific Coast, British retention of Vancouver Island, and the free navigation of the Columbia River would be acceptable to the Senate. Calhoun feared that the president's rock-like stance and nationalistic rhetoric might lead to a war in which Southern interests would be sacrificed. When he failed to dissuade the president from an aggressive policy in a private meeting on December 22,[36] Calhoun decided to assume the mantle of the opposition's leadership in the Senate. Over the next several months, Calhoun benefited from McLane's sharing his London dispatches. McLane, too, wanted a compromise.

When Congress opened its debate on the Oregon question in the final days of December 1845, it was strongly divided over the extent of national interest in that distant territory. On the Senate floor the Ultras vented their anger at the Southerners for having abandoned the Oregon cause once Texas annexation had been completed in June 1844. Others issued more hawkish statements. Senator Cass demanded an assessment of war preparedness, and Senator David R. Atchison (D., Mo.) called for the immediate establishment of a territorial government in Oregon. In the House the venerable John Quincy Adams (Whig, Mass.) led the charge for all of Oregon. Committed to Manifest Destiny and supporting the Eastern merchants' clamor for Pacific ports, Adams defended U.S. claims to Oregon in biblical terms: Americans should "be fruitful and multiply . . . and have dominion over the fish of the sea, and over the fowl of the air, and over every living thing that moveth on earth."[37] Pennsylvanian Lewis C. Levin (American Party) argued that by the right of "contiguity," the Americans had a right to claim Oregon. This "contiguity" was based upon "American institutions—on the spirit of republicanism, that permits not the contaminating proximity upon the soil that we have consecrated to the rights of man, and the sublime machinery of the sovereign power of the people; [and] the eternal laws of God."[38] A number of Whigs in both chambers joined Democrats to support Polk's policy as a fulfillment of the 1819 treaty with Spain.

As Congress commenced its discussions on Oregon, it gave little attention to the fact that Mexico had severed relations with the United States, refused to pay previously adjudicated claims to U.S. citizens, and recommitted itself to retaking Texas, or that Polk had ordered General Zachary Taylor and his 3,500 troops to relocate near the Texas border. The Texas issue continued to simmer throughout the Oregon debate. On the latter topic, following initial outbursts, Congress then focused on how best to serve notice to Britain, since the president offered no suggestion. Should a simple notice of abrogation be presented to the British? Should it include an offer toward a diplomatic solution? The Midwestern Ultras favored a simple notice followed by the active U.S. occupation of the entire Oregon Territory, and Senator Allen introduced a resolution calling for such action.

Soon a coalition of moderate Southern and Northeastern representatives emerged. They hoped to delay the notice of abrogation or to frame it in a way that invited a diplomatic solution at the 49th parallel. Included in this group were Benton, Calhoun, Webster, and Kentuckian John J. Crittenden. Benton advised everyone that the British did have legitimate claims to the Fraser River Valley.

Calhoun, who would come to play a leading role in policy formulation, argued that Polk's Oregon policy was pure folly and maintained that the Oregon Territory would, by the natural course of events, fall into U.S. hands. Following the annexation of Texas he had lost interest in Oregon and focused on protecting the trade relationship between Southern cotton planters and British textile manufacturers. Calhoun also questioned the legality of the U.S. claim to 54° 40' and reminded the president that while he had the right to suggest fixing the boundary at the 49th parallel, he also had the obligation to obtain Senate approval for any treaty containing such a proviso. Calhoun's measured response to the Ultras prompted Milwaukee newspaperman Rufus L. King to predict that the South Carolinian's leadership would save the nation from war. Webster, who charged Polk with indulging in "a monopoly of patriotic professions, and self gratification," viewed the Oregon Territory as unpromising and not worth the political risk.[39] Webster was willing to accept a compromise that limited the United States to south of the Columbia River: The needs of Eastern merchants could be satisfied with facilities in Puget Sound or at San Francisco, he argued. He feared that the emotions of national honor would disrupt sensible commercial relations. Crittenden warned that any hasty act would only harden the British position.

Calhoun met with Polk and his cabinet at the White House on January 10, 1846. Although he failed to convince the administration that a notice of abrogation closed the door to negotiations, he did impress upon Polk and his advisers that the clearest title was by discovery. Thus, the British could claim the Fraser River, the United States the Columbia; and the region in-between was open to question. Despite Polk's attitude, Calhoun was impressed with the president's observation that "Sir Robert Peel would be averse to going to war."[40] Calhoun came away confident that he could manage the situation and, in the process, enhance his own image in anticipation of the 1848 presidential nomination.

Polk not only confronted congressional opposition, but he also had to deal with Pakenham, who took advantage of the hardline-moderate split in Congress to approach Senator Benton in late December 1845 with a proposal that called for an extension of the 49th parallel to the Pacific, with the British retaining the right to free navigation of the Columbia River. Benton took the proposal to the president. At a cabinet meeting on December 23, Buchanan pressed the issue, but he failed to move the president and his colleagues to respond.[41]

About the same time, McLane's December 1 dispatch arrived in Washington, in which he urged the administration to accept Aberdeen's offer to arbitrate or otherwise face a British government and people prepared to defend their national honor. McLane's advice encouraged Buchanan to be more forceful in a cabinet meeting on January 10, 1846. This time, he persuaded the president to discuss with key senators a possible British proposal within the parameters of Pakenham's private offer to Benton.[42] Subsequently, Senators Allen and Hopkins Turney (D., Tenn.) advised the president to send such a British proposal forward. Pressed from all sides, Polk flinched, just as Buchanan thought he would. "For all his bravado," Buchanan believed that the president "would yield to the advice of the Senate should Britain offer a proposal."[43] Through Buchanan, the president informed McLane that a British proposal resembling his July 1844 offer would be sent to the Senate where favorable action was expected.[44] While awaiting London's response, Buchanan and Pakenham held contentious meetings, with each man defending his nation's interests.

During the same time, December 1845 and January 1846, Buchanan sent mixed signals to McLane in London. The official instructions reflected Polk's views: that unless the Senate recommended otherwise, nothing less than all of Oregon was acceptable; that joint navigation of the Columbia River, even for a seven-to-ten-year period, was nonnegotiable; that the Senate would reject a treaty that sacrificed Puget Sound and Admiralty Inlet; and that any British military buildup only threatened an end to the discussions. Buchanan's unofficial correspondence revealed a different attitude. In a private letter to McLane on February 26, 1846, the secretary of state reported that Benton's willingness to compromise was an important sign and instructed McLane to recommend that the British act promptly in order to capitalize on Benton's eagerness.[45]

Outside Washington, the euphoria that followed Polk's December 1845 message to Congress slowly receded, to be replaced by the voices of moderation. The *New York Herald* declared that the British government now understood that only the Hudson's Bay Company's greed prevented a compromise. Other newspapers, such as the *New York Journal* and the *National Intelligencer*, raised questions about the legality of the U.S. claims to 54° 40' and suggested that a compromise at the 49th parallel would be appropriate. The *North American Review* observed that the thirty-year-old Oregon debate was little more than an issue used by politicians who sought power for themselves. Most Americans, the journal concluded, had little interest in the barren wasteland. The New York *Journal of Commerce* was joined by newspapers in St. Louis, New Orleans, and elsewhere in calling for a compromise at the 49th parallel.[46] Public concern over a possible war with England made its way to print and in letters to congressmen. Even John Quincy Adams came under attack for clinging to the 54° 40' demand.

As the 1846 winter progressed, two Democratic factions favoring compromise surfaced in Congress. One was headed by Calhoun and George McDuffie, and the other by Benton and John A. Dix. Neither side wanted war, but for different reasons. Calhoun and his followers, both in the North and in the South, understood that war threatened their economic interests. Benton and his followers, largely from the Midwest, argued that the United States had no legal claim to the territory north of the 49th parallel. They also questioned the economic value of the entire Oregon Territory.

In early February 1846, Calhoun, confident of support from the Whigs and moderate Democrats, planned to introduce a resolution calling on President Polk to reopen negotiations with England with the objective of settling at the 49th parallel. On the Senate floor, Benton, a longtime advocate of compromise, spoke against proposals to increase military expenditures for the defense of Oregon because such action would only stiffen the British position. Others questioned the wisdom of sacrificing commercial relations with Britain to gain only a distant land. Benton and Archer, with Calhoun's approval, advised Pakenham that a partition of Oregon at the 49th parallel, with Britain granted control over Vancouver Island and full use of the Columbia River, would be acceptable to the Senate. While the public focused its attention upon the Senate debates, the Whigs and antiwar Democrats in the House approved a modified resolution providing for the abrogation of the joint occupation of Oregon along with a proviso calling for an amicable settlement of the dispute. In calling for a peaceful settlement, the House shifted responsibility back to President Polk.

In London, beginning in early 1846, the Peel administration also moved toward compromise. Most British statesmen dismissed Polk's December message to Congress as nothing more than Yankee bluster. London's *Morning Chronicle* reflected that opinion on December 27, 1845, when it noted that "while Polk . . . threatens us with war, he bribes us into peace."[47] Aberdeen appeared unmoved as he expressed confidence that a settlement would be reached in 1846. At the same time, several practical reasons converged to shape British policy.

The potato famine that began in Ireland in July 1841 had much wider ramifications than originally thought and prompted a call for the repeal of the protective Corn Laws so that additional grains could be imported. The debate over the Corn Laws soon expanded into an argument over free trade. Not only was there a need for food imports but also for Southern cotton to supply the British textile industry. At the same time, British manufacturers looked to the United States as an enticing market. While the British debate over repeal of the Corn Laws had little impact upon American thinking, it solidified the British argument that commercial relations with the United States were more important than the Oregon Territory.

Peel and Aberdeen also concerned themselves with the French. Although the French government had no designs on the Oregon Territory, there was friction on other issues in the Middle East and China. The Peel administration considered the possibility that the French might interfere with British interests elsewhere on the globe if Britain became involved in a war with the United States over Oregon, and in the Pacific Northwest, the Oregon Territory became less valuable to the British. Because of declining trade, not the increased American presence, the Hudson's Bay Company relocated its headquarters to Vancouver Island. In late 1844, Aberdeen declared that British shipping needs could be satisfied with control of the island, a reasonable division of the Juan de Fuca Strait, and equal access to the Columbia River, all of which fell below the 49th parallel.

With these factors in mind and understanding that the claims to all of Oregon were not clearly defined, Aberdeen mounted a public relations campaign in early 1846 to educate the British people that the territory was not worth the hassle, that the fur trade was dying, that the Columbia River offered little opportunity for heavy commerce, and that the United States had reasonable claims to Pacific Coast harbors. As a result, the British press shifted its attention from Oregon to Polk's tariff reform proposals. Major journals (*Edinburgh Review*, *Quarterly Review*, and *London Illustrated*) and subsequently newspapers (London *Times* and *Spectator*, *Manchester Guardian*, and Leeds *Mercury*) championed Aberdeen's cause and expressed a willingness to compromise. Simply put, the *London Illustrated* asserted on December 27, 1846, that Oregon did not merit the "expense of one year's war."[48] The press campaign also helped to temper British reaction to Polk's December 1845 message to Congress.

Beyond official British government circles, other pressures surfaced that contributed to the call for a compromise. Learning of the U.S. claims for the first time, some Britons questioned their government's position. The commercial sector clearly indicated that it would not support a war over Oregon. Speakers on the floors of both the House of Lords and House of Commons called for peace and pointed to the strong cultural ties between the two nations. The semi-official government newspaper, the *Times*, "leaked" Peel's suggestion that Pakenham offer a compromise solution along the oft-repeated theme: the 49th parallel to the Pacific, with Britain retaining all of Vancouver Island and rights on the Columbia River.

McLane reported these trends in a dispatch on February 3, but when it arrived in Washington later that month, Buchanan, Bancroft, and Polk focused not on the indications of compromise but on McLane's brief statement regarding the sailing of thirty British ships to North America. McLane's report "was not altogether of so pacific a character as the accounts given in the English newspapers had led me to believe," Polk fumed.[49] At its regular Tuesday meeting on February 24 and again the next day, the cabinet unanimously approved Buchanan's instructions to McLane: that he inform Aberdeen that "the door was not closed by anything which had heretofore occurred on the Oregon question." In so doing, the administration indicated its willingness to entertain a compromise at the 49th parallel, cession of all Vancouver Island to Britain, and the grant to Britain of limited, not perpetual, navigation rights on the Columbia River.[50] Aberdeen received further encouragement from Pakenham's report that Calhoun had indicated that no more than seven senators would oppose a compromise. Pakenham was convinced that the British threat of force had turned the tide, and therefore he advised the Foreign Office on February 26 that further military preparations were unnecessary.

As word about an impending compromise spread throughout Washington, a stream of congressmen and senators including Atchison, Cass, Calhoun, and Edward Hannegan visited the White House to confirm the rumors and to admonish Polk. The president failed to satisfactorily answer their queries. He refused to divulge his position, only to say that he remained committed to the principles found in the 1844 party platform and his December 1845 Annual Message to Congress. To Polk, these men were more interested in positioning themselves for the 1848 presidential election than in the fate of Oregon. " 'Forty-eight' has been with them the

great question, and hence the divisions in the Democratic party,"
the president observed.[51]

Given the rising crescendo of voices calling for compromise,
Polk now appeared willing to do so, but he remained adamant about
obtaining his cabinet's approval and the Senate's commitment to
any such plan. Although confident of the cabinet's backing, he lamented that the split in the Democratic Party left him "without
any certain or reliable support. . . . Each leader looks to his own
advancement more than he does to the success of my measures."[52]
For Polk, responsibility for the success or failure of the Oregon
question now rested squarely on the shoulders of the members of
Congress, and the Democrats "would be held responsible by the
country" because they commanded a majority in each chamber.[53]

The Senate debate took a crucial turn on March 16 when Calhoun, with the support of several Whigs and moderate Democrats,
declared in favor of a resolution calling for an end to the 1827 agreement in a form that encouraged an amicable settlement of the Oregon dispute. He also begged the Senate not to take any action that
invited war.[54] In support of Calhoun's proposal, Benton spoke for
three days. He explained that 54° 40' never existed in any agreement between the United States and Britain, that it was only mentioned in an 1823 U.S. proposal, and that it had made its way into
the 1824 agreement with the Russians. He also discounted the 1819
treaty with Spain as validating the line.[55] Cass spoke in opposition, but it was his last gasp. Effectively, the Ultras had been sty-
mied. By a 40-to-14 vote on April 16, the Senate approved a
moderately termed resolution drafted by Crittenden. In the last
week of April, Congress presented Polk with the directive to inform London that the United States intended to abrogate the 1827
arrangement on Oregon, but with the hope of amicably settling all
disputes regarding the territory. Within a week, the appropriate
instructions were en route to McLane. Polk wanted the congressional joint resolution taken all the way to Queen Victoria, but
McLane knew better and discreetly abandoned the idea.

As politicians in London and Washington inched toward an
agreement on Oregon, events on the Texas-Mexican border threatened to unravel the compromise. On May 9, three weeks after the
Senate vote for the joint resolution, John Slidell returned from
Mexico City to report that relations with Mexico had reached
an impasse. At the same time, Americans learned that U.S. troops
had engaged their Mexican counterparts on the Rio Grande. The
Mexican-American War had begun. The war posed a possible new

scenario, one in which Britain would abandon a compromise on Oregon to side with Mexico in order to thwart U.S. expansion to the Pacific. Fortunately, for Polk and the United States, that did not happen, but the prospect hastened the U.S. decision to compromise on Oregon.

In London in mid-April 1846, meanwhile, as the Senate completed its work on the joint resolution, Aberdeen moved forward with a treaty proposal. It satisfied the Americans' concerns, except that navigation of the Columbia River would remain open to all British subjects doing business with the Hudson's Bay Company. Ten days before news of the hostilities along the Rio Grande reached London, McLane sent the proposal to Washington with an appeal to Polk that he not reject it and instead treat it as an offer to reestablish negotiations.

When Aberdeen's proposal arrived in Washington on June 6, the Americans were hardly in a position to challenge it. The Mexican War denied them any leverage in dealing with Britain, either in suggesting modifications or calling for further discussions that might drive the British to a harder bargain or into the Mexican camp. But national honor moved Polk to hesitate over the Columbia River provisions. He relented only when he learned that the Hudson's Bay Company's charter would expire in 1859. The entire cabinet, except for Buchanan, agreed that the treaty should be submitted to the Senate with the understanding that if the Senate rejected it or refused to advise, war would follow. Such a thought was inconceivable. To fight two wars at one time was more than any sensible person could expect or imagine. Under the current international conditions, the administration expected the Senate's approval.[56] Throughout the cabinet discussions, Buchanan remained quiet. Although Buchanan feared that a lengthy and contentious debate might result in an unwanted war, Polk continued to think that he was currying favor with Western Democrats in anticipation of the 1848 party's presidential nomination. Polk found it a matter of "great misfortune that a member of the Cabinet should be an aspirant for the Presidency."[57]

Polk submitted the proposal to the Senate on June 10. Two days later the Senate, meeting in executive session, recommended approval of the British proposal by a 38-to-12 vote, two more than the required two-thirds for treaty ratification. When the Senate reconvened in open session on June 15, and with the nation already at war with Mexico, it debated the proposed treaty before passing it on June 18 by a 40-to-14 margin. The Ultras made one final, but futile, crusade for all of Oregon. They chastised Polk for cowering to the British and wondered how he could abandon territory to which the United States had clear title. Most indignant was William Allen, who stepped down as chairman of the Senate Foreign Relations Committee. Senator Benton played a major role in defusing the Ultras by pointing out that the treaty gave the United States all it had wanted and by cautioning that Britain was apparently prepared to go to war if a treaty could not be obtained.

Polk seemed to derive little satisfaction from the Senate vote. He merely recorded it in his diary with the observation that Congress approved "the first great measure of my administration, although not in a form that is altogether satisfactory or one that was preferred."[58] Polk assigned responsibility for the unsatisfactory agreement to several leading Democrats, including Benton, Calhoun, and Cass. The president claimed that these men were guided by their personal dislike of him and their determination "to defeat my measures and render my administration unsuccessful and useless."[59] Polk should not have been so disappointed. He had failed to indicate any acceptable alternatives to the stream of congressmen who had visited the White House since December 1845, despite all the indications that a compromise was favored by most of them. Polk remained committed only to the words found in the 1844 Democratic Party platform, his July 1845 offer to the British, and his Annual Message to Congress that December. In reality, Polk may have just been a victim of circumstances. "If he don't settle and make peace at forty-nine or some other parallel of compromise, the one side curses him," observed Senator Crittenden, and "if he yields an inch or stops a hair's breadth short of fifty-four forty degrees, the other side damns him without redemption."[60]

The proposed treaty reached London on June 29, just as Parliament repealed the Corn Laws and the Peel government gave way to a Whig administration formed by Lord John Russell. McLane handed the treaty to the new Foreign Secretary, Lord Palmerston, who had long been among the loudest critics of compromise. But the treaty satisfied British honor by including all that Aberdeen had proposed two months earlier: extension of the 49th parallel from the Rocky Mountains to the middle of the channel separating Vancouver Island from the mainland and then south through the Juan de Fuca Strait to the Pacific Ocean. South of the 49th parallel the waterway remained open to both parties. Control of Vancouver Island and use of the Columbia River were secured for the Hudson's Bay Company and for British subjects.

~

The context of events in 1846 indicated a complex situation for Polk. For him, the annexation of Texas during the previous summer did not end the contentious relations with Mexico, and eventually they led to war. Polk's domestic program — a lower tariff and independent treasury—remained stalled in Congress because of sectional and party differences. Added to the mix were the growing demands for a commercial treaty with Great Britain and the completion of the nation's Manifest Destiny with the incorporation of Oregon into the Union. Political dynamics left Polk with little room to maneuver.

From the time of his first overture to Britain in July 1845 until the settlement of the Oregon question nearly a year later, President Polk steadfastly demonstrated his desire to compromise. His unflinching public assertions to the contrary were offset by his determination to have Congress settle the issue. He understood the nation's sectional divisions: the Westerners' demand for all of Oregon, the Southerners' tepid support for it after the acquisition of Texas in June 1844; and the Northeastern merchants' clamor for Pacific Coast ports. Polk gave public support to all their causes. He also understood that without congressional approval, any deal struck with the British was doomed to failure. To circumvent that crisis, he charged Congress with determining the terms of abrogating the 1827 joint occupation agreement and sharing with the Senate in advance any British proposal to settle the crisis. To his credit, Polk adroitly manipulated the political dynamics to his advantage.

Polk also benefited from the dynamics of British policy. Although the government in London shuddered at the implications of a continental America, it understood the reality of the day and the prospects for the future. From the start, Foreign Secretary Lord Aberdeen indicated his willingness to compromise on the Oregon issue; and had it not been for Pakenham's rash decision in July 1845, Polk's initial offer may well have brought the problem to an earlier conclusion. In the year that followed, Aberdeen understood that Britain had lost influence in both Texas and Mexico, and that Oregon was of diminishing economic value. And like Polk, he faced domestic opposition to the thought of defending a distant land. Rather than territory, trade with America came to the forefront of British considerations. By early 1846, Aberdeen was prepared to compromise. The U.S. acquisition of Oregon, however, did not satisfy the American need for satisfactory ports on the Pacific Coast, nor did it satisfy the expansionists' desire for more land. They had already focused their attention on California.

Notes

1. Richardson, *Messages and Papers*, 5:2231.

2. Bevans, *Treaties*, 11:528–36.

3. Ibid., 12:41–48.

4. John M. Belohlavek, "Race, Progress, and Destiny: Caleb Cushing and the Quest for American Empire," in Sam W. Haynes and Christopher Morris, eds., *Manifest Destiny and Empire: American Antebellum Expansion* (College Station: Texas A&M University Press, 1997), 29.

5. Robert Greenhow, *The History of Oregon and California* (Los Angeles: Sherwin and Fruetel, 1970, reprint of 1844 edition), 363–64.

6. Frank Thistlethwaite, *America and the Atlantic Community: Anglo-American Aspects, 1790–1850* (New York: Harper and Row, 1963).

7. Quoted in David M. Pletcher, *The Diplomacy of Annexation: Texas, Oregon, and the Mexican War* (Columbia: University of Missouri Press, 1973), 314.

8. Bevans, *Treaties*, 12:82

9. Richardson, *Messages and Papers*, 5:2047–48.

10. Quoted in Weinberg, *Manifest Destiny*, 110.

11. Norman A. Graebner, *Empire on the Pacific: A Study in American Continental Expansion* (Claremont, CA: Regina Books, 1989), 38.

12. Quoted in Weinberg, *Manifest Destiny*, 387.

13. Richardson, *Messages and Papers*, 5:2111.

14. Ibid., 5:2187–92.

15. Quoted in Howard Jones and Donald A. Rakestraw, *Prologue to Manifest Destiny: Anglo-American Relations in the 1840s* (Wilmington, DE: Scholarly Resources, 1997), 246.

16. Quoted in Robert V. Remini, *Andrew Jackson and the Course of American Democracy, 1833–1845* (New York: Harper and Row, 1984), 513.

17. Frederick Moore Binder, *James Buchanan and the American Empire* (Selinsgrove, PA: Susquehanna University Press, 1994), 66–67.

18. Moore, *Works of Buchanan*, 6:194–204.

19. Quaife, *Diary*, 1:155.

20. Moore, *Works of Buchanan*, 6:231–34.

21. Quaife, *Diary*, 1:5.

22. Quoted in Jones and Rakestraw, *Prologue to Manifest Destiny*, 222.

23. Quoted in Weinberg, *Manifest Destiny*, 145.

24. Quaife, *Diary*, 1:63.

25. Graebner, *Empire on the Pacific*, 125–26.

26. Quaife, *Diary*, 1:74.

27. Benton, *Thirty Years*, 2:669–73.

28. Quaife, *Diary*, 1:107–8.

29. Quaife, *Diary*, 1:64–65.

30. Fred I. Israel, ed., *The State of the Union Messages of the Presidents, 1796–1966* (New York: Chelsea House, 1967), 1:647.

31. Quaife, *Diary*, 1:110–11 and 115–16.

32. Ibid., 129.

33. Ibid., 139 and 147–48.

34. Ibid., 147–48.

35. Binder, *Buchanan*, 78.

36. Quaife, *Diary*, 1:131–32.

37. Quoted in William Earl Weeks, *John Quincy Adams and American Global Empire* (Lexington: University Press of Kentucky, 1992), 197.

38. Norman A. Graebner, ed., *Manifest Destiny* (Indianapolis: Bobbs-Merrill, 1968), 96.

39. Quoted in Maurice G. Baxter, *One and Inseparable: Daniel Webster and the Union* (Cambridge, MA: Harvard University Press, 1984), 379

40. Quaife, *Diary*, 1:159–62.

41. Ibid., 135–36.

42. Ibid., 162.

43. Binder, *Buchanan*, 89.

44. Ibid., 79

45. Ibid., 80.

46. Graebner, *Empire on the Pacific*, 133–37; Pletcher, *Diplomacy of Annexation*, 333–44.

47. Quoted in Pletcher, *Diplomacy of Annexation*, 314.

48. Quoted in Jones and Rakestraw, *Prologue to Manifest Destiny*, 236.

49. Quaife, *Diary*, 1:244–46; Moore, *Works of Buchanan*, 6:377–83.

50. Quaife, *Diary*, 1:245–46 and 249–53.

51. Ibid., 345.

52. Ibid., 265.

53. Ibid., 295–96.

54. John C. Calhoun, *The Works of John C. Calhoun*, 6 vols. (New York: Appleton, 1853–1855), 4:258–90.

55. Extracts of Benton's speech are found in William M. Meigs, *The Life of Thomas Hart Benton* (New York: Da Capo Press, 1970), 305–12.

56. Quaife, *Diary*, 1:451–55.

57. Ibid., 297.

58. Ibid., 348.

59. Ibid., 280.

60. Chapman Coleman, ed., *The Life of John J. Crittenden*, 2 vols. (New York: Da Capo Press, 1970), 1:235.

4

The Beckoning of California Seaports

Great Britain had her eye on that country [California] and intended to possess it if she could, but . . . the people of the United States would not willingly permit California to pass into the possession of any new colony planted by Great Britain or any foreign monarch, and that in reasserting Mr. Monroe's doctrine I had California and the fine bay of San Francisco as much in view as Oregon.
—James K. Polk, October 24, 1845[1]

Prior to the spring of 1845, California did not receive much attention from the expansionists, but when they focused on this region soon thereafter, the national objectives for the area south of Oregon already had been defined by New England merchants and Pacific travelers. These men identified San Francisco Bay as the most important port of call; and, in fact, it had become the object of international rivalry among the Atlantic powers, prompting U.S. policymakers and the public alike to anticipate a European presence at their back door. Thus, Polk's application of the Monroe Doctrine to California reflected knowledgeable opinion at the time.

The movement to acquire California did not spring from the mind of Polk but rather evolved from a long and complex history that dated to Spanish colonization. Although the *conquistadores* traversed parts of California during Spain's early conquest of the New World, not until the late eighteenth century was the region tied to the Viceroyalty at Mexico City due largely to the missionary activities of the Jesuits and Franciscans. From the beginning, California lived by its own resources. Mexico neglected the region following its independence from Spain in 1821, leaving the mission economy to disintegrate, the Indians to the effects of various European diseases, and the priests to the mercy of local civil authority. Beginning in the nineteenth century a few foreign visitors touched upon the California coast, and soon villages appeared at Yerba Buena, Santa Cruz, Monterey, Santa Barbara, Los Angeles, and San Diego.

In the absence of central authority over California an international rivalry developed. The Russians came first, with settlements as far south as Fort Ross (1812), just north of San Francisco. By the mid-1820s poor finances and the distance that hampered transportation and communication between the Pacific Northwest and St. Petersburg caused the Russians to abandon their enclaves along the Pacific Coast. A French expedition visited the region in 1786, and by the mid-1830s four French merchant ships annually plied their way along the California coast. The French government appointed as consul at Monterey M. Gasquet, who saw unlimited economic potential in California, but his government lacked the political will and the ability to pursue any further activities in the region.

Britain's interest in California dated to the voyages of George Vancouver in 1792. Subsequently, British seamen, travelers, and officials focused on the significance of San Francisco Bay. The Oregon-based Hudson's Bay Company sent reconnaissance expeditions into the unsettled parts of northern California, and its agents hunted furs and purchased livestock in the San Francisco Bay area during the 1830s and 1840s. The 1841 report of Sir George Simpson, chief of the Company's operations in the Pacific Northwest, described San Francisco's harbor as the finest in the region and stated that, along with San Diego, it would be a valuable commercial asset to Britain. Also, in the late 1830s various schemes surfaced that offered British bondholders land in California. Throughout the decade, Simpson continued to report on the increased American presence there. Despite the pressure from British bondholders and encouragement from diplomats in the field, Foreign Secretary Lord Aberdeen had little interest in pursuing the establishment of a British outpost in California that entailed any diplomatic confrontations with the United States or any heavy expenditures that would require new taxes.

The Americans never fully understood French or British intentions, but what they knew or conjectured disturbed them. In particular, they feared that the Hudson's Bay Company would gain a monopoly on San Francisco Bay, thereby effectively destroying U.S. commerce in the Pacific. The Americans also concluded that the Mexican government would grant the British either special privileges or the right to establish a colony in California.

American interest in California dated to the 1790s, about the same time that the Polk family settled in Maury County, Tennessee. At first, New England merchants and seamen, known as Boston men, hunted sea otters for their pelts in the offshore waters. When that trade became nearly extinct in the 1820s, they ventured into the cattle and sheep hide-and-tallow trade, which reached a peak in 1838. Trade rapidly declined thereafter due to the decimation of the herds, local taxes and regulations in California, and competition from Cuba. Still, when Polk entered the House of Representatives in 1825, American merchants had established trading posts in the coastal towns from Yerba Buena in the north to San Diego in the south. The towns became dependent upon the sea for their survival, not only for export but also for the importing of every conceivable need—hardware, cutlery, clothing, furniture, and boots and shoes—to be sold for exorbitant prices with profits reaching 300 percent and more. Yankee merchants came to dominate the coastal towns and inland trade.

Americans also made contact with China as early as 1789. By 1820 some $5 million worth of goods from East Asia made their way into the American market. The lure of this trade contributed to a growing interest in California's coastal ports. Among the most notable of the merchants was Thomas O. Larkin, who arrived in Monterey in 1832 with $500. By the end of the decade he was lending money to the local government. (There is no evidence that he worked for the U.S. government during this time, but his refusal to take out Mexican citizenship and his lavish Fourth of July celebrations raised suspicions.)

Interest in the interior of California developed slowly after the first expeditions crossed the Sierras in 1826. Over the next decade, as Polk's political career blossomed in Washington, American explorers, fur trappers, and opportunity seekers trekked across the mountains into the Sacramento and San Joaquín valleys. The economic downturn that struck the United States in 1837 impacted severely upon the Midwest in 1839 and contributed to a new stream of pioneers moving west. Although most of these settlers went to Oregon, some drifted south into California, particularly after 1841.

The strongest non-Mexican influence in the interior was a German-Swiss, John A. Sutter, who fled to America to escape his creditors. He obtained a land grant from the California government in 1840 and built a fort and stockade on the upper Sacramento River. His quasi-feudal settlement, New Helvetia, welcomed many weary travelers in the 1840s. But, unlike Larkin, Sutter was debt-ridden. After the discovery of gold in California in 1849, newcomers overran his holdings and he went into bankruptcy.

Sutter's Fort, New Helvetia, California

Almost all of the Americans in California lived quietly and on good terms with the local government officials and the Spanish-Mexican *rancheros*. Well into the 1830s the American and other foreign communities, more interested in turning a profit than engaging in local politics, remained small, scattered, and generally peaceable, although dissension among the Mexican officials at times affected them. For example, in 1836 a relatively able clique led by Juan Bautista Alvarado, Mariano Vallejo, and José Castro seized power, which prompted American trappers to talk of another revolution patterned after Texas. Alvarado silenced these mutterings and managed to maintain his regime for a few years. In 1840 he arrested about one hundred American and British coastal-area residents on unproven charges of conspiracy and shipped them off to Mexico, where they were imprisoned. This incident created alarm in Mexico City and officials issued orders forbidding immigration into California, but there was no way of enforcing them.

In the late 1830s accounts by American travelers and occasional press notices gradually increased popular knowledge about California. The literature reached its peak between 1844 and 1846. While commerce was the focus of Richard Henry Dana's *Two Years Before the Mast* (1840), his description of the Pacific Coast proved most important. In 1842, Richard J. Cleveland's *Narrative of Voyages and Commercial Enterprises* remarked on the importance of San Francisco Bay. John C. Frémont's *Report of the Exploration to the Rocky Mountains in the Year 1842 and to Oregon and North California in the Years 1843–1844* (1845) went through several printings before the Mexican War broke out in 1846. Captain Charles Wilkes's *Narrative of the United States Exploring Expedition* (1845), Robert Greenhow's *History of Oregon and California* (1844), and Thomas Farnham's *Travels in California and Scenes on the Pacific Coast* (1845) all shared the common theme of pleasant lifestyles, the potential for opportunity, and the region as a gateway to the Pacific trade. Equally important were their graphic and critical evaluations of the coast from San Francisco to San Diego.

In addition to these accounts, efforts by California residents contributed significantly to the national awareness of the possibilities awaiting Pacific-bound settlers. For example, in 1840 and 1841, John J. Warner, a longtime resident of California, visited the East Coast where he lectured and published articles urging the annexation of the region and the construction of a transcontinental railroad. Also during the early 1840s, Larkin wrote a series of letters on the Bay area that appeared in New York's *Herald* and *Journal of Commerce* and Boston's *Daily Advertiser*.

The U.S. government's interest in acquiring California, or any part thereof, paralleled the increasing presence of Americans in the territory. In 1819, Secretary of State John Quincy Adams discussed access to the California ports with the Spanish minister to the United States, Luis de Onís, but it was only an aside to the larger questions regarding the Texas boundary and the Northwest Territory. In 1827, as president, Adams instructed the U.S. minister to Mexico, Joel Poinsett, to inquire about the purchase of Texas but with the inclusion of California. These ineffective initial efforts paled by comparison to those pursued by President Andrew Jackson, who clearly had his sights set upon the California ports as part of his vision of a continental empire. He made generous financial offers to the Mexican government for the acquisition of all of California, or at least the San Francisco Bay area, but Jackson's efforts only contributed to the ever-deepening resentment of the Mexicans toward the United States.

Jackson's interest in Pacific Coast ports came at a time when the value of East Asian trade and that of the Boston men with

California were at new peaks. Also, by the mid-1830s fur trappers reaching out of the Missouri Valley cut trails into California, which would soon be used by westward-moving pioneer settlers. These factors persuaded Jackson to link Texas, California, and domestic politics. Concerned about sectional rivalries, he suggested to the Texas minister in Washington, William Wharton, that Texas must claim California in order "to paralyze" the Northern and Eastern opposition to annexation.[2] Nothing came of the suggestion because the Texans refused to make the connection. The president also linked California to the possible British alliance with Texas, which would result in the two nations "contending for California" and possibly find the United States at war with Britain "to safeguard the American west."[3] Clearly, Jackson understood the significance of California; and from then until Polk's presidency, those who dreamed of a coastal empire focused on the addition of the California ports and, eventually, of the entire territory. Those observers who anticipated expansion to the Pacific, including Polk, foresaw a British threat to a U.S. presence in the territory.

Although Jackson's successor, Martin Van Buren, expressed no interest in western expansion, including California, he did nothing to prevent the continued flow of Americans into the territory. Also during Van Buren's administration, policymakers fixed upon Great Britain as an obstacle to U.S. western interests because the British advised the Mexicans to accept the loss of Texas, if for no other reason than to save California from U.S. penetration. Significantly, the U.S. Navy's interest in the Pacific ports led to Van Buren's approval in 1838 of the Wilkes expedition from Hampton Roads, Virginia, to the Pacific Coast. At a cost of several million dollars, the fleet spent nearly three years exploring the coast and, to the joy of the Boston men, provided a detailed description of every port from San Francisco through the Juan de Fuca Strait (when the ships returned east in the summer of 1841). Wilkes also predicted that California would separate from Mexico, annex Oregon, and "perhaps form a state that is destined to control the destinies of the Pacific."[4]

As the American knowledge of California increased, so too did the perception of an anticipated British threat to the region. The public vented its anger in 1837 when it learned of the British bondholders' colonization scheme and again in 1839 with the publication of Alexander Forbes's *History of California*, which advocated that the London government support the plan. The book inspired fears in the United States that English aggression was imminent. At the same time, the expansionist-minded press left no stone unturned. *Niles Register Weekly*, for example, spread exaggerated, and often contradictory, rumors about the Hudson's Bay Company's monopolies, Anglo-Mexican treaties, and foreign naval expeditions to seize San Francisco. An 1840 editorial in the *Baltimore American* charged that the British sought the acquisition of California to carry out their pretensions in Oregon, to make the Rocky Mountains the western boundary of the United States, and to control the Pacific ports in order to dominate the Asian trade.[5] Thus, in 1841, during his East Coast lecture tour, John Warner found audiences receptive to his warnings that the English were negotiating with Mexico to purchase San Francisco, if not the whole California province. Warner cautioned that the United States could not let this territory fall into the hands of another power, which alone was sufficient reason for its annexation. "Is it not important, then, that instead of permitting it to fall into the hands of our most dangerous rivals, it should be united to our own country?" he asked.[6] While the British made it clear that they were determined to prevent the United States from obtaining California, U.S. policymakers and the public alike failed to understand that the London government never intended to acquire California for itself. The Americans assumed that the ports were a prize coveted by every power.

~

As Polk began to lick his political wounds after his unsuccessful bid for the Tennessee governorship in 1841, California emerged as a national issue. By the time he reemerged in the political limelight in 1844, the California question had become inextricably linked to the Oregon and Texas questions.

President John Tyler revealed a keener interest in California than had either of his two predecessors. In a special message to Congress on June 1, 1841, two months after President William Henry Harrison's death, Tyler invited the Western settlers "to come and settle among us as members of our rapidly growing family . . . and to unite with us in the great task of preserving our institutions and thereby perpetuating our liberties."[7] His secretary of state, Daniel Webster, appreciated the potential of the California ports; but since he was not an expansionist, he could not decide whether they should belong to the United States or become part of an independent Pacific nation. Furthermore, Webster did not share the expansionists' suspicions about European intentions on the Pacific Coast. He appeared determined to ensure an equal footing there for American merchants. Webster also understood that Mexico's nationalism and its resentment of the United States prevented the purchase of California.

Tyler's minister to Mexico City, Waddy Thompson, significantly contributed to the president's awareness. Thompson's dispatches emphasized the importance of the ports, particularly "Upper California" with its magnificent harbor opening toward the Pacific trade. He also anticipated that the territory's fertile valleys were "destined to be the granary of the Pacific." He repeated previous assertions that England and France had their sights set on the territory and that the United States should prevent its loss to either nation.[8] Already piqued at the loss of Texas and knowing that many Americans had their sights set on California, the Mexicans further stiffened their resistance to U.S. advances as the result of an almost comic-opera incident in the fall of 1842. Responding to unconfirmed reports that a U.S.-Mexican war was imminent and that Mexico had ceded California to Britain for $7 million, Commodore Thomas ap Catesby Jones, the commander of the Pacific Squadron, acted on his own. With two warships, Jones arrived at Monterey on October 19, 1842, where he secured the surrender of the surprised Mexican garrison and raised the American flag over the fort. When reliable dispatches arrived the next day to inform Jones of his mistake, he solemnly ordered the lowering of the flag and apologized to local authorities. The incident concluded with banquets and dances given by Jones and Larkin in hopes of relieving the embarrassment. Although there were no reprisals against the Americans residing in Monterey, Mexican officials and European diplomats in Mexico City found it difficult to accept Minister Thompson's explanation that Jones had acted without orders. The incident passed, but Mexican suspicions of U.S. intentions lingered.

For a short time thereafter, U.S. interest shifted to Oregon and Texas. Still, California remained an important piece of the expansionist puzzle. California, Oregon, and Texas made their way into the Webster-Ashburton negotiations in the spring and summer of 1842. Feeling the temper of the times, Secretary Webster demonstrated his willingness to trade the Oregon Territory for choice seaports. Under the terms of his proposed "Tripartite Plan," Mexico would recognize Texas independence, Oregon would be settled at the Columbia River, and, in return, Britain would use its influence to persuade Mexico to cede Upper California, including San Francisco Bay, to the United States. In a separate overture to the Mexicans, Webster sought the acquisition of San Francisco Bay and whatever part of California came with it. Neither the British nor Mexicans showed any interest in pursuing either offer, but the incidents further confirmed Mexican suspicions about the United States.

Throughout 1843 and into early 1844, as Polk plotted his political comeback and U.S. government and public attention focused on Texas and Oregon, events in California continued to build toward a crisis. New waves of American immigrants headed across the Rocky Mountains. While most pioneers settled in Oregon, many of them reached the Sacramento and San Joaquín valleys after enduring severe hardships and marauding Indians along new routes and shortcuts to the Pacific Coast. By 1844 the recognizable California Trail branched off from the better-known Oregon Trail in what is present-day Idaho. Sutter's Fort became an increasingly important stop in the long trek westward. As 1845 began, it was clear that more American settlers would enter California over the next few years.

The lure of California resulted from the success stories sent back East by earlier settlers. Equally, if not more important, were the explorations of John C. Frémont, an ambitious young Army lieutenant who married the daughter of Senator Thomas Hart Benton. During 1842, Frémont led an expedition into the area west of South Pass in Wyoming. Realizing the geographic and propaganda value of Frémont's findings, Benton helped him to organize a second expedition, which set out from St. Louis in 1843 to explore large areas of the present-day states of Utah, Nevada, and Oregon, proceeded through the San Joaquín Valley to San Francisco Bay, and returned to St. Louis in August 1844. His report of the trip made both him and California household words in the United States.[9]

Although their numbers did not markedly increase during the early 1840s, the British increased their presence in California. Merchants engaged in the East Asian trade prodded the government in London to secure ports along the Pacific Coast, and British agents in California reported back to London on the growing American communities and the ever-increasing Mexican inability to control the territory. The British actions only served to keep the Americans on the alert and prompt the Mexican president, General Santa Anna, to consider restrictions on further immigration into California and on the foreign residents already there. Santa Anna backed down in the face of pressures exerted by foreign diplomats in Mexico City, including Thompson, although it is doubtful whether the restrictions could have been enforced. Mexico City's control of its peripheral territory was almost nonexistent.

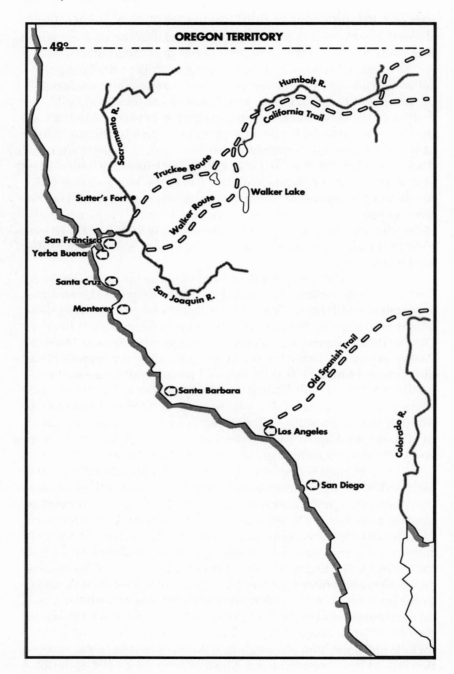

California in the 1840s

Due to the vacuum in authority, in the spring of 1844 representatives of the competing interests attempted to make a case with their home governments. The able deputy from Upper California to the Mexican congress, Manuel Castañada, took every opportunity to extol the province's resources, exhort against foreign penetration, and plea for more supplies and troops until he became such a nuisance that few other deputies would speak to him. In Monterey, Larkin kept a close watch over British activities and suggested to Washington that the best way to offset the British would be to revive Webster's "Tripartite Plan." For their part, the British and French diplomats in Monterey and Mazatlán sent home anxious reports about American emigration and land purchases. The British vice-consul in Monterey went so far as to suggest that a protectorate be established over California, while the French consuls urged King Louis-Philippe to forestall the British and the Americans.

In Washington, Secretary of State John C. Calhoun, who was devoting most of his attention to Texas, instructed his special agent, Colonel J. Gilbert, to include an offer to purchase California during his discussions with Santa Anna in May 1844. In London, Foreign Minister Lord Aberdeen acknowledged that Britain could not provide a protectorate for California, but he also admitted that it would not look favorably upon the region coming under the control of a third party, particularly the United States. The French government had no desire to become involved in the affairs of this distant territory.

In the spring of 1844, as Polk's political star again began to ascend and the Texans moved toward annexation to the United States, Aberdeen launched a major diplomatic campaign to permanently link California to Texas. He attempted to persuade the Mexicans to recognize the independence of Texas in return for a British and French guarantee of Mexico's northern borders, specifically California. The initiative quickly collapsed in the face of France's ambivalence and Mexico's refusal to part with any territory. Mexico could not come to grips with Texas's independence and its anticipated annexation to the United States. At the same time the Mexicans feared both British and American imperial ambitions.

Significantly, Aberdeen's campaign began just as the United States focused on securing California. Former President Jackson reflected the popular opinion at the time. In his 1844 letter-writing campaign to congressmen urging them to work for the annexation of Texas and a favorable settlement in Oregon, he warned that the

British coveted California. Jackson argued that Britain, either in possession of Texas or in an alliance with it, would work to limit U.S. interests in California. He urged the annexation of Texas and, with it, the acquisition of California, for national security purposes.[10] The *New York Herald* sounded the same alarm on July 2, 1845: "Should Texas be annexed, the next movement of Great Britain will probably be to negotiate with Mexico for the purchase of California. . . . In this she will be successful unless intercepted by our government."[11]

~

While Polk may have coveted California at the time of his inauguration in March 1845, he did not have a plan to acquire it. The only indication of Polk's early interest was his approval of the War Department's plan to send Frémont on a third expedition across the Rocky Mountains into the Great Basin and possibly California. The organizers of the trip were Navy Secretary George Bancroft and Senator Benton, Frémont's father-in-law. And shortly after his inauguration, Polk told Bancroft that among the four great objectives of his administration would be "the acquisition of California."[12] As time passed, Polk revealed his methodology: buy California from Mexico; and, failing that, encourage its residents to seek annexation to the United States.

In May 1845, two months after Polk's inauguration, news of the December 1844 revolt in Los Angeles against Governor Manuel Micheltorena reached Washington. The revolt illustrated the federalist-centralist struggle that characterized Mexican politics at the time and permitted the rebels to proclaim an independent California for a brief period. It was of little consequence to the Americans residing in California, however; they continued to pursue their usual activities. But news of the revolt set off alarm bells among the U.S. press, public, and administration. Expansionist editors of the *New York Sun*, *New York Herald*, and *Washington Union* worried about the welfare of the American residents and demanded that the Polk administration take steps to ensure their safety. Furthermore, the press speculated that an independent California would be so weak that it would invite a British or French takeover.

In particular, the Americans were concerned about any British designs on San Francisco. If England gained control of that port city, "she would be the mistress of the seas—not for a day but for all time," claimed the *American Review*.[13] Unaware of the lack of

British and French interest in acquiring California territory, the newspapers recommended the appointment of an aggressive U.S. consul to Monterey to offset the foreign influence. Polk shared that concern: "In reasserting Mr. Monroe's doctrine I had California and the fine bay of San Francisco as much in view as Oregon," he told an approving Senator Benton during a private conversation on October 24.[14] The public furor convinced the British and French ministers in Washington that the Americans would take California in the near future.

Polk understood the value of the California ports to American commerce, but his preoccupation with the Texas and Oregon questions prevented him from taking an aggressive stand at that moment. His instructions to Commodore John D. Sloat in June 1845 reflected his caution. Polk directed Sloat to take San Francisco and any other California ports that his forces could seize, but only upon learning with certainty that Mexico had attacked the United States.

In October 1845, with the Texas annexation complete, Polk's California policy took form. On October 11, Secretary of State James Buchanan received a dispatch from Larkin written three months earlier. Larkin asserted that he had definite information about a Mexican expedition en route from Acapulco, led by an unidentified European and financed by the Hudson's Bay Company, to impose centralized Mexican authority over the territory, and that the local British merchants would pay for the quartering of the troops. Although exaggerated, Larkin's message was in part confirmed by separate messages that arrived that same day from the U.S. diplomats in Mexico City, William S. Parrott and John A. Black. These communications addressed a purported proposal from California that sought federal status within the Mexican system, which also interested the British.[15]

Secretary of War William Marcy subsequently received a private letter from his friend Aaron Leggett, residing in California, who indicated that the European residents in the territory were planning a British guarantee of California's independence from Mexico with the promise never to join the United States. The four reports alarmed Buchanan and Polk, neither of whom knew that the Mexican expedition was not European-led and that it was about to collapse, that the Hudson's Bay Company had already decided to withdraw, and that the British vice-consuls were nothing more than listening posts for the London government.

Based on the information at hand and after consulting with his cabinet, on October 17 the president completed new instructions for Larkin, Sloat, and General Zachary Taylor. Larkin, who had been U.S. consul since May 1844, now became Polk's special agent and was ordered to avoid completely the struggle between Mexico and the Californians and only to advise Washington of the danger threatened by any European intrigue. Polk also determined that if the Californians won their independence from Mexico and made known their desire to join the Union, the U.S. government would move quickly. Clearly, the instructions reflected the Texas model. In an accompanying letter, Secretary Buchanan asked Larkin to exert his influence in thwarting any attempts made by foreigners to acquire control of California because it would deny the Americans residing there the "blessings of liberty."[16] Although Larkin's instructions did not anticipate war, Polk was nevertheless prepared. He had Navy Secretary Bancroft dispatch Commodore Robert F. Stockton, commander of the USS *Congress* stationed at Norfolk, to join Sloat, who remained under orders to seize the California ports in case of war with Mexico. Stockton, considered an expansionist, had played a major role in the protection afforded to Texas by Polk six months earlier when annexation hung in the balance.[17]

Next, Archibald H. Gillespie, a young marine lieutenant, was selected as the messenger to deliver the Polk and Buchanan messages to Larkin and Sloat. Disguised as a merchant by Bostonians, Gillespie was to cross the border at Veracruz, Mexico, rather than take the time-consuming cross-country trek or accompany Stockton on the high seas. Before Gillespie's departure, Polk spoke privately with Senator Benton, who apparently convinced the president to add his son-in-law to the list of the recipients of Gillespie's message. Gillespie came away from his meeting with Polk with the impression that Larkin was to persuade the Californians to declare their independence and voluntarily petition for annexation.[18] Most controversial were the instructions to Frémont, a record of which does not exist. Important for future consideration, however, is the fact that Frémont, who acted as a law unto himself, had not ingratiated himself with the Mexican authorities in California and often left the impression that he served as the U.S. government's expansionist agent.

Polk's instructions to Larkin, Sloat, and Frémont remain the subject of controversy. Polk clearly indicated that he was trying to place the United States in a strong position to deal with several contingencies: 1) continued nominal Mexican rule over California, 2) a local revolt for independence, or 3) war with Mexico or a European power. Secretary Bancroft later recalled that he and Polk did not anticipate war, but with the presence of any European warships in California waters U.S. forces needed to be on the alert, particularly if Mexico decided to seize San Francisco or any other port before the Europeans acted.[19] Despite the importance of Gillespie's mission, he did not depart for California until November 16 and did not arrive there until six months later. In the interim, the California issue virtually disappeared from public discussion as the Oregon and Texas questions moved front and center.

President Polk initiated his effort to purchase California with the dispatch of John Slidell to Mexico in November. For the New Mexico territory, Polk was willing to pay $5 million above the American claims for damages suffered in Texas at the hands of the Mexicans; if the settlement included San Francisco, $20 million; and $25 million if it included Monterey. [20] Significantly, he expressed interest only in the California ports, and only in San Francisco and Monterey. Polk's aspirations to purchase any part of California momentarily ended with Slidell's humiliating welcome upon his arrival in Mexico City in December. The acquisition of California had to await the peace treaty that officially ended the war with Mexico.

While Gillespie made his way to California across Mexican territory and Slidell squirmed in Mexico City, Frémont arrived in mid-December with about fifteen of his exploring party at Sutter's Fort, where he waited until late January 1846 for the remainder of his troops. In the meantime, Frémont received a temporary pass from Sutter, who served as the local magistrate, so that he could make several trips to the San Francisco area to purchase horses and other supplies and establish contact with Larkin. Frémont also informed the local Mexican authorities that once he was reunited with his full contingent, his exploratory trip would continue, but he did not indicate whether it would be north into Oregon or farther south in California.

In February, with his full contingent, Frémont moved south to the coast near Monterey. This unauthorized action raised the suspicions of the local authorities, who ordered Frémont to leave California at once or be arrested and forcibly expelled. Larkin, Polk's special agent, was as apprehensive about Frémont as were the locals, but he did not know whether the lieutenant was acting on his own or under government orders. Fearing a conflict in which the Americans would suffer, Larkin suggested to Frémont that he evacuate the area, which he did abruptly and without explanation on March 9. Frémont moved his men back to Sutter's Fort and then up the Sacramento River into Oregon.

As Frémont lingered in California over the winter of 1845–46, Lord Aberdeen, well aware of Polk's designs on the territory, made it clear within his government's circles that he had no intention of preparing for war with the United States over Oregon or Texas, much less California. Aberdeen did not reveal his decision to either the Americans or Mexicans, each of whom continued to operate under the assumption that the British would intervene, but it impacted significantly upon the Mexican government, which, without external assistance, could do nothing to preserve its distant territory.

During that same winter, California's political factionalism became most acute. In Los Angeles the residents selected a good-natured farmer, Pío Pico, to serve as the nominal governor after the overthrow of Micheltorena in December 1844, but Pico enjoyed little support in the north. There, local leaders such as José Castro, Juan Bautista Alvarado, and Mariano Vallejo had similar aspirations. Elsewhere in California the spirit of separatism from Mexico was rampant. Only the anticipation of a wave of new American immigrants prompted Pico in late April to call for a conclave of local authorities for June 15 at Santa Barbara. Pico also informed the British consul at Monterey that he intended to have the leaders declare California independent and to solicit British protection from the Americans. It did not matter that Pico and the consul were ignorant of British policy. The course of events would separate California from Mexico before the scheduled June 15 meeting.

~

In mid-April 1846, about the same time that Pico called for the Santa Barbara meeting, Gillespie arrived in California. He actually had reached Commodore Sloat's base at Mazatlán in February; but with no apparent reason for haste, Gillespie was in no hurry to depart for California. On April 17, Larkin learned of his new instructions to encourage the peaceful incorporation of California into the United States. In fact, he had already begun to move in that direction. Now, buoyed by Polk's instructions, the jubilant Larkin prepared a more accurate assessment of the local situation for Secretary Buchanan. This time, he did not exaggerate the British threat and placed greater emphasis on the weakness of the local leaders. He also drew up encyclopedic descriptions of the resources and principal residents of California. Ever anxious to alert Easterners to the territory's assets, Larkin undertook a letter-writing campaign to various New York newspapers. His effort only reenforced the Easterners' perception of California's riches.[21]

Larkin also sent letters to his merchant friends along the Pacific Coast, informing them about Polk's instructions, about Slidell's rejection in Mexico City, and about the arrival of Captain John B. Montgomery and the USS *Portsmouth* at Monterey. Larkin concluded that the only alternatives open to the residents of California were either a war for independence or better political terms from Mexico, something he deemed most unlikely. In fact, Larkin expected the American flag to be flying over California by July 4.

Others shared Larkin's opinion about the commercial importance of California. For example, in January 1846, New York's *American Review*, a Whig publication, described the agricultural potential of northern California, the attractiveness of San Francisco Bay, and the threat that either British or French occupation would bring to the United States. To impress readers with the sole importance of maritime interests, the essay cast southern California into the bin of geographical wastelands. And in reflecting the Manifest Destiny spirit of the time, it argued that for "California, to become the seat of wealth, and power for which Nature has marked it, [it] must pass into the hands of another race" (meaning the United States) because "it was the only republic of mark on the face of the Earth."[22]

As Larkin pursued his tasks, Gillespie caught up with Frémont near the California-Oregon border during the first week of May. He gave Frémont Polk's written and oral instructions along with letters from Frémont's wife and father-in-law, Senator Benton. The nature of what followed is open to debate, but definitely Gillespie and Frémont hastened south to Sutter's Fort where they camped among recent American arrivals. Stirred by unconfirmed reports about the outbreak of war between the United States and Mexico, along with rumors that the local officials planned to set the Indians upon the Americans in order to eliminate them, both the newcomers and Frémont's troops appeared anxious for action.

What Frémont did next remains obscure, but it was enough to touch off a revolt against the local authorities that began on June 10. Probably he intimated to the settlers that he had the support of the U.S. government, although he was not yet aware that Congress had declared war on Mexico. The Americans captured Sonoma, took Mariano Vallejo and others prisoner, and proclaimed the Bear Flag Republic, symbolized by a flag depicting the crude figure of a bear.

The movement spread to the San Francisco Bay area with Frémont in command. There he joined with Captain Montgomery, who moved the *Portsmouth* to San Francisco. By the end of June, Frémont's forces engaged in several minor skirmishes with local troops, resulting in a few casualties. Still, the rebels controlled much of northern California between San Francisco and Sacramento.

San Francisco, California, about 1845

Rumors of the Bear Flag movement spreading southward pre-cipitated the final engagement. On July 5, Sloat received word from Montgomery aboard the *Portsmouth* that Frémont and the Bear Flaggers had joined forces and that the Mexican officials might be planning a campaign to eliminate the American settlers. Montgom-ery, Sloat, and Larkin conferred on a course of action. Sloat averred that he would rather be criticized for taking action than sitting idle. Therefore, he and Larkin drew up a proclamation to the Califor-nians, declaring the province annexed to the United States as a con-sequence of the war and extending U.S. authority over them. On July 7, a detachment of 250 marines landed at Monterey, marched to the customshouse, and raised the American flag while the three warships fired a twenty-one-gun salute. A few days later, Montgomery repeated the same ceremony at the small settlement of San Francisco before an assembly of some thirty residents and a few dogs.[23]

Admirers of Frémont argue that the Bear Flag revolt saved California from the British until American regulars could use the war to justify a formal occupation. Consul Larkin, who was on friendly terms with both Castro and Vallejo, suspected that Frémont and Gillespie had conspired to prevent the peaceful incorporation of California into the Union. Thus, Larkin remained cool toward the Bear Flag Republic.

At first, the U.S. conquest of California went well. In August, Commodore Stockton, who had succeeded Sloat the preceding month, joined forces with Frémont and Gillespie and attacked Los Angeles. They wrested the capital from Pío Pico, but Gillespie's subsequent tactless administration led to continued fighting until the arrival of Colonel Stephen W. Kearny in December 1846. Kearny and Stockton retook Los Angeles on January 10, 1847, and three days later the local leaders submitted to American rule in the so-called Cahuenga Capitulation. According to this document the Californians surrendered their arms and promised to obey American laws and refrain from enlisting in the Mexican army. The Cahuenga Capitulation completed the U.S. conquest of California. What remained was its incorporation into the United States. Although that would come with the Treaty of Guadalupe-Hidalgo, Polk determined its acquisition seventeen days after the declaration of war against Mexico on May 13, 1846, when he announced to his cabinet that "the United States should be in possession of California at the time peace was made."[24]

Secretary Buchanan disagreed with Polk and his cabinet colleagues that all of California should be acquired. Earlier, as a senator, Buchanan had spoken about the value of ports on the West Coast, trade with China, and the constant threat of a British presence in California,[25] but in 1846 he feared that its acquisition as a prize of war would draw a response from the British and French. He also thought that the acquisition of all of California would cause sectional tensions at home. Therefore, Buchanan argued that only northern California, with its harbor at San Francisco, were necessary. Otherwise, Northern Whigs, the abolitionists, and the Calhoun faction would be antagonized sufficiently to block acquisition. As the war against Mexico progressed, Buchanan fell in line behind Polk in the demand for the entire territory.

The British observed the entire affair. When Sir George Seymour and his squadron arrived at Monterey in mid-July 1846, the American flag was firmly implanted. Seymour thought that the American seizure resulted from a war farther to the east but understood that he could offer no more than provisional occupation. He also concluded that the Bear Flag movement caused great resentment among the locals, and, with Washington a great distance away, California would soon become an independent state. Under these conditions, Seymour concluded that British control would be impossible without a large commitment of troops and loyal immigrants, neither of whom was on the horizon. Without British interests or honor at stake, Seymour departed for Hawaii a week after his arrival.

Meanwhile, in Washington, as Congress debated Polk's message for war with Mexico, the president met with his cabinet to discuss California. Polk told his advisers that he was not conducting the Mexican war "with a view to acquire either California or New Mexico," but that in any subsequent treaty he expected, "if practicable, [to] obtain California and any other portion of the Mexican territory as would be sufficient to indemnify our claimants on Mexico, and to defray the expenses of war."[26] Although the president initially focused on the ports at Monterey and San Francisco, his advisers and New England merchants constantly bombarded him with reminders about the value of Los Angeles and San Diego. As news of the American victories in California reached Washington in late summer 1846, Polk wrote his brother that the longer the Mexican war lasted, the greater the indemnity, and that would require additional territory. By December 1846, Secretary Buchanan was convinced that Polk would seek the annexation of New Mexico and all of California at the war's end in order to satisfy American claims.[27]

~

With Polk's election in November 1844 the British understood that American expansion westward was at hand, and it included California. They also understood American apprehension about foreign encroachment on the Pacific Coast, which the United States considered its own. The Americans were equally apprehensive. In the tense atmosphere of the 1840s it was difficult to convince most of them, including Polk, that the British did not covet the California ports. Furthermore, with strained relations over Texas, Oregon, and Maine, even the faintest rumor of a British move created a furor in official and nonofficial circles.

In California after 1840, the Monterey and San Francisco colonies existed as Mexican outposts over which the central government had negligible control or influence. News from Monterey reached Mexico City only twice per year. Government officials from Mexico City who were sent north found themselves treated as strangers and only bided their time while awaiting another assignment. Local revolts destroyed all but a slight semblance of civil government. These revolts, however, were not really efforts at independence but instead attempts by desperate men in search of power and the spoils of victory. After 1841 there was no functioning government in California and the *presidios* at Monterey and San Francisco lay in shambles. Travelers to the region agreed that San Francisco had drifted beyond the control of Mexico. The Frenchman Duflot de Mofras believed that the town could be taken by any nation willing to send a corvette and two hundred men, and the London *Times* asserted that conquering San Francisco would be as easy as taking a desert island. Indeed, most people believed that California eventually would pass to another nation. The question was, when and how would that happen?

For the United States, the American pioneers who poured over the mountains to the Pacific Coast in the 1840s, not President Polk's policy, proved to be the decisive factor. And as the U.S. press increased the public's awareness about California, Polk pursued a cautious agenda. Not until after the admission of Texas into the Union did the American people lose all respect for Mexican territorial integrity and Polk launch his drive for the California coast. Still, events in the territory, to which American military commanders were linked, provided for California's independence but not its annexation to the United States. That step awaited the outcome of the war with Mexico.

Notes

1. Quaife, *Diary*, 1:71.
2. For a discussion of President Andrew Jackson's efforts regarding California see Manning, *Diplomatic Correspondence, IAA,* 8:1–77, 239–40, 180–81, 202–6, and 216–18.
3. Quoted in Remini, *Jackson*, 494.
4. Graebner, *Manifest Destiny*, 36.
5. Pletcher, *Diplomacy of Annexation*, 98.
6. Hubert Howe Bancroft, *History of California*, 7 vols. (San Francisco: The History Company, 1886–1890), 4:295.

7. Richardson, *Messages and Papers*, 5:1892.

8. Manning, *Diplomatic Correspondence, IAA*, 8:483–85.

9. John C. Frémont, *Report of the Exploration to the Rocky Mountains in the Year 1842 and to Oregon and North California in the Years 1843–1844* (Washington, DC: Gales and Seaton, 1845).

10. Remini, *Jackson*, 494.

11. Quoted in Norman A. Graebner, "American Interest in California, 1845," *Pacific Historical Review* 2:1 (February 1953): 16.

12. McCormac, *Political Biography*, 351.

13. Quoted in Graebner, *Empire on the Pacific*, 88.

14. Quaife, *Diary*, 1:71.

15. Manning, *Diplomatic Correspondence, IAA*, 8:169–70 and 733–36.

16. Quaife, *Diary*, 1:169–71.

17. For Buchanan's instructions to Larkin see Moore, *Works of Buchanan*, 6:275–77. For Bancroft's instructions to Sloat see Edwin A. Sherman, *The Life of the Late Rear Admiral John Drake Sloat* (Oakland, CA: Caruth and Caruth, 1902), 51.

18. John A. Husey, "The Origins of the Gillespie Mission," *California Historical Society Quarterly* 19 (March 1940): 48–53.

19. Pletcher, *Diplomacy of Annexation*, 284.

20. Quaife, *Diary*, 1:33–35; Manning, *Diplomatic Correspondence, IAA*, 8:180–84.

21. Manning, *Diplomatic Correspondence, IAA*, 8:841–44.

22. Quoted in Graebner, *Manifest Destiny*, 144–52.

23. Given time and distance, Polk did not learn of California's independence until September 1, 1846, when dispatches from the British legation in Mexico City arrived at the legation in Washington, DC, and out of courtesy were delivered to Buchanan. Quaife, *Diary*, 2:107–8.

24. Quaife, *Diary*, 1:438.

25. Shomer S. Zwelling, *Expansion and Imperialism* (Chicago: University of Chicago Press, 1974), 25–29.

26. Quaife, *Diary*, 1:397.

27. Binder, *Buchanan*, 95–99.

5

Mr. Polk's War and Peace

Mexico has passed the boundary of the United States, has invaded our territory and shed American blood upon American soil . . . notwithstanding all our efforts to avoid it . . . we are called upon by every consideration of duty and patriotism to vindicate with decision the honor, the rights, and the interests of our country.
—James K. Polk, May 11, 1846[1]

President Polk placed responsibility for the outbreak of war with Mexico in 1846 squarely on the Mexicans. He argued that his diplomatic efforts since coming to office in March 1845 were aimed at bringing a rightful settlement to the issues that separated the governments in Washington and Mexico City. According to Polk, the Mexicans rebuffed his every effort to seek accommodation—an accommodation that satisfied U.S. expansionist interests. But did Polk understand that Mexican nationalism militated against the loss of territory, no matter how little control the government at Mexico City might hold over those distant lands? By design or accident, did Polk back the Mexicans into a corner from which they could do nothing but attack?

Three contentious issues characterized U.S.-Mexican relations when Polk assumed the presidency: 1) the Texas boundary; 2) claims by U.S. citizens against the Mexican government; and 3) the status of California. Of the three, the Texas problem proved to be the most important, and within a year it would bring the United States and Mexico to the brink of war.

Shortly after moving into the White House, Polk pledged that the Texas Republic's boundary claims to the Rio Grande would be upheld and that an invading army would not be permitted to occupy any territory east of the river. Following Texas's legislative approval of annexation to the United States in June 1845, Polk demonstrated his determination to defend that boundary by ordering General Zachary Taylor to move his troops from Louisiana into Texas and directed additional naval forces into the Gulf Coast region.

Although Polk appeared clear and resolute about the location of the Texas border, he was vague about where the U.S. Army might go. He did not specify a place for Taylor to encamp. Only after Polk's special agent to Texas, Andrew Jackson Donelson, caved in to local pressure did the president direct Taylor to station his troops at San Antonio and Corpus Christi, the latter adjacent to the Nueces River. Although Taylor also was told to move as close to the Rio Grande as prudence dictated, at the moment the general refused to budge from Corpus Christi. He took Donelson's advice that it was "better for us to await the attack than incur the risk of embarrassing the question of annexation with . . . the immediate possession of the Territory to the Rio Grande."[2]

In response to rumors that Mexican forces were marching toward the Rio Grande, the president emboldened the U.S. position in August by reinforcing the general's contingent. As a result of the rumors, Taylor was informed that Washington considered any Mexican crossing of the Rio Grande an act of war. Subsequently, the general learned that Polk considered even a Mexican attempt to cross the river an act of war.[3] For Polk and some members of his cabinet, Taylor's presence at the Nueces River meant that the U.S. government supported and guaranteed Texas's claims to the land between the Nueces and the Rio Grande. Polk reasoned that this show of force would deter the Mexicans from acting. In effect, he engaged in a risky game of troop deployment that he claimed was intended to deter Mexican aggression, not invite it. For the moment his strategy worked.

The tension caused by the Texas boundary dispute was compounded by the refusal of Mexico City to make payments on the nearly $3 million in adjudicated claims by U.S. citizens against the Mexican government. Added to the mix of issues was the U.S. desire for ports in California, separated from Texas by a vast tract of land known generally as New Mexico. When Polk and the expansionists could not accept a gaping hole in the pattern of continental extension, New Mexico soon became a large piece of the Manifest Destiny puzzle. Eventually, Polk would justify acquisition of these lands as part payment for the claims of U.S. citizens. These issues, coupled with the apparent military stalemate along the Rio Grande in the early fall of 1845, did not deflect either the ambition of the expansionists to support the Texas boundary claim at the Rio Grande or their determination to acquire New Mexico and California. These issues seemed to make armed confrontation with Mexico inevitable, a perception strengthened by Polk's stance on behalf of expansionism. Against this backdrop the president followed a diplomatic path that the Mexicans could only view as arrogant and brazen as the stationing of U.S. troops in Texas.

Shortly after his inauguration in March 1845, Polk dispatched William S. Parrott to Mexico City in hopes of encouraging officials there to accept the inevitability and reality of Texas's annexation. Parrott arrived filled with optimism that Mexico would not only settle the Texas boundary issue but also sell New Mexico and California. He also understood that Polk was equally prepared to go to war to obtain his objectives. As the Mexican government deliberated Polk's offer, the U.S. consul general in Mexico City, John A. Black, made a goodwill gesture by ordering the American warships out of Veracruz.

Although Parrott remained in Mexico City for several months, he never grasped the depths of the nationalism or the significance of the federalist-centralist argument that contributed to the country's ongoing political instability. Instead, he sent optimistic reports about the Mexican political situation back to Washington. Because the Mexican government had never "seriously contemplated" war, Parrott was confident in late August that a U.S. commissioner would be "hailed with joy" and, with "comparative ease, settle over a breakfast" the issues that divided the two countries.[4] In addition to Parrott's dispatches, Polk received other encouraging words from Mexico. For example, one report indicated that General Mariano Arista, commander of the troops at the Rio Grande, proposed to settle the boundary dispute through negotiations. Another report, received by Navy Secretary George Bancroft, alleged that the Herrera government was becoming increasingly stable and that the public furor over Texas had subsided. And the British minister in Mexico City, Charles Bankhead, encouraged the Mexicans to accept the American offer to negotiate all outstanding issues between them.

At the time, however, the reality of Mexican politics belied the signals received in Washington. The administration of José Joaquín Herrera was beset by internal turmoil and isolated internationally. President Herrera governed over a nation where banditry and violence spread across the countryside and rumors abounded that the federalists were about to instigate a civil war. The French minister had left the country; and from London, Mexico's minister, Tomás Murphy, sent copies of newspapers that reported that Britain would not supply the foreign aid needed for the recovery of Texas.

President Herrera decided to go forward cautiously. Following deliberations with his advisers, he had Foreign Minister Manuel de la Peña y Peña inform Black that his government would receive a commissioner to settle the present dispute in a peaceful manner. The status of that envoy and the meaning of "present dispute" would prove to be important. To the Mexicans, the term "commissioner" was not synonymous with "minister," former legation secretary Benjamin E. Green informed the State Department. And the Mexicans interpreted the words "present dispute" to mean that discussions would be confined to the Texas problem.

Encouraged by the optimistic messages coming to Washington, on September 16, Polk and his cabinet opted to send a minister to Mexico City on the condition that the Mexicans agree to receive a diplomat with full powers to settle all outstanding issues between the two countries—Texas, U.S. claims, and the territory west of Texas to the Pacific. Regarding the diplomat's status, Polk claimed that Parrott failed to clearly define it, and he expected the next group of dispatches from Mexico City to clarify the issue in order "to guard against the danger of having our Minister rejected or not received by Mexico."[5] Apparently the clarification never came.

For the delicate mission to Mexico City, Polk selected John Slidell, a former Louisiana congressman who spoke fluent Spanish. It mattered little, for when Slidell departed for Mexico, he did so as envoy and minister plenipotentiary, not as the commissioner requested by the Mexicans. Slidell's task was made even more difficult when Polk assigned Parrott as secretary of the Mexico City legation, despite the fact that Peña y Peña had expressed his personal dislike for him. Slidell sensed the futility of the mission when he told Secretary of State James Buchanan that he did not expect a war with Mexico despite its blustering threats to the contrary; but at the same time, Slidell did not anticipate Herrera's negotiating away any territory, no matter what the price.

On November 10, with his cabinet's approval, Polk signed Slidell's instructions and issued him a private letter. The lengthy instructions did not mention the annexation of Texas, the major issue on the Mexican agenda. Instead, Polk addressed the intertwining issues that concerned the expansionists. He first gave a long recital of the American claims against the Mexican government, which had reached over $3.3 million in late 1843 and which he proposed to liquidate as part of a general boundary adjustment. Next, Polk defended the Rio Grande as Texas's legitimate boundary but acknowledged that it did not include the upper Rio Grande Valley or Santa Fe. Still, the cession of all of New Mexico would remove a trouble spot and source of Indian raids too remote for the Mexican government to control. As to California, Polk clearly stated that he would strive to prevent its cession to another foreign power such as Britain or France. In the end, Slidell was to offer to settle all debts and to pay $5 million for Mexico's recognition of the Rio Grande as the Texas boundary and the cession of New Mexico. Polk agreed to raise the payment to $20 million for the addition of northern California, including San Francisco and Monterey. He determined that money was no object, particularly for the acquisition of California, whose future would promise an infinite return on the investment. Polk and his cabinet deemed this offer a fair and generous one.[6]

In his private letter to Slidell, Polk emphasized his desire to annex New Mexico and California, and he urged Slidell to obtain an agreement before Congress adjourned in March. The president also hinted that war would follow if the differences between the two countries were not resolved peaceably. The United States would have no choice but to "take redress for the wrongs and injuries we have suffered into our own hands and I will call on Congress to provide the proper remedies," Polk informed Slidell.[7] The *Washington Union*, which echoed the administration's opinion, editorialized that if the Mexican government failed to negotiate, Congress would most likely declare war. Despite the threatening language, Polk wrote his brother that "there will be no war with Mexico."[8] Rather, he anticipated that the penniless and factionalized Herrera regime would capitulate to U.S. expansion, despite the weight of Mexican nationalism.

When Slidell arrived in Mexico City on December 6, he brought with him instructions to renew normal diplomatic relations under the assumption that the annexation of Texas was a fait accompli and that the Herrera government was prepared to negotiate away a further loss of the national territory. Instead, Slidell faced a rude awakening. Rumors about American troops marching on Matamoros set off a jingoistic response that gripped the Herrera government and the press alike. The Americans were described as miserable colonists, adventurers, and speculators. Despite near bankruptcy, the jingoism prompted War Minister Pedro María Anaya to press the congress to underwrite funds for military preparedness. Simultaneous with Slidell's arrival, the pamphlet *El amigo del pueblo* revealed the U.S. plan to acquire New Mexico and California and, in order to prevent such a loss, called for the overthrow of the Herrera government.[9] Unbeknown to Slidell and Herrera, such a change was on the horizon.

The atmosphere in Mexico City made Slidell's task an impossible one. Foreign Minister Peña y Peña hesitated to meet with Slidell because he was not expected until January and then only as a commissioner, not a full minister. Moreover, Peña y Peña's dislike for Parrott was so strong that he declared the new secretary persona non grata. Still, Peña y Peña did not want to cut off the possibility of a diplomatic solution to the Texas problem. Although unprepared to negotiate at the time of Slidell's arrival, Peña y Peña gained time by submitting Slidell's credentials to the Council of Government for consideration. The Council's response focused on Slidell's title and the scope of his instructions. As they had indicated earlier, the Mexicans were prepared to receive only a commissioner to discuss only the current dispute over Texas, not a full minister to discuss the sale of New Mexico and California. Thus, Peña y Peña asked Slidell to obtain new credentials, a new title, and the task of discussing solely the Texas issue that threatened hostilities between the two nations.

Peña y Peña's response angered Slidell, who in turn vented his frustration on Buchanan and Polk. To the secretary of state he wrote that only a hostile act by the United States would sway the corrupt and ignorant Mexican leaders into accepting reality. Privately to the president he asserted that a war would be the most realistic way to settle Mexican affairs despite his conviction that the promise of British aid had bolstered Mexico's resistance to the U.S. initiatives.[10] Obviously, Slidell was unaware of the fact that the British already had informed the Mexicans that no aid would be forthcoming. Over the next several months he failed to make any progress. In the meantime, events in Mexico and the United States overtook the possibility of any settlement.

In Mexico, the centralist-federalist political argument that had plagued the nation since its independence in 1821 was not fully appreciated by either Parrott or Slidell. The controversy intensified in the fall of 1845 as rumors circulated regarding the possible overthrow of the Herrera government. The president did not help his own cause in December 1845 with the distribution of a letter to the state governors informing them that despite the existence of a just cause for war against the United States over Texas, Mexico was in no position to prosecute one: it lacked the resources and the allies. Furthermore, he noted that Texas had no real value to Mexico unless Mexicans populated the territory, which was unlikely to happen. And finally, a war against the United States would advertise the national weakness and invite further American aggression.

Despite the validity of the argument, Herrera's letter caused many of the centralists to rally around General Mariano Paredes y Arrillaga, who wanted to reestablish monarchical rule, preferably by a member of the Spanish royal family. A monarch, Paredes reasoned, would bring order to the chaos, end the bickering among the political factions, and enable the Mexican government to confront the Americans with a greater degree of strength. Finally, on January 2, 1846, Paredes marched into Mexico City just as Herrera fled, but the change in leadership did not put an end to Mexico's political conflicts, nor did it improve relations with the United States. Rumors persisted in both Mexico and on the European continent that Britain and France supported the monarchy's restoration. The rumors reinforced Polk's belief that the British wanted to thwart any settlement of U.S.-Mexican problems. He failed to comprehend contemporary British politics as he tended to blame the London government for all that went wrong for him in Mexico.

Also contributing to the deterioration of Mexico's relations with the United States was Paredes's tendency to interpret the escalating tensions between Washington and London over Oregon to his own advantage. When copies of Polk's December 1845 Annual Message to Congress arrived in Mexico City a month later, it reinforced the Mexican belief in the probability of an Anglo-American war. That view became more entrenched during the winter of 1845–46 when neither Polk nor the U.S. press gave much attention to the ongoing Mexican crisis. Paredes hoped that an Anglo-American conflict over Oregon would save his nation from disaster. He also was encouraged to stay his course by the Spanish minister to Mexico City, Salvador Bermúdez de Castro, himself part of the monarchist plot. In addition, the jingoistic Mexican press continued to stir up nationalism and, in so doing, ignored the country's unpreparedness for war. These newspapers described the United States in unkind terms: a colossus with feet of clay, its prosperity dependent upon British trade rather than its republican government; and as a nation of immigrants, a country without a national identity or spirit.

In reality, the Oregon problem impacted adversely upon U.S.-Mexican relations over Texas. While the U.S. preoccupation with Oregon contributed to the Mexican resistance to negotiating over Texas, Paredes and his advisers misjudged Polk's determination regarding Oregon. The Mexicans were not aware of Polk's ability to separate the issues, which became evident during the second week of January 1846, when Polk learned of Slidell's cool reception in Mexico City. At that time the president was angered by Senator John C. Calhoun's push for a compromise on the Oregon question that led to the Senate's postponement of its debate over that territory. Coupled with the possibility of war with Britain over Oregon, wisdom should have dictated restraint in regard to Mexico. Not for Polk. He compartmentalized Oregon and Mexico into separate boxes and stressed the point to Buchanan in a cabinet meeting: "I told him there was no connection between the Oregon and Mexican questions."[11] He determined to press forward with Oregon while simultaneously dealing with the Mexican problem. At the same time, the Oregon issue diverted the American public's attention away from Texas. Not until the spring of 1846 did the public realize how close it stood to war with Mexico.

Regarding Mexico, Polk directed two new initiatives. On the diplomatic front he had Buchanan send new instructions to Slidell on January 28, 1846. The president now warned that if the Mexican government refused to see Slidell as minister, "then demand your passport . . . and return to the United States." And if that happened, Polk concluded that he had no choice but "to submit the whole case to Congress and call upon the nation to assert its just rights and avenge its injured honor."[12] On the military front, Polk directed Taylor to move from Corpus Christi to a position on the north bank of the Rio Grande near Matamoros. Should the Mexicans declare war or otherwise act in a hostile fashion, the president instructed Taylor to respond accordingly. These bold initiatives, Polk wrote his brother, were taken to strengthen the negotiating hand, not to provoke a conflict. He was convinced that President Paredes's blustering was solely "to enable himself to take power";[13] and, once confronted with a U.S. show of force, the Mexican chief executive would back down.

Before Slidell and Taylor received their new instructions, Alexander J. Atocha, a naturalized Spanish-American, a supporter of Santa Anna, and an ingratiating adventurer with a long record of speculation in Mexico, gave Polk another opportunity. He called upon the president on February 13 and 16 with Santa Anna's offer to grant the Americans a generous boundary, running from the Rio Grande to San Francisco Bay, in exchange for $30 million. To accomplish this feat, Santa Anna encouraged Polk to take aggressive steps that would rattle Paredes and prompt the elite and the Church hierarchy to invite Santa Anna back to Mexico. The ever-opportunistic Santa Anna misunderstood contemporary political dynamics. The Mexican aristocracy and Catholic Church officials, along with other reactionaries, remained committed to Paredes and, like him, were determined to resist any further American encroachments and abhorred the sale of peripheral lands.

While Polk dismissed Atocha as an unreliable person who "would betray any confidence reposed in him" when it was in his interest,[14] the president also misunderstood Mexican political dynamics. He dismissed Santa Anna's offer as a gambit destined to fail, but at the same time he shared Santa Anna's belief that Paredes could be cajoled into making concessions. In an attempt to sway Paredes, Polk proposed to withdraw Slidell from Mexico City to a U.S. naval ship in the Gulf of Mexico, but he failed to persuade his cabinet. In these deliberations, Secretary Buchanan argued that Slidell's absence from the Mexican capital would only hinder the flow of information and therefore hinder the decision-making process. Secretary Bancroft reported that the Paredes administration wanted a peaceful solution to all the issues, a view reinforced by Slidell's reports about the bankruptcy of the Mexican government and the continuing revolts in the countryside.[15] And, as always, there was Oregon. The British war preparations required the Polk administration to face the need for compromise. Unable to obtain the cabinet's approval, Polk abandoned this aggressive step.

Amid the political posturing in Mexico City and Washington, Slidell, on his own initiative, relocated to Jalapa, where he received new instructions in late February. With his title and purpose reaffirmed, he concluded that Mexico must now choose between peace and an open break with the United States. In delivering the message to the new foreign minister, Joaquín Castillo y Lanzas, Slidell demanded an answer within two weeks. Why not? Given the Mexican government's financial straits, the resignation of implacable Yankeephobe war minister Juan N. Almonte, the mere promise from the British of moral support, and ongoing strife in the countryside, Slidell confidently rationalized that Paredes had no choice but to capitulate to negotiations.

Other forces, however, were at work. To the Mexicans, General Taylor's move to the Rio Grande and the presence of U.S. naval ships offshore near Veracruz only reaffirmed American bellicosity. Minister Bermúdez de Castro, still hopeful for the monarchist plan and the possibility of arbitration by a friendly power, encouraged Castillo y Lanzas to delay his response. And from London, Tomás Murphy reported that because the British government did not want California in American hands, it would help the Mexicans once the Oregon question was settled.

These encouraging diplomatic reports reinforced Paredes's determination not to cave in to U.S. pressure. On March 12 his government repeated its refusal to receive Slidell as minister. Paredes also presented Slidell with a history of the Texas problem, fixing blame for the 1836 war for independence and U.S. annexation in 1844 upon the calculated intrigues of the government in Washington. And if war were to come, that too would be the responsibility of the United States.[16]

Not to be outdone, Slidell responded in kind, summarizing the long history of American claims against Mexico and the latter's failure to face reality. On Texas, he pointed to Jackson's neutrality in the 1830s, Mexico's inability to reconquer the territory, and its refusal to recognize the republic in 1845. If war ensued, it would be a function of Mexico's reluctance to negotiate and its decision to publicly insult the U.S. government.[17] Understanding the impossibility of his task, Slidell asked for his passport. Two weeks later, on March 31, he sailed from Veracruz to the United States.

Slidell was so focused on his mission's objectives that he misread the political scene. He erroneously blamed British Minister Bankhead for the continued rumors of a monarchist plot without mentioning the Spanish minister, Bermúdez de Castro. He was not sure if his final rebuff came because Paredes feared his political opponents or if he anticipated European aid. Slidell was not alone in misunderstanding Mexican politics. The American consuls at Mexico City and Veracruz continued to send Washington conflicting reports, including the observation that a substantial number of federalists favored negotiations with the United States.

With the diplomatic impasse, Paredes finally ordered General Pedro Ampudia to lead reinforcements northward, where General Taylor and his 4,000 men had settled on the north bank of the Rio Grande, near present-day Brownsville, Texas. Taylor also made contact with the naval reinforcements in the Gulf of Mexico and established a supply depot at the mouth of the Rio Grande at Point Isabel. At his main encampment, Taylor commenced the construction of a fort, knowing full well that the Mexicans had considered his incursion an act of war.

After his arrival in the area on April 12, General Ampudia demanded that Taylor and his troops retreat north to the Nueces River within twenty-four hours. Taylor refused, instead ordering the naval ships to blockade the mouth of the Rio Grande as a defensive measure, an act that could only be justified by a state of war. The stakes rose higher after General Mariano Arista replaced Ampudia. Skirmishes left casualties on both sides, and finally, on April 25, the Mexicans entrapped sixty-three of Taylor's men while on reconnaissance. Sixteen were killed, a few escaped, and the remainder were taken to Matamoros for imprisonment. Taylor reported to Washington the next day that "hostilities may now be considered as commenced."[18] He also called upon the governors of Texas and Louisiana to send him an additional 5,000 troops. Another ten days would pass before Taylor's report reached Washington.

~

As events unfolded along the disputed Texas-Mexican border, Polk remained optimistic about his peace initiatives and clung to the expectation that the Mexican officials would receive Slidell. At a cabinet meeting on March 28, and unaware that Slidell had already given up, the president shared his belief that Slidell would succeed and claimed that the only genuine obstacle might be the availability of money with which to pay the Mexican government. With the exception of Buchanan, the cabinet agreed with Polk's suggestion that $1 million most likely would persuade Paredes to negotiate the surrender of the Western territories. Although Buchanan thought it unlikely that Congress would provide such a sum, he joined his colleagues in approving the president's intention to confer with several senators about the likelihood of a special appropriation, using as a precedent Thomas Jefferson's 1806 request for a secret fund to facilitate the acquisition of West Florida.[19]

Polk immediately conferred with William Allen (D., Ohio) and Thomas Hart Benton (D., Mo.). The former pressed the president to meet with John C. Calhoun, a leading skeptic on Western expansion beyond Texas, and they met at the White House on March 30. Although Calhoun favored a quick treaty with Mexico, he did not commit himself to supporting a special appropriation. When he returned to the White House four days later, Calhoun advised Polk that the time was not right to seek such funding. Later the same day, Allen warned Polk that without Calhoun's support, the measure would not be well received in the Senate because tempers were already frayed over the Oregon issue. As a result, Polk postponed his plan for enticing the Mexican government to negotiate.

The situation became more bleak on the evenings of April 6 and 7, when the early March dispatches from Slidell and Black arrived at the White House to inform the president of Slidell's frustrations and the demand for his passport. Subsequently, the cabinet agreed with the president that should Slidell return home empty-handed, the administration had no choice but "to take the remedy for the injuries and wrongs suffered" by the Americans at the hands of the Mexicans.[20]

At that moment, Polk may have favored a declaration of war, but the enormity of such an action warranted caution and delay. Something of greater magnitude than Slidell's failed mission was needed to ask Congress for a war declaration. A Mexican attack upon Taylor would offer Polk such an opportunity, but it also had its risks. If the American troops were defeated in a major battle, it would strengthen the will of the antiexpansionists. Reports of a possible federalist revolt against the Paredes administration also influenced the president because he understood that the federalists favored negotiations with the United States. The prominence of the Oregon debates before Congress momentarily lessened the importance of other issues. Polk elected to wait, hoping for more recent and optimistic news from Mexico. During the wait, however, warfare broke out along the disputed border.

On April 16, Congress approved the resolution to terminate the joint occupation of Oregon. Polk correctly speculated that the British would now compromise on the situation in the Northwest and therefore free him to devote full attention to the growing crisis with Mexico. Still, Polk's advisers cautioned against any action until Slidell returned to Washington with a complete report. Beginning on May 6, however, events moved rapidly. On that day, Polk learned from Taylor that Mexican reinforcements had arrived just south of the Rio Grande and that he had blockaded the mouth of the river. On the next day the president received word from Louis McLane in London that the British were prepared to resume talks over Oregon, which reinforced Polk's determination to deal more firmly with Mexico. On May 8, Slidell returned to Washington and met with Polk and Buchanan at the White House. After Slidell reviewed circumstances in Mexico City, the three men agreed that the United

States had no alternative but "to take redress of the wrongs and injuries which we had so long borne from Mexico."[21] Polk concluded that it would only be a matter of time before he presented Congress with an appropriate message.

On Saturday, May 9, Polk passed the point of no return. That morning he reviewed the situation with his cabinet, and everyone agreed that if the Mexicans attacked Taylor, Polk immediately should send a war message to Congress. At the same meeting, the cabinet also agreed to assist the president in drafting the war message at its regularly scheduled meeting on the next Tuesday, attack or no attack. They would be denied the luxury of time. At 6 P.M. that evening, four hours after the cabinet adjourned, the adjutant general called at the White House with Taylor's April 26 dispatch reporting the Mexican attack upon his reconnaissance party. Polk immediately reconvened his cabinet, which agreed to send a war message to Congress on Monday. That evening a few congressmen who learned of Taylor's dispatch also called on Polk to express their support.[22] By Sunday morning, May 10, all of Washington knew of the attack, and Polk understood that he needed to have his war message ready the next day if he were to capitalize upon the public's indignation.

Polk and Navy Secretary Bancroft began drafting the message early Sunday morning; and after Polk took time out to attend church with his family, the two men were joined by Secretary of State Buchanan. Before they completed a draft that evening, a parade of congressmen visited the White House to offer advice and learn of Polk's decision. On Monday morning, May 11, the president revised the message one more time, and at noon he sent it to Congress.

In his message, Polk laid responsibility for war at Mexico's doorstep for its refusal to deal honorably with the American claims that "have been accumulating [for] a period of more than twenty years," which "inseparably blended itself with the question of [the Texas] boundary." Referring to the Slidell mission, Polk explained that two Mexican heads of state refused "the offer of peaceful adjustment of our difficulties." He justified Taylor's presence on the Rio Grande by explaining that with the annexation of Texas, the United States "recognized the country beyond the Nueces as a part of our territory" and the Rio Grande "as the southwestern boundary" of Texas. And because the Mexicans threatened Americans by sending troops along this "exposed frontier," Polk asserted that the United States had no choice but to protect Texas. Hence, Taylor was

sent on a defensive mission with clear instructions not to act unless the Mexicans attacked, which they did. Clearly, the president
asserted, the Mexicans "invaded our territory and shed American
blood upon the American soil."[23] Because a state of war already
existed, Polk asked Congress to recognize its existence and to appropriate a large sum of money for its prosecution.

Polk anticipated some furor in response to the message, but
little came from the House of Representatives, and then only from
a small group of abolitionist Whigs led by John Quincy Adams,
who described the war as "unrighteous" and called for "the unilat-
eral withdrawal of American forces from Mexico."[24] Garret Davis
(Whig, Ky.) angrily charged that "it is our own President who began this war" by sending Taylor to the Rio Grande. The opposition
did not prevail. Instead, the House Military Affairs Committee put
forth its proposal calling for a $10-million appropriation for the
necessary 50,000 volunteers who would be called up to defend the
nation. Jacob Brinkerhoff (D., Ohio) called for a quick and complete victory and inserted into the military appropriations bill a
statement echoing Polk's assertion that war already existed by an
act of Mexico. After minimal debate, the administration's supporters pushed through the war declaration with the Brinkerhoff preamble by a 174-to-14 vote.

The Senate greeted the war message with greater resistance.
While there was strong sentiment among both Democrats and
Whigs to reinforce Taylor's contingent, several senators challenged
the president on different fronts. Benton and Calhoun, for example,
criticized Polk for sending Taylor to the Rio Grande where he faced
immediate danger. John M. Clayton (Whig, Del.) repeated Garret
Davis's assertion in the House that by sending Taylor to the Rio
Grande, Polk actually provoked war without consulting Congress.
Calhoun addressed the broader question of constitutional authority. According to him, the president had constitutional authority to
defend the country militarily but not to conduct offensive military
actions, which required congressional approval. "Only Congress
could declare war," Calhoun asserted; and then he asked, had Taylor conducted defensive or offensive military operations? While the
debate raged, Calhoun suggested the immediate sending of reinforcements to Taylor while other congressmen wanted a debate over
defensive and offensive military measures.[25] Kentucky's Senator John Crittenden put together the Whig case with some thought-
ful questions. Mexicans had shed American blood, to be sure, but
on whose soil and under what circumstances? And if the Mexicans

believed that the U.S. government had insulted them, why not in-
tensify the diplomatic effort rather than abandon it? [26]

In the face of the Calhoun-led opposition, Polk needed to retain the loyalty of the Democratic senators. Influential expansionist
senators such as Allen, Lewis Cass, and Sam Houston immediately
sprang to the president's defense, but Benton's support was considered crucial. On that Monday evening, May 11, Benton conferred
with Polk and Secretary of War William Marcy at the White House
in an attempt to ascertain the projected cost of the war in terms of
both money and men. The president did not give a firm answer,
instead preferring that the Senate accept the House bill that recognized the existence of war. Benton, who believed that the House
had acted too quickly, left the White House in a frustrated and de-
fiant mood and for the moment refused to commit himself to Polk's
course of action. Benton was willing to support a defensive war
but in this instance "did not think that the United States territory
extended beyond the Nueces."[27] Throughout the remainder of the
evening, Polk engaged other Democratic senators at the White
House, and they came away more supportive of his position. On
Tuesday morning, Frank Blair, a veteran Jacksonian, informed
Benton that he had best conform to the party's wishes or find his
political career in ruins. Benton yielded and convened his Military
Affairs Committee, which subsequently reported that it would support the House war bill. Allen's Foreign Affairs Committee did the
same.

Shortly after noon on Tuesday, May 12, the full Senate began
its debate on the war measure, but it quickly degenerated into one
of charges and countercharges about loyalty to the nation, Polk's
policy, and his interpretation of events. Finally, amid flared tempers, the war bill passed by a majority of 40 to 2. This apparently
widespread support in Congress for war with Mexico was a mis-
leading view of the decision's popularity. A healthy debate over
the president's message had not occurred. Rather, the Democrats
who controlled the House restricted the time of debate to two hours
and refused the Whigs' demand for additional time to study the
materials that Polk had submitted with his war message. Young
Illinois congressman Abraham Lincoln introduced the "spot resolutions," which challenged the president to show the exact spot
where American blood had stained American soil. Others bitterly
called it Mr. Polk's War.

Much of the war's unpopularity was attributable to the question of extending slavery into any of the territories that the United

States might acquire as a result. Polk rejected that argument and, instead, emphasized that the war's origin had not concerned slavery; he asserted that it had become an issue only because of the actions of his sinister and wicked domestic opponents. The debate centered on the attempt by antislavery groups to pass the so-called Wilmot Proviso. House Democrat David Wilmot of Pennsylvania sought to bar slavery from any areas taken from Mexico and affixed the measure as a rider to the war appropriations bill of August 1846. Northern support was not sufficient to override the opposition of Southern Whigs and Polk Democrats, but it did not prevent Wilmot and others from repeatedly introducing the proposal over the next few years. The Wilmot Proviso never passed Congress, but it caused heated debates over slavery and the preservation of the Union.

Insofar as public opinion could be measured, it reflected the diverse opinions found in Congress. While most Americans appeared stunned by the sudden clamor for war, a large number of patriotic expansionists demanded prompt, unquestioning support for the president and the endangered troops. On June 1, the day that Polk signed the war bill, a mass meeting of nearly twenty thousand people was held in Philadelphia to express their support for the president. The *New Orleans Commercial Bulletin* declared that the "United States [had] borne more insult, abuse, insolence and injury from Mexico . . . than one nation ever before endured from another." [28] Following the initial euphoria, a national sentiment in support of the war developed. Eventually, demonstrations, posters, and speakers spread throughout the Ohio Valley and across the South exhorting young men to enlist for the noble cause against the Mexicans. With the campaign came expressions of dislike for the contemptuous Mexican people. Others blasted the British for allegedly standing behind the Mexicans and encouraging them to refuse legitimate American demands.

Similarly, war opponents presented a variety of arguments. Both Whigs and Democrats, especially in the Northeast, warned that Polk had exploited national patriotism to conduct a war of conquest designed to obtain more slave territory. Renowned writer and abolitionist Ralph Waldo Emerson of Massachusetts warned that "because the cotton thread holds the union together," war with Mexico would raise the issue of slavery to such heights that it would result in the destruction of the Union. Other antislavery spokesmen such as Joshua Giddings of Ohio lamented that Polk had violated every principle of international law and moral justice in provoking the war. Pacifists grumbled that the path to America's greatness lay in peaceful expansion, not in war, while commercial journals fretted over the decline in New Orleans and Gulf Coast trade during the months leading up to the conflict. Calhoun fretted that Polk's actions on the Rio Grande might squelch the opportunity for obtaining Oregon and bring England and France into the war on Mexico's side. The *Niles Register* viewed Polk's strong-arm methods toward Congress as "a distortion of the Constitution."[29] The Whigs were especially uneasy, aware that opposition to the War of 1812 had dealt a death blow to the Federalist Party. At the same time the Whigs were dismayed to see their arguments for a strong national government and president snatched away by a Democrat.

The Whigs were not alone in their criticism of Polk's method. Senator Benton, a Democrat, accused the president and his advisers of intriguing for war. "Never have the men at the head of government . . . [been] more addicted to intrigue," he asserted. While they professed to be "men of peace," they saw "war as a necessity" to achieve their purposes. "They wanted a small war, just large enough to require a treaty of peace," Benton concluded.[30]

Polk, then, had obtained his war bill under the pretense of public enthusiasm and by use of coercive tactics that exploited partisan loyalty and Whig patriotism. Its passage did not put an end to discussion in Congress, for on the day that the Senate approved the bill, a debate in the House on the annual appropriation for West Point degenerated into an argument over the Rio Grande boundary. During the following weeks, opposition to the war entered into several congressional discussions on other topics. Polk had his war; now, it was up to him to win his goals before the mercurial public turned against him.

Although the outbreak of war produced an immediate groundswell of popular support across the United States, the nation was ill prepared for the challenge before it. Most of its 10,000-man army lacked battlefield experience and were in small units scattered at remote outposts along the Western frontier. Equally unprepared was the nation's fledgling industrial base and infrastructure; neither had been designed with a frontier ground war in mind. Despite the state of national unpreparedness and the administration's haste to overcome it, the president understood the need to wage a vigorous war to a speedy conclusion. Political considerations dictated a short, not a prolonged, conflict. The situation demanded strong leadership, and President Polk proved equal to the challenge despite the fact that nothing in his political career had prepared him for the task.

The administration's first challenge focused on a military strategy. Within two weeks of the declaration of war the cabinet approved Polk's plan for a two-pronged attack against Mexico at two vital points: Santa Fe, New Mexico, in the Southwest, and Mexico's northern provinces below the Rio Grande. At the end of May, Polk added a third objective: the sending of an expeditionary force to seize California. In addition, the president ordered the U.S. warships already stationed off the coast of Mexico to blockade Veracruz and other principal ports. Once these objectives were secured, Polk expressed confidence that the Mexican government would sue for peace. In fact, he did not expect the war to last more than 90 to 120 days.[31] His lively interest in the conduct of the war continued to produce plans and strategies, but there were no important deviations from the original concept set down in mid-May 1846 until the decision in the fall of 1846 to launch an expedition at Veracruz.

As the president developed his war strategy, Secretary Marcy prepared the army to fight a war on foreign soil. He directed the infrastructure needed to provide the army with logistical support. In a short time, factories worked around the clock to manufacture the instruments of war. At the same time, a sense of national duty, if not adventure, prompted an estimated 200,000 men to respond to Secretary Marcy's call for 50,000 volunteers to meet the anticipated needs of the army. So many men attempted to enlist in Tennessee that the selection had to be made by lottery. The quotas of some states were filled so quickly that young men moved to neighboring states to enlist.

General Taylor's military successes along the Mexican frontier contributed to the popular support for Polk in May and June 1846. Fighting along the Rio Grande intensified immediately after the outbreak of war, where, although heavily outnumbered, Taylor had the advantage of better training, weaponry, and supplies over the Mexican army commanded by General Mariano Arista. In particular, artillery proved to be significant as the Mexican ranks were pounded with high-explosive shells. Taylor's troops occupied Matamoros on May 18, but the general did not advance because he awaited reinforcements, supplies, and clear directives from Washington. In the meantime, opposition to the war in the United States intensified.

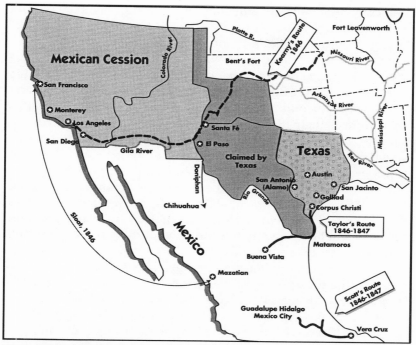

Major campaigns of the Mexican War, 1846–47

The popular euphoria on behalf of the war effort faded for several reasons. As the public learned of the living conditions endured by the volunteers at the Texas staging camp near Camargo, the administration came under attack for unpreparedness. Due to the mass influx of soldiers, the camp was quickly overrun by filth and disease, made increasingly unbearable by Texas's blistering summer heat. Another source of political discontent followed the passage in July of the war appropriations bill, which provided that the organization of volunteers into battalions and regiments be done by the states but that the leadership of the brigades and divisions be completed by the federal government. Within days, congressmen swarmed to the White House seeking commissions as brigade and division commanders for themselves and their constituents. "The pressure for appointments . . . is beyond anything I have witnessed since I have been President," Polk recorded in his diary.[32] His strong partisan feelings prompted him to fill many of these requests with loyal Democrats, despite the promise of equal treatment for the Whigs. Of course, when the Whigs received assignments, the

Democrats became disgruntled; and as a result, members of both parties questioned Polk's policy.

The president faced a greater problem at the national level, where the army's officer corps was dominated by Whigs, including the top-ranking officer, General Winfield Scott. As ardent a Whig as Polk was a Democrat, Scott gave indications of his political ambitions before the outbreak of war, and many of his party's leaders viewed him as their 1848 presidential nominee. Polk had no desire to enhance Scott's image and hence his political career, but he felt obliged to offer him the command because of his rank. Polk disliked Scott from the start, and the relationship between the strong-willed president and his general quickly deteriorated. On May 13, the day of Scott's appointment, Polk confided to his diary: "Though I did not consider him in all respects suited for such an important command, yet being commander-in-chief of the army, his position entitled him to it if he desired it."[33]

Following a strategy meeting the next day between Polk, Marcy, and Scott, the president described his commanding general as too visionary. A week later, Polk became highly incensed over a minor matter concerning a Captain Hutter, who wanted an appointment that Scott refused. The oversensitive Polk interpreted the affair as an indication of the general's hostility toward the appointment of Democrats and found Scott "recklessly vindictive in his feelings toward the administration" and personally "disrespectful . . . to the President."[34] Polk immediately informed Marcy that he had no confidence in Scott's willingness to carry out the administration's plans and views, and he lamented that he was being compelled to wage a war with Scott as overall commander. Polk, who always insisted on unquestioning obedience from his subordinates, complained that Scott sought to block pending legislation before Congress that called for the appointment of two additional generals to the army. The bill passed, but the Whigs managed to reduce the number to one major general and two brigadiers. The bill infuriated Secretary Marcy, who charged that he was fighting two fires: one against the Mexicans, the other in Washington.

Scott was equally offended by the president's demand that he move up the timetable for initiating the campaign against Mexico. Whereas Polk wanted prompt action, Scott wanted to wait until September when the troops would be better organized and trained and the war matériel in place. Scott, however, paid a high price. At a special meeting called by Polk on May 25, the cabinet reached a decision to relieve Scott of his role as field commander. Instead, he would coordinate the war from a desk in Washington. Not even a profuse written apology from Scott persuaded Polk to change his mind. The president turned to Zachary Taylor as Scott's replacement.

As the war strategy took shape during late May and early June, Polk also faced questions about his territorial objectives. *Washington Union* editor Thomas Ritchie, a good friend of the president, may have exaggerated the administration's goal when he wrote in late May that "we shall invade her [Mexico's] territory, we shall seize her strongholds, we shall even take her capital," because Polk had yet to publicly explain his objectives.[35] At a special cabinet meeting on the evening of May 13, the same day that Polk signed the war declaration, Secretary Buchanan sought to determine the president's territorial aims. He presented a draft of a circular letter to U.S. ministers abroad that stated that the United States disavowed territorial ambitions beyond securing the Rio Grande as the Texas boundary.

The proposed letter ignited a heated discussion among Buchanan's colleagues and drew a rebuke from Polk, who would not renounce any territorial ambitions. "We had not gone to war for conquest," Polk told his cabinet, "yet it was clear that in making the peace we would . . . obtain California and such other portion of the Mexican territory as would be sufficient to indemnify our claimants on Mexico . . . [because] the Mexican government had no other means of indemnifying us."[36] The president drafted a substitute letter that left no doubt about his war aims, particularly in the West. He intended for New Mexico and California to become part of the United States. But Polk made it clear that he could not publicize his territorial ambitions because they might stir up public opposition at home and encourage foreign nations to provide aid and comfort to Mexico. The president's outburst, however, did not stop Buchanan from continuing to express his apprehension about territorial annexations.

Congress also questioned Polk's territorial objectives. In July the president, for the second time, asked Congress for a special discretionary fund of $2 million to be used to facilitate negotiations with Mexico. Polk explained that he was not conducting a war of conquest, but at the same time he would not identify publicly the territories that he would demand as indemnification for American claims and war costs. Thus, the so-called Two Million Dollar Bill referred only to the boundary adjustment between the two countries, although there was little doubt in the minds of many observers that Polk intended the money for the acquisition of California and New Mexico.

In the House of Representatives, Whig and Democratic congressmen who thought that they had been stampeded into approving the declaration of war used the Two Million Dollar Bill as an opportunity to renew the debate on the administration's aims. Northern Whigs charged that the bill was designed to promote the extension of slavery. As mentioned earlier, the accusation prompted Pennsylvania's David Wilmot to propose the prohibition of slavery into any territory acquired from Mexico. His proposal struck a responsive chord not only among Northeasterners but also among those representing fledgling industries and small farms concerned about the political implications of adding slave states. These groups combined to add Wilmot's proviso to the Two Million Dollar Bill.

Although many of Wilmot's followers were motivated by concerns over the extension of slavery, Wilmot himself still smarted from the party's denial of the 1844 presidential nomination to his idol, Martin Van Buren, and from the belief that Polk had played an important part in that denial. Wilmot also opposed the administration's tariff proposal and its refusal to fund many internal improvements. In addition, he was angered by Polk's willingness to compromise on Oregon, but not Texas, a sure sign of sectional politics. Whatever his reasons, Wilmot's proviso drove a wedge between the Free Soil and proslavery wings of the Democratic Party, threatening not only Polk's territorial ambitions but also the Union itself. Subsequently, the Two Million Dollar Bill passed the House by a 87-to-64 margin, with Wilmot's proposal attached, but a Southern filibuster prevented it from coming to a vote in the Senate before the session ended.

Polk expressed great disappointment at Congress's rebuff of the Two Million Dollar Bill, and he was equally perplexed by the Wilmot Proviso. To Polk, who, as we know, compartmentalized issues, there was no connection between slavery and making peace with Mexico. Polk's failure to make that connection encouraged his congressional opponents. Henceforth, they used the Wilmot Proviso to wage an unrelenting war against the beleaguered president and expanded their arguments beyond the slave issue to include assertions that the Mexican War was unconstitutional, corrupt, and, in fact, immoral.

If Polk initially misjudged the extent of domestic opposition, he also underestimated the determination of the Mexican leadership to resist American aggression. The military plan that Marcy and Scott had devised brought immediate success. By early July, Taylor had secured northern Mexico, Frémont and Sloat had over-run Monterey and San Francisco, and Kearny faced little opposition as he approached Santa Fe. These quick victories revealed Mexico's weaknesses. Lacking even the rudiments of an industrial base, the Mexican government could not supply its own army; in fact, most of its weaponry was outdated and in disrepair. The army itself reflected the nation's political instability and deep racial divisions. The officer class consisted largely of professional soldiers from the ruling elite and from Europe while the rank and file was composed of irregularly paid and poorly fed peons, many of them Indians and *mestizos* who spoke little or no Spanish. The government for years had resorted to impressment to staff its garrisons, but they were plagued by high rates of desertion. Polk saw only the shortcomings but failed to perceive that nationalism would defy the military reality. The presence of American troops on its home soil increased Mexico's determination to resist.

Given the military successes along the Rio Grande and in California, the Polk administration concluded that Mexico lacked the will to fight. On July 27, Polk sent a letter to Mexico City offering to initiate peace negotiations.[37] At the same time that he was willing to undermine that government, he decided to approach deposed Mexican leader Santa Anna, who was residing in Havana. Polk dispatched John Slidell's half-brother, Alexander Slidell Mackenzie, to Cuba to ascertain whether Santa Anna would negotiate peace with the United States and whether he could manage to assume the leadership of Mexico. Only six months earlier, Polk had distrusted Santa Anna when he approached the president through Alexander Atocha.

Once in Havana, Mackenzie committed to writing the three alleged goals of President Polk: 1) Santa Anna's restoration to power; 2) an insistence upon the Rio Grande as the Texas boundary; and 3) a willingness to pay handsomely for part of California. About a year and one-half later, Polk claimed that he had not sent any specific message to Santa Anna, particularly written instructions with Mackenzie. Polk argued that Mackenzie had exceeded his authority by composing the memorandum and presenting it to the Mexican general.[38] While the truth remains unknown, Santa Anna certainly professed peaceful intentions and some support for unidentified territorial cessions to the United States.

Mackenzie came away from Havana convinced that peace was at hand, as was President Polk after receiving his report. As previously arranged, Santa Anna passed through the U.S. naval blockade at Veracruz in early August and arrived in Mexico City on August 16. In the meantime, the volatile political situation in the capital resulted in the ouster of General Paredes and the installation of a provisional government headed by General José Mariano Salas, who quickly rejected Polk's July 27 offer to negotiate and instead welcomed Santa Anna's return from exile. As he had in the past, Santa Anna again reneged on his promises to the Americans. He proceeded to organize an army with which to launch a counteroffensive against the United States.

In response, Polk stiffened his resolve. If Mexico would not negotiate away unspecified territory, the United States would take it by force. Taylor was directed south from the Rio Grande to Monterrey, Mexico, where he arrived with his 6,000 troops on September 19. There he found the Army of the North, now under the command of General Ampudia, dug in and prepared to defend the town in a battle that began on September 21. Within three days the American and Mexican forces were fighting in the streets of Monterrey, and Ampudia asked to negotiate. Taylor initially demanded unconditional surrender but stepped back because his own troops' morale and discipline were poor after the three days of hard combat. Taylor therefore permitted Ampudia to leave Monterrey peacefully with some of his arms and equipment. Because of poor communications with their respective capitals, both generals agreed to an eight-week armistice, with the stipulation that it could be rescinded if either government later found its terms unsatisfactory.

Although Taylor became a national hero and his successes prompted two biographies by the year's end, relations between the general and the president spiraled downward. Polk charged that Taylor had grievously erred when he allowed Ampudia to retreat— a move that gave the Mexicans the opportunity to regroup and make another stand. Polk instructed Taylor to terminate the armistice immediately, but "under existing circumstances . . . [he] should not advance beyond Monterrey" for logistical reasons.[39] The relationship was further aggravated by Taylor's increased desire for greater rewards at a time when he was being touted by the Whigs as a possible presidential candidate in 1848. Having sidelined one Whig general to keep him from making political capital from the war, Polk now found to his dismay that he had created another one.

In the prosecution of the Monterrey campaign, Polk also tried to woo the residents of northern Mexico to the American cause. For example, Taylor was instructed to pay for all supplies requisitioned by his army at a fair market price, Catholic priests were employed to assure the locals that their customs and beliefs would not be attacked, and propaganda was aimed at the region's long-standing distaste for the central government at Mexico City, but all these efforts failed. The American troops, particularly the Texan volunteers who sought revenge for the death of their colleagues at the hands of other Mexican armies, plundered the villages and committed atrocities. Taylor was disinclined to deal with the separatists, and the racial attitudes of the American troops overshadowed the administration's goodwill gestures.

~

Despite the impressive victories during the first six months of the war, the Mexican government did not come to the bargaining table as Polk had anticipated. Instead, its recalcitrance fanned the opposition's flames across the United States. Whigs intensified their criticism of Polk's leadership, but cognizant of the Federalists' experience during the War of 1812, they did not question the right to conduct a war against Mexico. The Whigs had to tread very carefully or risk being characterized as friends of the enemy. Members of the party were uncomfortable voting for troops, weapons, and supplies while at the same time protesting against the war effort. They were also caught by disagreements among themselves over the proper course of action to take regarding the war itself. Because the Whigs did not control either chamber of Congress until its thirtieth session, their role became essentially one of delaying, stalling, criticizing, and hampering the administration whenever possible. Beyond that, the Whigs did little to stop the war effort or the administration's march toward its territorial goals. The Whigs' more extreme element staked out a strong antiwar position, usually coupling it with an antislavery position.

Special interest groups within the Democratic Party also militated against Polk's war policies. Many Southerners followed John C. Calhoun, whose expansionist goals had been satisfied with the acquisition of Texas. This group opposed further territorial conquests. Van Burenites, such as Pennsylvanian David Wilmot, argued that Polk had sold out to Southern interests. Irritated by the Wilmot Proviso, Polk at the time, however, failed to see its wider ramifications, but neither did many other politicians of that day. As the slave issue received increased attention, it contributed to the nation's widening sectional divisiveness.

Because of his leadership position, Calhoun's activities received greater attention. In December 1846 he conferred with Polk at the White House. Although both men agreed that the Western territories were unfit for slavery, Calhoun adamantly opposed government restrictions placed upon its expansion into that region, arguing that the future residents should determine the issue. He also opposed the anticipated invasion of Mexico at Veracruz, believing that it would be too costly and possibly lead to an interminable conflict. Instead, he proposed a string of American military posts in Mexico to ensure indemnification.[40] On a personal level, Calhoun, piqued at Polk's desire to create a new lieutenant generalship earmarked for Thomas Hart Benton, could not tolerate advancing the Missouri senator's career. Already at odds over Calhoun's position on Oregon, the two men parted ways in January 1847, when Polk requested congressional support for ten new regiments. Fearing that the president embraced the current "All-Mexico Movement," Calhoun introduced Senate resolutions against the conquest and annexation of Mexico. Until the arrival of the peace treaty in 1848, the South Carolinian remained an outspoken critic of the president.

Outside Washington, Polk confronted widespread opposition, particularly in the Northeast, where Whig newspapers and journals kept up a relentless attack on the administration. Their motives were transparent as they found no merit in Polk's actions while taking special care to praise the military genius of Taylor and Scott. The Whig press, like its political brethren, had to temper its strong stance against the war, since most readers fully supported it as a natural by-product of Manifest Destiny. Still, in October 1847 the *American Review* charged that "a civilized and Christian people regard an unnecessary war, in the middle of the nineteenth century, a spectacle of backsliding and crime over which angels may weep."[41]

Other groups, such as the New England abolitionists, found ample reasons to protest the war. Some extremists even wished for the success of the Mexican troops. As could be expected, members of the pacifist movement raised their objections to the war, although division crept into their ranks. One group, led by George Beckwith, opposed it because it was not defensive in nature; another, under the leadership of Elihu Burritt, radically opposed all war. Thomas Corwin demanded: Why should the "mothers of America . . . [be] asked to send another of their sons to blow out the brains of Mexicans" to meet the U.S. demand for indemnity?[42] Closely allied with the abolitionists and the pacifists were the clergy in the Northeast's

Unitarian, Congregational, and Quaker churches, but elsewhere religious dissent against the war was virtually nonexistent. In fact, in the South and West, the clergy offered support. Despite their opposition, these groups shared the concern that Great Britain might come to Mexico's rescue. In the end, however, the opposition groups had little impact because they failed to overcome the public enthusiasm for the war and because they failed to offer alternatives to Polk's policies.

If the war protesters did not shake the administration's confidence, the November 1846 congressional elections did. In sixteen state contests in the North and Midwest, the Whigs gained more than two dozen seats. While the war itself was not an election issue, the perception that it was being fought to extend slavery westward militated against the Democrats. Equally important to the voters were local concerns and other issues, such as the Walker Tariff and the independent Treasury system. In sum, the recent battlefield victories did not translate into political gains for the Democrats.

~

Confronted with a military stalemate, a contentious Congress, and public opposition, Polk discussed with his cabinet the possibility of opening a second front on October 10, 1846, the day before news of General Taylor's victory at Monterrey reached the White House. But Taylor's refusal to force the unconditional surrender of the Army of the North gave new meaning to the plan. Polk sought input from the former U.S. consul at Veracruz, F. M. Dimond, whose detailed analysis and suggested strategy encouraged the president. With the Democratic losses in the November election, Polk understood that he could not wait much longer for the Mexicans to come to the bargaining table. Only an aggressive attack to the interior, Polk reasoned, would force them to accept defeat.

Throughout November, Polk sought a wide range of opinions, after which he and his cabinet concluded that sending Taylor south through the arid land of Mexico's high plateau presented immense logistical problems. A second front westward from Veracruz also was very risky. To date, the American troops had fought in only sparsely populated areas, but an attack on the Mexican capital and its population would meet greater resistance. Furthermore, the steamy lowlands in the Veracruz region harbored tropical diseases that would raise the fatality rate and, in turn, dampen troop morale. Marching westward from Veracruz into the mountains was another logistical nightmare. Despite the obstacles, on November 17 the cabinet agreed to the Veracruz operation. Polk remained cautious, knowing that if peace did not come after the capitulation of Veracruz, he was "in favor of taking Mexico City if we have sufficient force in the field to do it."[43]

Selecting a commander was another problem for Polk. By this time he had lost confidence in General Taylor for his failure to pursue the enemy aggressively. To send General Winfield Scott, his old nemesis with presidential ambitions, to battlefield victory would only serve to enhance those ambitions. "If I had the power to select a General I would select Col. Benton to conduct this expedition," Polk angrily told his cabinet, but he offered the position to Scott.[44] At a White House meeting on November 18, Scott was overcome with emotion as he accepted the command and pledged to work harmoniously with the president.

While plans went forward to equip the 10,000 troops whom Scott would take with him, Polk also decided to extend the olive branch to Mexico City. In an effort to bring closure to the crisis, the president undertook three diplomatic missions. Two ended in failure. The first effort came in March 1846 with the appointment of journalist and businessman Moses A. Beach as a special agent, who served with no specific instructions except to "collect and furnish useful information" to the administration, although he did confer on several occasions with Secretary Buchanan. At the time of his appointment, Polk noted that Beach might "misconstrue his authority . . . and it may be possible . . . that he will make a treaty with them." [45] Beach arrived in Veracruz in early January 1847 and, shortly thereafter, in Mexico City. After conferring with Consul Black, other Americans residing in the capital, and some Catholic Church officials, he informed Polk that the parameters of a peace treaty had been framed. Surprised by the news, Polk asserted that Beach had exceeded his authority. There matters stood until April, when Beach returned to Washington to collect $3,000 for his services.

Upon Beach's arrival in Mexico City in January, the wily *caudillo* Santa Anna entered the diplomatic equation for the third time within a year. His spokesman, Alexander J. Atocha, again came to Washington with Santa Anna's offer to conclude a peace agreement. Atocha met with Secretary Buchanan and Senator Benton, but not with Polk, who interpreted Atocha's mission as a sure sign that the Mexicans wanted a settlement—one that would satisfy the Americans' appetite for the Texas boundary at the Rio Grande and the California Territory. With caution, Polk initiated his second diplomatic effort. The president agreed to send a peace delegation to Mexico with full power to negotiate an end to the war and a lifting of the blockade. When Atocha returned to Mexico City in late February, however, the political landscape had changed. Acting President Valentin Gómez Farías, representing those who opposed caving in to the United States, published Polk's response to Atocha in such a way as to make the U.S. demands unreasonable. Farías's refusal to negotiate convinced Polk that only Mexico's military defeat would resolve the crisis.

Landing of the troops at Veracruz, Mexico, in March 1847

In the meantime, Scott prepared his troops for the invasion of Veracruz, which they captured on March 19, seventeen days after landing. Scott's army then won hard-fought battles at Cerro Gordo and Puebla and was prepared for an assault on Mexico City, where he would face the major arm of the enemy army under Santa Anna. During the same month, Colonel Alexander W. Doniphan departed from Santa Fe, going down the Rio Grande to El Paso to occupy Chihuahua.

When Polk learned of Scott's victory at Veracruz on April 10, he anticipated Mexico's capitulation. Scott's success contributed to a sense of urgency within the administration to define its peace terms and dispatch a peace commissioner. This goal became Polk's third diplomatic effort. Over the next several days the cabinet hammered out the peace demands: the Rio Grande as the Texas boundary, and the cession of New Mexico and California. At the insistence of Treasury Secretary Robert Walker, the president agreed to the demand that American citizens receive transit rights across the Isthmus at Tehuantepec, but with the proviso that it not be an absolute necessity for the successful conclusion of a treaty. After haggling over compensation to Mexico for its lost territories, the cabinet authorized up to $30 million unless the negotiators agreed to a smaller amount.[46] For the mission the cabinet selected Nicholas Trist, Secretary Buchanan's chief clerk, who spoke fluent Spanish and who departed immediately in order to accompany Scott's army to Mexico City. Although Polk professed that he wanted the Trist mission kept secret from the public and the Whig press, he informed his friend Thomas Ritchie, the editor of the *Washington Union*, so that he could properly prepare the nation should success be forthcoming. Still, the details of the Trist mission first appeared in the *New York Herald*.

With illusions of grandeur, Trist arrived in Veracruz on May 6. Shortly thereafter, he and Scott were at odds; each man's huge ego was bolstered by a fierce independence. In particular, Scott felt betrayed by the president for sending a special emissary. Until July, when Scott reached out to Trist, they avoided each other to the point of not talking, instead penning lengthy letters of complaint to Washington. After July, a mutual respect and deep friendship developed resulting in a spirit of cooperation that Polk came to mistrust.

In August, Trist and Scott concluded that Santa Anna understood the futility of the Mexican military effort and decided to advance him $10,000 on a $1-million payment for the successful conclusion of a peace treaty. The wily Mexican general kept the money but did not respond to the peace overtures. This approach to Santa Anna so infuriated Polk that he used it as ammunition to seek Trist's and Scott's recall.[47] In the meantime, as the outraged Scott, who had marched toward the capital, prepared to assault the city on August 23, Santa Anna signaled that he wished to negotiate. A cease-fire was put in place to give Trist an opportunity to reach a settlement. When Santa Anna refused Trist's conditions for peace, Scott lifted the cease-fire and proceeded to storm Mexico City. On September 13, Scott's troops took the fortress at Chapultepec and on the next day seized control of the entire city.

Two days later, Santa Anna resigned and was replaced by a provisional government.

In part due to the distance between Polk in Washington and Scott and Trist in Mexico, the period between September and December 1847 produced awkward decisions on both fronts. In cabinet meetings on September 7 and 14, Polk expressed his displeasure with both Scott and Trist for failing to bring success on either the military or diplomatic front. In particular, he complained about Trist's willingness to sacrifice Lower California and to adjust the Texas boundary. Cabinet deliberations continued until October 6 when Secretary Buchanan was instructed to recall Trist. In so doing, Buchanan informed Trist that if he had completed a treaty before the letter of recall arrived, he was to bring it to Washington with him; otherwise, he was to immediately suspend his talks with the Mexicans.[48] Scott was instructed to take harsher measures against the Mexican people and do everything possible to eradicate guerrilla warfare. Subsequently, Polk considered asking Congress to immediately annex New Mexico and California and to establish territorial governments there, but he believed that only Mexico's military defeat would resolve the crisis and permit the completion of U.S. expansion to the Pacific Coast.

Trist ignored his recall notice when it arrived in mid-November; instead, on December 6, he wrote a sixty-five-page letter to his superiors explaining why he would remain in Mexico. For the most part, Trist feared that if Polk became consumed by the All-Mexico Movement, the United States would find itself in an interminable war in which the monetary and human costs could not be calculated. He argued that if a more conservative government emerged in Mexico City, it would be less likely to consent to even the minimum U.S. demands.[49] Thanks largely to infrequent communications, from late November 1847 until February 1848, Polk remained unaware of Trist's maneuverings in Mexico City and the obstacles put in his way.

In early January 1848, Polk received Trist's November missive at a time when he had already determined to replace Scott with General William O. Butler. Infuriated with the diplomat's failure to follow instructions, the president, predisposed to conspiracies anyway, was now convinced that Scott and Trist were acting together. At the time, Scott faced a court of inquiry for removing Polk's long-standing friend, Gideon Pillow, from his command. As for Trist, Polk considered having Butler forcibly evict him from Mexico and impose some sort of punishment, but the cabinet demurred on the possibility that Trist might conclude a treaty that accomplished Washington's objectives. Polk, then acting alone, dispatched a special courier on January 26, instructing Butler to oust Trist from Mexico and send him home. The courier arrived on February 2, the same day that Trist and the Mexican commissioners put their signatures on the final peace agreement at Guadalupe Hidalgo outside of Mexico City.

The terms of the Treaty of Guadalupe Hidalgo satisfied the minimum requirements laid down by Polk in April 1847: the United States received title to New Mexico and all of California and recognition of its annexation of Texas with the border at the Rio Grande. In return, the United States agreed to pay Mexico $15 million and assume its citizens' damage claims set at $3.25 million.[50] The money paid to Mexico was less than the president originally had contemplated, but it was still a large amount since Polk considered the territorial gains an indemnity for a war caused by Mexico. On the other hand, the money enabled the Mexican government to tell its people that it had forced those funds from the United States. The payment also helped to absolve the American conscience of charges of imperialism.

The treaty arrived in Washington on February 19, and for the next two days Polk and his cabinet considered the document completed by their dismissed envoy. While the president favored it because it satisfied his war objectives, he confronted several obstacles on the path to ratification. Secretaries Buchanan and Walker held out for more territory and were rumored to be working with the Senate to effect its rejection. Polk faced a new and reluctant Congress. The Whigs had captured control of the House of Representatives in the November 1846 election, and it was likely that if Polk rejected the treaty, Congress "would not grant either men or money to prosecute the war," thus forcing Polk to withdraw the U.S. troops already in Mexico.[51] In January 1848 the Senate already had approved a Calhoun-initiated resolution denouncing the war as unnecessary and unconstitutional and placing blame on Polk for having started it.

Given the extent of the congressional opposition, Polk faced the possibility of having to withdraw his troops from Mexico with nothing to show for the effort, a fact that would bolster Whig chances of capturing the White House in the 1848 election. Thus, with a guarded recommendation for its approval, Polk submitted the Treaty of Guadalupe Hidalgo to the Senate on February 22 with the notation that "the cessions of territory made by [Mexico] to the United States [are an] indemnity . . . for the satisfaction of our injured citizens, and the permanent establishment of the boundary" of Texas. He also promised to the Mexican citizens living in the newly acquired territories the "free enjoyment of all the rights of citizens of the United States, according to the principles of the Constitution." [52] What Polk did not say was equally important. He avoided a discussion of the divisive issues over the extension of slavery into the new territories and the acquisition of the Pacific Coast ports.

For several days thereafter, rumors abounded about the Senate's possible treaty rejection. At one point a coalition of fifteen Whigs wanted to return all lands west of the Rio Grande to Mexico, while eleven Democrats favored enlarging the conquered territory to include all or part of the provinces of Chihuahua, Coahuila, Nuevo León, and Tamaulipas in northern Mexico. Polk also confronted the All-Mexico Movement, which gained momentum in the late fall of 1847. Democrats from New York and the Western states led the movement and justified their position on the basis of Manifest Destiny. John O'Sullivan's *Democratic Review* called upon the United States to take all of North America, while New York's *Herald* and *Sun* and the *New Orleans Picayune* agreed that the Mexican people needed American guidance because they could not govern themselves. The *New York Evening Post* was more direct when it described the Mexicans as aborigines who could not exist independently next to the United States. Polk realized that the All-Mexico Movement could prolong the war and undermine U.S. objectives. Fortunately for the president, the movement reached its peak about the time that Trist's treaty arrived in Washington. Although the movement's spokesmen made some noises in the days that followed, they soon joined the dwindling minority that opposed the treaty

The tide of opposition ebbed, and by March 2, Polk was confident that the Senate would approve the treaty. For all their bluster, the opposition groups fell apart during the Senate vote on March 10. Twenty-six Democrats joined twelve Whigs to approve the Treaty of Guadalupe Hidalgo by a 38-to-14 margin. The task of delivering the ratification to Mexico fell to Attorney General Nathan Clifford.

During the early spring of 1848, Scott's army occupied the beleaguered Mexico City. The central government had moved to Querétaro, where it continued to be plagued by fiscal insolvency and weakened authority over the outlying provinces. Its weakness threatened acceptance of the Treaty of Guadalupe Hidalgo, but news from New Mexico that its residents had voted to join the United States and the promise of a $3-million payment upon ratification persuaded many national legislators. After a brief and, at times, rancorous debate, the congress voted on May 25 to ratify the treaty.

Later that same day, Clifford arrived in Querétaro to a mixed welcome. While government officials greeted him warmly, the citizens who lined the streets stoned his carriage. Clearly, the Treaty of Guadalupe Hidalgo inflamed Mexican nationalism. The two governments exchanged ratifications on May 30, and Polk declared the treaty in effect on July 4. When he learned of the Mexican ratification, he noted that only Democrats called at the White House to congratulate him.[53]

~

The Treaty of Guadalupe Hidalgo completed U.S. continental expansion except for a small strip of land on the southern border of New Mexico and Arizona (which was acquired from Mexico in 1853[54]), but it left the Polk administration with the question of how to administer the additional territories. The president hoped that Oregon, New Mexico, and California would be admitted to the Union with the "question of slavery . . . left to the people of the new States when they came to form a State constitution for themselves."[55] Only after a bitter debate in both chambers of Congress, which focused on the extension of slavery into the new state, was Oregon admitted to the Union in August 1848. Finally, both the House and the Senate agreed that because it lay north of the 1820 Missouri Compromise line, Oregon would be admitted free of slavery. However, Polk made it clear that he would veto any legislation that determined the extension of slavery into the New Mexico and California territories because he firmly believed that the state residents had the right "to regulate their own domestic institutions, and the Congress could not prevent this."[56] As a consequence of the congressional stalemate, Polk feared that California would become an independent nation, a prospect that apparently pleased incoming President Zachary Taylor. On his inauguration day, March 5, Taylor remarked to Polk that both Oregon and California "were too distant to become members of the Union and that it would be better for them to be an independent government."[57] The embattled Congress did not come to grips with the issue until 1850.[58] Polk, who hoped to end his administration with sectional harmony, instead found the nation bitterly divided over the future of the "peculiar institution."

In addition to the administration of the Western territories, Polk also faced the possibilities of extraterritorial expansion on Mexico's Yucatán peninsula and on Spain's island of Cuba before he left office. On the periphery of Spanish interests, the Yucatán was the least modernized part of the Spanish world, and the Mayan Indians residing there refused to be assimilated into the culture. Following Mexico's independence in 1821, the Yucatecans continued to resist centralized authority, this time from Mexico City, and even briefly functioned as an independent state (1839–1843). Thereafter, the Yucatecans' allegiance to Mexico City remained questionable. At the local level since colonial times, a dichotomy existed between the ruling white, or *criollo*, minority and the Mayan majority. Tensions between the two peoples permeated Yucatecan society and politics.[59]

In 1846 the Yucatán province again seceded from the government in Mexico City and maintained a neutral stance during the war with the United States, but the racial tensions soon erupted into violence. A caste war threatened to topple the *criollos* from their privileged position. In April 1848 the independent Yucatecan *criollo* government turned to the United States for assistance, without which, the *criollos* claimed, they soon would be exterminated by the Indians. Informal requests were soon transformed into an official offer of annexation to the United States.[60] The Yucatecan government made similar proposals to Britain and Spain. The Polk administration faced not only the issue of a local insurrection but also the possibility of an increased European presence in Mexico.

As was his custom with such issues, Polk took the Yucatán problem to his cabinet. There, Buchanan and Walker forcefully argued for sending arms and ammunition to the Yucatecans. In fact, Walker favored annexation of the Yucatán, while Buchanan opposed it. Polk confided to his diary that he shared Walker's position, but for the moment he favored offering only military assistance provided that it did not make its way into other parts of Mexico.

Polk also rationalized that the threat of foreign intervention called for prompt action, which required congressional approval. In his April 29 message to the legislators, Polk cited the Monroe Doctrine as the basis of any policy decision: "Whilst it is not my purpose to recommend the adoption of any measure with a view to the acquisition of the 'dominion and sovereignty' over Yucatán, yet according to our established policy, we could not consent to a transfer of this 'dominion and sovereignty' either to Spain, Great Britain or any other European power."[61] The president left it to Congress to adopt measures that would prevent the Yucatán's affiliation with a European power.

In referencing James Monroe's 1823 declaration, Polk drifted from his predecessor's intention. Clearly, Monroe had concerned himself with any new European colonization or forceful interference with established governments in the Western Hemisphere, not the solicitation of annexation, but times had changed since 1823. The April 29, 1848, Polk's Doctrine, as it came to be called, could be justified on the grounds that any method of European interference constituted a threat to hemispheric security. In this instance, the United States needed to prevent the transfer of the Yucatán to any European power.

The crisis on the Mexican peninsula sparked a sharp debate both outside and inside Congress and became involved in partisan politics. Fortunately, for the United States, Mexico had ratified the Treaty of Guadalupe Hidalgo just as Congress began its debate. The Senate Committee on Foreign Relations briefly deliberated on Polk's proposal. On May 4 its chairman, Edward Hannegan (D., Ind.), reported to the full Senate the committee's recommendation that the United States temporarily occupy the Yucatán.

Outside Congress, ultraexpansionists anticipated further U.S. penetration into the Central American isthmus. John O'Sullivan, author of the term Manifest Destiny, extolled the virtues of the peninsula's hospitable people, who deserved the benefits of U.S. annexation. More practical men such as the *New York Sun*'s Moses Beach envisioned the Yucatán as part of a larger acquisition to provide for the construction of a rail line across the isthmus of Tehuantepec.

On the Senate floor, Hannegan was joined by other Democrats— Michigan's Lewis Cass, Texas's Sam Houston, Mississippi's Jefferson Davis, and Virginia's Henry Foote, Illinois's John Bagby, and Florida's James Westcott—to assault the alleged British plot to occupy the Yucatán. Hannegan, Cass, and Westcott focused on Britain's commercial intentions to link the Atlantic and the Pacific. Houston compared the Indian menace on the Yucatán to that of Texas. All expressed the fear that a continued British presence on the peninsula would ultimately threaten U.S. security.

Senator Calhoun led the Whigs in opposition to any U.S. presence on the Yucatán. He was joined by Kentucky's John Crittenden, Massachusetts's John Davis, Maryland's Reverdy Johnson, and New

Jersey's Jacob Miller in charging that any U.S. intervention on the peninsula was an unwise extension of Monroe's 1823 message. These senators asserted that the expansionists exaggerated the British threat just as they had done with Texas and California. The administration had no evidence of British efforts to influence the separation of the Yucatán from Mexico. The Whigs also gained support from conservative Democrats.

Polk's hope for congressional action quickly faded. Fortunately, a confrontation between the executive and the legislature was averted. On May 17, Hannegan withdrew his proposal when he learned that a peace treaty had been concluded between the adversaries on the Yucatán. About the same time, Lord Palmerston made it clear that the British government had no designs upon the peninsula. Thus, when the caste war erupted again in the 1850s, neither the United States nor Great Britain became overly concerned.

The episode on the Yucatán revived U.S. interest in Cuba and again gave rise to the fear that the British might acquire the island. Despite the grievances against Spanish rule, the Cuban *criollo* class did not seek independence when their brethren on the Latin American continent separated from Spain between 1810 and 1823, largely because Cuba's slave-based society differed vastly from that on the mainland. Separation from Spain would most likely mean freedom for the slaves. In the generation after 1823, Cuba's economic link to the United States tightened as many *criollos* found compatibility with the Southern cotton planters. These Cubans increasingly expressed a desire to be annexed by the United States, particularly following the slave revolts on the island in 1843 and 1844. The *criollos* became convinced that Spain could no longer maintain order.

Until the 1840s, U.S. policy toward Cuba rested on a principle set down by President Thomas Jefferson in 1808 when he reacted to an unfounded report that the island was about to be transferred to Great Britain. Jefferson explained that such a transfer threatened the security of the South and the Gulf Coast. Thereafter, the United States preferred a Cuba controlled by a weak government in Madrid to that of a stronger European power. Polk agreed. If the United States failed to acquire it, "it might fall into the hands of Great Britain."[62]

In the 1840s the island took on new importance as Southern slave owners looked toward Cuba as a place where additional states could be created in order to preserve a political balance in Congress. This prospect was particularly clear after it became known that the Western territories acquired from Mexico in the Treaty of Guadalupe Hidalgo would not support a slave-based economy. In 1847, O'Sullivan and Beach met while visiting Havana. For their own purposes, each man became an advocate of the *criollo* cause for annexation. Once stateside, Beach, a railroad tycoon as well as the owner of the *New York Sun*, popularized the annexation of Cuba through editorials, while O'Sullivan quietly approached Secretary Buchanan to suggest that the United States offer $150 million to Spain for the island, at the same time suggesting that Britain had its covetous eye upon it. In the meantime, Cubans led by Narciso López plotted an insurrection.

Drawing no response from Buchanan, O'Sullivan appealed directly to President Polk. On May 10, 1848, with the Mexican treaty now ratified, O'Sullivan and expansionist Senator Stephen A. Douglas (D., Ill.) met with the president. Polk was persuaded by the argument and presented the issue to his cabinet. Between May 30 and June 17, Polk and his advisers discussed the Cuban situation. During that same time, dispatches from the U.S. consul in Havana reported on the ever-increasing possibility of an armed rebellion, and O'Sullivan again called on Polk to encourage military action. Rumors also circulated that U.S. troops still in Mexico wanted to join the insurrectionists.

Although Polk was "decidedly in favour of purchasing Cuba and making it one of the States of the Union," he vetoed military action.[63] Instead, he suggested to his cabinet that the United States offer Spain $100 million. Thanks to the persuasiveness of Secretary Walker, who also favored annexation of Cuba, the cabinet finally approved Polk's plan. The U.S. minister in Madrid, Romulus Saunders, then approached the Spanish government.[64] The American offer only served to incite Spanish nationalism. Under absolutely no circumstances was Cuba for sale, asserted Foreign Minister Emeterio S. Santovenia. In fact, he told Saunders, rather than see Cuba transferred to any other power, Spain preferred "seeing it sunk in the ocean."[65] Even without Madrid's rejection, the Cuban problem would have ended with the election of Zachary Taylor to the presidency in 1848. He took office at a time when the expansionist zeal had passed its zenith in the United States.

Like the policy regarding the Yucatán and Cuba, U.S. policy toward Central America in the late 1840s was predicated upon alleged British interests. Most Americans knew very little about Central America, and those who were knowledgeable viewed it as a distant land wracked by political turmoil and plagued by cultural backwardness. Not so for the British. Beginning in the mid-1830s their minister to Central America, Frederick Chatfield, promoted his country's interests across the isthmus, and the British superintendent at Belize proclaimed a protectorate over Nicaragua's Mosquito Coast. Throughout the period, U.S. agents William S. Murphy and Henry Savage begged Washington to check the growing British presence; so too did the government in Guatemala City, but their pleas fell upon deaf ears at the State Department. American prestige reached its lowest point in the region in 1847 when the Guatemalan government refused to invite Savage to its Independence Day celebrations. The United States finally broke its silence in June 1848, two months after the Treaty of Guadalupe Hidalgo concluded the Mexican War. Secretary of State Buchanan took notice of Savage's reports and became alarmed at the expanded British presence in Central America.[66] A course of action awaited the arrival of the Taylor administration.

~

With the annexation of Texas in June 1845, President Polk accepted the state's claim to the Rio Grande as its boundary with Mexico and, in so doing, determined to defend it. Over the next year, Polk also added the California and New Mexico territories to the list of U.S. acquisitions. Events in California and pressure from commercial interests in the Northeast encouraged the president to do so. Logic dictated that the gaping hole between Texas and California not be left out.

To complete U.S. continental expansion, Polk was convinced that he could badger the Mexicans into accepting his demands, first by a show of military force in Texas and then by offering generous compensation to the bankrupt Mexican government. After all, Polk concluded, if he had successfully withstood the British over Oregon, he certainly could force the weaker Mexicans to capitulate. But Polk misjudged the strength of their nationalism. No matter its financial and political weakness, Mexico would not accept the loss of territory to its northern neighbor; its government refused to recognize the loss of Texas. The Mexicans were as determined to retain their peripheral territories as the United States was anxious to acquire them. Given the distance between their positions, war between the United States and Mexico appeared inevitable, and the attack upon Taylor's troops along the Rio Grande on April 25, 1846, was an event waiting to happen.

The course of the war was equally predictable, given the weight of U.S. capabilities compared to those of Mexico. Its length can be attributed only to indecision on Washington's side, first by Taylor after his initial victories in northern Mexico, and then by Polk in launching a frontal assault on Mexico City. On the diplomatic front, however, Polk remained committed to the acquisition of new territories and may have rationalized that these lands were compensation for U.S. claims against the bankrupt Mexican government. Polk's reasoning mattered little either to the Mexicans, who lost half of their national domain, or to the expansionists, who were satisfied with a continental America.

Notes

1. Richardson, *Messages and Papers*, 6:2292.
2. Manning, *Diplomatic Correspondence, IAA*, 13:444.
3. Sellers, *Polk: Continentalist*, 260–62.
4. Manning, *Diplomatic Correspondence, IAA*, 8:745.
5. Quaife, *Diary*, 1:36.
6. Manning, *Diplomatic Correspondence, IAA*, 8:172–82.
7. Richard R. Stenberg, "President Polk and California: Additional Documents," *Pacific Historical Review* 10:2 (May 1941): 217–18.
8. Quoted in Pletcher, *Diplomacy of Annexation*, 290.
9. Manning, *Diplomatic Correspondence, IAA*, 8:775.
10. Ibid., 785–803.
11. Quaife, *Diary*, 1:398.
12. Manning, *Diplomatic Correspondence, IAA*, 3:788.
13. Quoted in Pletcher, *Diplomacy of Annexation*, 365.
14. Quaife, *Diary*, 1:230.
15. Ibid., 1:238.
16. Manning, *Diplomatic Correspondence, IAA*, 8:818–23.
17. Ibid., 824–29; Moore, *Works of Buchanan*, 6:294–306.
18. Quoted in Dean B. Mahin, *Olive Branch and Sword: The United States and Mexico, 1845–1848* (Jefferson, NC: McFarland and Company), 73.
19. Quaife, *Diary*, 1:305–9.
20. Ibid., 319.
21. Ibid., 382.
22. Ibid., 384–90.
23. Richardson, *Messages and Papers*, 6:2287–92.
24. Weeks, *John Quincy Adams*, 195.
25. Sellers, *Polk: Continentalist*, 417.
26. Coleman, *John J. Crittenden*, 1:240–43.
27. Sellers, *Polk: Continentalist*, 418.
28. Quoted in Weinberg, *Manifest Destiny*, 163.
29. Emerson, quoted in Sellers, *Polk: Continentalist*, 477; *Niles Register*, quoted in Pletcher, *Diplomacy of Annexation*, 391.
30. Benton, *Thirty Years*, 2:680.
31. Ibid., 680–81.
32. Quaife, *Diary*, 1:412.

33. Ibid., 396.
34. Ibid., 414.
35. Quoted in Paul H. Bergeron, *The Presidency of James K. Polk* (Lawrence: University of Kansas Press, 1987), 77.
36. Quaife, *Diary*, 1:397.
37. Manning, *Diplomatic Correspondence, IAA*, 8:193–94.
38. The record of Mackenzie's meeting with Santa Anna is found in Jesse S. Reeves, *American Diplomacy under Tyler and Polk* (Gloucester, MA: Peter Smith, 1967), 299–307.
39. Quaife, *Diary*, 2:198–202.
40. Ibid., 282–84 and 292–93.
41. Quoted in Graebner, *Manifest Destiny*, 173.
42. Ibid., 164.
43. Quaife, *Diary*, 2:241–42.
44. Ibid., 246.
45. Ibid., 476–77.
46. Manning, *Diplomatic Correspondence, IAA*, 8:201–7.
47. Quaife, *Diary*, 1:245–46.
48. Quaife, *Diary*, 1:159–66 and 186–87.
49. Manning, *Diplomatic Correspondence, IAA*, 8:984–1020.
50. Bevans, *Treaties*, 9:791–806.
51. Quaife, *Diary*, 3:347–51.
52. Richardson, *Messages and Papers*, 6:2444 and 2534.
53. Quaife, *Diary*, 3:485.
54. Friction between the United States and Mexico continued after 1848 regarding the southwestern boundary and alleged support by both sides for the Indians, who raided American and Mexican settlements in the area. The problem was complicated by the discovery of gold in California in 1848, which increased the demand for the construction of a transcontinental railroad. In May 1853 the U.S. minister to Mexico completed a treaty with President (again) Santa Anna for the purchase of the disputed strip of territory and the release of the United States for the damages inflicted by the Indian raids.
55. Quaife, *Diary*, 4:286.
56. Ibid., 288.
57. Ibid., 375.
58. The Compromise of 1850 provided for the admission of California into the Union as a free state; the organization of governments for the New Mexico and Utah territories, with the proviso that the residents would eventually determine the slave issue; the settlement of the Texas boundary, for which the U.S. government provided Texas with $10 million to settle its debts with Mexico; and the abolition of the slave trade, but not slavery, in the District of Columbia.
59. Manning, *Diplomatic Correspondence, IAA*, 8:974–76.
60. Ibid., 1071–78.
61. Richardson, *Messages and Papers*, 6:2432.
62. Manning, *Diplomatic Correspondence, IAA*, 11:54–65; Quaife, *Diary*, 4:469.
63. Quaife, *Diary*, 4:446.
64. Manning, *Diplomatic Correspondence, IAA*, 11:53–64.
65. Ibid., 458.
66. Ibid., 2:869–93.

Conclusion

> In less than four years the annexation of Texas to the Union
> has been consummated; all conflicting title to the Oregon Ter-
> ritory . . . has been adjusted, and New Mexico and Upper Cali-
> fornia have been acquired by treaty. . . . [These] great results
> . . . will be of immeasurable importance in the future progress
> of our country . . . [to] preserve us from foreign collisions, and
> . . . pursue . . . our cherished policy of peace with all nations,
> entangling alliances with none. . . . The present condition of
> the country is similar . . . to that which existed immediately
> [at] the close of the war with Great Britain in 1815.
> —James K. Polk, December 5, 1848[1]

President Polk's final State of the Union message to Congress brimmed with pride over the triumphs of his administration. By December 1848 the nation had fulfilled its Manifest Destiny with the acquisition of Texas, California, New Mexico, and Oregon; and, compared to the political ambiance of Europe and Mexico at that time, a sense of domestic tranquility also prevailed. Polk's confidence, however, did not conceal the fractured country over which he governed. The sectional and political strife that surrounded the debates regarding Westward expansion remained. The "era of good feelings" that characterized the years immediately after the War of 1812, and in which he commenced his political career, did not exist in the 1840s.

When Polk arrived at the White House in March 1845, he was characterized as a man with limited experiences, a narrow vision, and a stubborn determination to have things his own way. He also shared the Jacksonian call for a strict interpretation of the Constitution and saw himself, as president, as more representative of the people than any other federal official. The latter perception gave Polk the confidence to assume a leadership role rather than defer to Congress. Many observers asserted that he failed to appreciate the socioeconomic changes that had occurred in the nation since

James K. Polk, 1845

1820, when he began his public career, and that had played out in the political arena thereafter.

His domestic program reflected his Jacksonian roots: a lower tariff, an independent Treasury system, and federal support for infrastructure projects that dealt only with international commerce or national defense. Congress was slow to act on all three measures. The 1846 Walker Tariff contained more protectionist features than the president wanted, but he recognized that Congress would not produce anything different. The establishment of an independent Treasury in late 1846 pleased Polk, but he had no time to gloat because the nation was engaged in a war with Mexico. Throughout his presidential term, he won out over Congress in the struggle for internal improvements.

Polk did not understand that America had greatly changed in the generation that spanned his political career before entering the White House in 1845. Sectional interests regarding trade, banking, and internal improvements became more apparent; and in the more democratic America of the 1840s, politicians vociferously defended their constituents. Polk clung to principles that guided the nation's early development but that did not meet the demands of the 1840s. Compared to the other presidents and congressional leadership of the 1840s, it is doubtful whether another chief executive could have been more successful.

In foreign affairs, however, Polk clearly understood the nation's sense of Manifest Destiny and ignored his narrow view of the Constitution regarding the acquisition of new lands but, like his contemporaries, misjudged British intentions. In 1845 he shared the opinion of many Americans that Great Britain's goal was to thwart the young nation's every initiative. Polk's foreign policy also benefited from the conflicted internal political dynamics of other nations, while at home he understood the need to obtain a broad consensus in order to achieve his objectives.

Polk had been an advocate of territorial expansion and expressed the same confidence in America as did the proponents of Manifest Destiny. He believed that its citizens, with their culture superior to others, would spread its benefits across the continent. As they did so, these people had the right to expect the government in Washington to protect them from foreign threats to their security and well-being. Polk also understood the economic and political reasons for the South wanting to annex Texas, for New England merchants coveting ports on the Pacific Coast, and for small farmers needing to obtain land in the vast Western expanse. These reasons overrode the idealistic considerations of Manifest Destiny as the United States completed its continental expansion.

Although their motivations differed, the expansionists clearly identified their objectives—Texas, the Southwest, California and Oregon. Given the political environment of the day, the pragmatic Polk understood the need to forge a national consensus out of sectional diversity. He did not attempt to achieve that consensus by cajoling the public or Congress but rather by astute political maneuvering. While his cabinet reflected the varied sectional interests—James Buchanan represented the emerging industrialism of the Northeast, Robert Walker the mono-agriculture of the South, and Polk himself a border state—the president's insistence that his advisers reach a consensus on every issue not only reflected Polk's strong will but also gave the appearance of administrative unity to the public and to Congress.

Once the administration enunciated a position, Polk remained noncommittal to all inquisitive congressmen who came calling at the White House. Many interpreted his reticence as a sign of Polk's stubbornness, but in reality he forced the legislators to propose alternatives acceptable to the national interests and upon which they could agree. Polk pursued the same strategy regarding treaties; he sought the Senate's advice and consent prior to submitting a proposed treaty for its consideration. In reality, Polk's hard-line stance forced the opposition and the divided congressional representatives to offer alternative policies. And, if they bickered and failed to reach an agreement among themselves, they, not Polk, would be criticized for failure. He thus shifted responsibility from himself to the representatives of the divided nation.

Polk signaled his intentions immediately upon assuming the presidency in March 1845. Since its independence in 1836, Texas had sought admission to the United States, but Presidents Andrew Jackson and Martin Van Buren avoided the issue, in large part out of concern for inciting sectional controversies. Not so President John Tyler, who extracted from Congress a joint resolution for Texas's annexation on the eve of the Polk presidency. Polk could have undone Tyler's work but did not. Instead, Polk, who favored annexation, gained the approval for such action from every cabinet designee prior to appointment. Immediately after becoming president, Polk dispatched Andrew Jackson Donelson on a mission to pave the road for Texas's admission into the Union. If the effort failed, Polk could excuse himself for carrying out his predecessor's congressionally approved policy. If he succeeded, which he did, Polk could claim credit.

Oregon provides the best example of Polk's political skills. Amid the jingoism to take all of Oregon to 54° 40' in the spring of 1846, Polk told every congressman who called at the White House that he was committed to the same, despite the fact that nine months earlier the president had indicated his willingness to compromise at the 49th parallel. Polk understood that for nearly a generation the Northeast's commercial interests focused on the Pacific Coast ports, first in Oregon and then in California. The lure of trade with East Asia was too appealing. When American pioneers poured into Oregon in the 1840s, Midwestern congressmen determined that Oregon should be incorporated into the Union, just as Texas had been. Southern politicians, understanding that the addition of so-called free states threatened their section's well-being, resisted the Westward movement. Polk grasped the parameters of the problem and therefore was anxious to know in advance what terms of settlement the Senate would approve. Ever confident that the British would not go to war over the distant territory, Polk stood firm with the government in London while waiting for the Senate to determine its position, which it did in the spring of 1846. Polk claimed victory for a triumph already secured.

Again, sectional interests guided Polk's California policy. Northeastern merchants looked to San Francisco and Monterey, not the entire territory. In fact, not until 1845, as pioneers in significant numbers veered south off the Oregon Trail into California, did Midwesterners recognize the potential of the region. At the same time, spokesmen for the Southern states saw the commercial potential to be gained from the California ports, but they had little interest in anything more. The vast New Mexico territory went largely unnoticed in the discussions of the day, although merchants operating out of Missouri and Texas recognized its economic value, and the administration its importance to national security. California leaped to prominence just as the United States entered its war with Mexico, and Polk quickly placed both territories on the list of wartime objectives without consulting Congress. California and New Mexico were to be part of any peace treaty negotiated with Mexico; and again, the divided Congress would have to deal with the issue.

Polk's Mexican policy demonstrated the shortcomings of his political style and the triumph of American sectionalism. With Texas's annexation completed, Polk needed to clarify the new state's boundary with Mexico, to settle the claims of U.S. citizens against the Mexican government, and to seal the fate of California. Critics, then and now, assert that Polk knew that Mexico's nationalism prevented the surrender of any additional territory and that its bankrupt treasury and underdeveloped economy precluded the meeting of any financial obligations. As Polk increased the pressure, Mexico had no choice but to resist with force. Overlooked in this argument is the fact that Mexico's weakness became a rallying point for the proponents of Manifest Destiny. The U.S. expansionists argued that the political and financial instability of Mexico was the legacy of Spanish colonialism, and the lack of development since 1821 was caused by the inferiority of its people. An American presence could correct all that; and, if not, some European power would and, in the process, threaten U.S. frontier security. Polk articulated these thoughts in his public statements. When war finally broke out in the spring of 1846, Polk's appeal to the American people was based on the patriotism of Manifest Destiny—a patriotism that soon disappeared as criticism of the war intensified.

The Mexican War itself revealed the nation's division. Northeastern and Southern Whigs opposed an extended war that threatened their commercial linkages to Great Britain. And rather than look at the potential markets offered by the new states that would be carved from the conquered territory, these same Whigs feared for their political lives. These new states most likely would become home to Free Soil small farmers, whose representatives in Congress would oppose their commercial interests, and to the Southern "peculiar institution" of slavery.

The 1848 Treaty of Guadalupe Hidalgo completed U.S. continental expansion and provided Mexico with $15 million in compensation that helped to salve the American conscience. Polk, however, never gained preapproval of the treaty. The climate had changed, and he was no longer confident of his control over the political arena. He fretted that the treaty's opponents might be too strong. The Whigs now controlled the Senate, and sectional divisiveness had reached a new high. The Senate approved the Treaty of Guadalupe Hidalgo not because of Polk's political finesse but because it satisfied the varied sectional interests and the demands of Manifest Destiny that the United States stretch from the Atlantic to the Pacific.

Throughout the expansionist period, Polk constantly anticipated British hostility and interference. He was convinced that the British sought not only to block U.S. expansion in Oregon and California but might also use force to achieve their objectives. Polk also anticipated a British threat to the Southern frontier through a presence in Texas and support for Mexico in resisting U.S. advances. While reports from American emissaries in Mexico and California heightened Polk's fears, he chose to ignore contrary intelligence from London. Granted, the British government did not look with favor upon a United States stretching from the Atlantic to the Pacific, but its policies were realistic. The British understood that with the Hudson's Bay Company in decline, the need for all of Oregon was not compelling and that, in fact, the best shipping harbors lay at Vancouver Island, not along the Pacific Northwest coast. Unless it was willing to make a military commitment, the London government expected the Americans to soon come to dominate Oregon and California. Moreover, the corruption of the Mexican government undercut the British investment in shoring up the regime in Mexico City, and Whitehall withdrew its prop before the Mexican War started.

Despite misjudging British intentions, Polk benefited from the domestic pressures that affected the government in London. As the 1840s progressed, the British economy worsened, which reduced the popular interest in foreign adventures. At the same time, the commercial sector increased its demand for free trade and a concomitant end to protective tariffs. The textile industry, largely dependent upon Southern cotton, shrank from a fight with its chief supplier; and, at the same time, urban food shortages increased the demand for U.S. grains. To the north, Ireland was again boiling in discontent, and on the continent French friendship was not assured. With public attention focused upon domestic issues, British voters were in no mood to support increased taxation to underwrite an aggressive foreign policy in a distant land. These conditions left Prime Minister Robert Peel and his foreign secretary, Lord Aberdeen, in a compromising mood.

The weakness of Mexico's central government also contributed to Polk's success. Since its independence in 1821, the government in Mexico City had little control over its northern states and even less control over those more distant at Santa Fe and Monterey. During the same time, the conflict over control of the central government often evolved into personal conflicts. As a result, Mexico was politically disorganized, financially destitute, and unprepared to fight the Americans over Texas, the Southwest, or California in 1846. Patriotism was its most potent weapon but, by itself, insufficient to defend the national territory from U.S. aggrandizement.

In the end, Polk completed the U.S. continental expansion with the exception of the territory acquired by the 1853 Gadsden Treaty. His early successes—the completion of Texas's annexation and the Oregon treaty—demonstrated his political skill and the benefits of British policy. Although he brought the New Mexico and California territories into the Union by 1848, Polk could no longer manipulate the political arena. The nation's political fiber strained under sectional differences that continued until the War between the States erupted in 1861.

Polk left Washington on March 6, 1848, a day after Zachary Taylor's inauguration as the twelfth President of the United States. Despite their mutual dislike that dated to the early days of the Mexican War, Polk and Taylor remained civil to each other throughout the inaugural ceremony. Instead of politics, Polk anxiously anticipated his return to Tennessee for the first time in four years. During his presidency he had disposed of the family property in Maury County and purchased the Nashville home of his former mentor, Felix Grundy. Although Polk expected to lead an active life in retirement, the burdens of office had taken their toll. He looked far older than his fifty-two years. In fact, his health, never robust, declined over the four years of his presidency, and the circuitous route home further drained him. By prearrangement, Polk's monthlong trip took him through Richmond, Virginia; Wilmington, North Carolina; Charleston, South Carolina; Savannah, Georgia; Mobile, Alabama; and then New Orleans before going up the Mississippi River to Memphis and finally to Nashville.[2] Shortly after he reached home in early April 1849, a cholera epidemic that began in New Orleans spread northward through the Mississippi's tributaries. In broken health, Polk succumbed quickly and died on June 15, 1849.

Polk did not take the nation's expansionist spirit with him. In the decade after his death, Americans looked to the Caribbean, Central America, and the Pacific, but no additional territory was acquired until after the Civil War. In the 1890s the United States again felt the spirit of Manifest Destiny as it embarked upon an expansionist program that placed the nation squarely at the center of international events in 1898. In the ongoing process of expansion, Polk was only one of many agents, albeit a very important one.

Notes

1. Richardson, *Messages and Papers*, 6:2483–84.
2. Polk describes his trip home in Quaife, *Diary*, 4:377–416.

Bibliographical Essay

The literature regarding President James K. Polk and the events of his time is abundant; therefore, only the most salient works are cited here. To understand the controversies over Polk's presidential capabilities and his responsibility for and conduct of the Mexican War, one should turn to James Van Horn, "Trends in Historical Interpretation: James K. Polk," *North Carolina Historical Review* 42:4 (1965): 454–64. Although this essay is in need of updating to reflect more recent literature, it provides a framework for understanding the Polk historiography.

Biographies are an excellent starting point for those wishing to gain an understanding of Polk and his period. The most recent, Sam W. Haynes, *James K. Polk and the Expansionist Impulse* (New York: Longman's, 1997), gives a favorable account of Polk's political career with equal treatment allotted to various topics. The most complete study of Polk's political career is Charles G. Sellers, *James K. Polk: Jacksonian, 1795–1843* (Princeton: Princeton University Press, 1957), and *James K. Polk: Continentalist, 1843–1846* (Princeton: Princeton University Press, 1966). Sellers's anticipated third volume would complete the study. Although dated, Eugene I. McCormac, *James K. Polk: A Political Biography* (Berkeley: University of California Press, 1922), is still useful. Two more recent volumes that focus upon Polk's presidency are Charles A. McCoy, *Polk and the Presidency* (Austin: University of Texas Press, 1960); and Paul H. Bergeron, *The Presidency of James K. Polk* (Lawrence: University of Kansas Press, 1987). The latter two studies are important for their emphasis on Polk's domestic policies and administrative style. Two contemporary accounts are Lucien B. Chase, *History of the Polk Administration* (New York: George P. Putnam, 1850); and John S. Jenkins, *James Knox Polk and a History of His Administration* (Auburn, AL: James A. Alden, 1851). Both praise Polk's accomplishments. Important for its information about the president's family and administration is Anson and Fanny Nelson,

Memorials of Sarah Childress Polk, Wife of the Eleventh President of the United States (New York: Anson D. Randolph and Company, 1892).

Primary source materials regarding Polk's political career are abundant. His correspondence is available on microfilm at the Library of Congress in Washington, DC: Papers of James K. Polk, 67 reels. Eight volumes of these materials have been edited by Paul H. Bergeron et al., *The Correspondence of James K. Polk* (Nashville: Vanderbilt University Press, 1969–1993). For the fourteen years that Polk spent in Congress one should consult *The House Journals*, *The Congressional Globe*, and the *Register of Debates*; these same sources also are important for an examination of the events during the Polk presidency. The most important source for the presidency itself is Milo M. Quaife, ed., *The Diary of James K. Polk, During His Presidency, 1845 to 1849*, 4 vols. (Chicago: A. C. McClurg and Company, 1910), which gives Polk's detailed account of events on a daily basis. Allan Nevins has edited a shorter version of the diary, which also includes an analytical introduction: *Diary of a President* (New York: Longmans, Green and Company, 1929). Volume four of James D. Richardson, comp., *A Compilation of the Messages and Papers of the Presidents, 1789–1899* (Washington, DC: U.S. Congress, 1917), reproduces Polk's public statements during his presidential term. These sources provide the framework for his political ideology.

While the first volume of the Charles Sellers biography, mentioned above, offers the best account of Polk's early years on Tennessee's frontier, other relevant discussions are found in Albert V. Goodpasture, "The Boyhood of President Polk," *Tennessee Historical Quarterly* 7 (1921–22): 38–50; Tennessee Historical Commission, *Tennessee, Old and New*, vol. 1 (Kingsport, TN: Kingsport Press, 1946); and Stanley J. Folmsbee, Robert E. Coslew, and Enoch C. Mitchell, *History of Tennessee*, vol. 1 (New York: Lewis Historical Publishing Company, 1960).

Other aspects of Polk's life that are important for understanding the eleventh president include a discussion of his religious views, which are described by John B. McFerrin, *A History of Methodism in Tennessee* (Nashville: Southern Methodist Publishing House, 1869). John S. Bassett informs us about Polk's plantations in *The Southern Plantation Overseer, as Revealed in His Letters* (New York: Negro Universities Press, 1968). Like other presidents of his time, Polk attempted to use the press to his own advantage. This concept is explored by Culver H. Smith in *The Press, Politics, and Patronage: The American Government's Use of Newspapers, 1789–1875* (Athens: University of Georgia Press, 1977).

The place of the trans-Appalachian frontier in the larger context of Jeffersonian America can be found in Malcolm Rohrbough, *The Trans-Appalachian Frontier: Peoples, Societies, and Institutions, 1775–1850* (New York: Oxford University Press, 1978); Drew McCoy, *The Elusive Republic: Political Economy in Jeffersonian America* (Chapel Hill: University of North Carolina Press, 1980); and Lance Banning, *The Jeffersonian Persuasion: Evolution of Political Ideology* (Ithaca: Cornell University Press, 1978).

An overview of the America in which Polk completed his political career is described by Glyndon G. Van Deusen, *The Jacksonian Era, 1828–1848* (New York: Harper Brothers, 1959); Edward Pessen, *Jacksonian America: Society, Personality, and Politics* (Homewood, IL: Dorsey Press, rev. ed. 1978); and Arthur Schlesinger, Jr., *The Age of Jackson* (Boston: Little, Brown and Company, 1945). More recent interpretative studies include Charles G. Sellers, *The Market Revolution: Jacksonian America, 1815–1846* (New York: Oxford University Press, 1991); and Harry L. Watson, *Liberty and Power: The Politics of Jacksonian America* (New York: Hill and Wang, 1990).

The economic differences that developed in the various sections of the United States from the 1820s through the 1840s are described in Stuart Bruchy, *The Roots of American Economic Growth, 1607–1861* (New York: Harper and Row, 1965). Thomas Cochran provides an overview of industrial development in *Frontiers of Change: Early Industrialism in America* (New York: Oxford University Press, 1981). A portrait of the socioeconomic issues on the Midwestern frontier is found in Paul W. Gates, *The Farmer's Age: Agriculture, 1815–1860* (Armonk, NY: M. E. Sharpe, 1960). Gavin Wright thoroughly analyzes the economic development of the Old South in *The Political Economy of the Cotton South: Households, Markets, and Wealth in the Nineteenth Century* (New York: Norton, 1978). The standard picture of slavery from its defenders is presented by Ulrich B. Phillips, *Life and Labor in the Old South* (Boston: Little, Brown and Company, 1929). For a contrasting view see Robert Fogel and Stanley Engerman, *Time on the Cross: The Economics of American Negro Slavery* (Boston: Little, Brown and Company, 1976). The analysis of American society by Alexis de Tocqueville, translated from the French by Henry Reeves, *Democracy in America* (New Rochelle, NY: Arlington House, 1966), remains an important commentary on the United States during this time.

The Jacksonian period also ushered in the emergence of political parties and witnessed a marked increase in political participation by the people. Studies addressing these developments include

Joel H. Silbey, *The Shrine of Party: Congressional Voting Behavior, 1841–1852* (Pittsburgh: University of Pittsburgh Press, 1964); Richard P. McCormick, *The Second American Party System: Party Formation in the Jacksonian Period* (Chapel Hill: University of North Carolina Press, 1966); and two studies by Michael F. Holt: *Political Parties and American Political Development: From the Age of Jackson to the Age of Lincoln* (Baton Rouge: Louisiana State University Press, 1992), and *The Rise and Fall of the Whig Party: Jacksonian Politics and the Onset of the Civil War* (New York: Oxford University Press, 1999). An older, but useful, study is E. M. Carroll, *Origins of the Whig Party* (Durham: Duke University Press, 1925).

In the changing of America, from Jeffersonian agrarianism to Jacksonian Democracy, Polk commenced his political career, first as a congressman from Tennessee and subsequently as governor of the state. In addition to the biographies mentioned above, other works that address Polk's early political career include Paul H. Bergeron, *Antebellum Politics in Tennessee* (Louisville: University Press of Kentucky, 1982); and Oliver P. Temple, *Notable Men of Tennessee from 1833 to 1875: Their Times and Their Contemporaries* (New York: Cosmopolitan Press, 1912). The political feud between Polk and John Bell revealed much about the changing socioeconomic landscape of the state. Joseph H. Parks, *John Bell of Tennessee* (Baton Rouge: Louisiana State University Press, 1950), and Norman L. Parks, *The Career of John Bell as Congressman from Tennessee, 1827–1841* (Nashville: Joint University Libraries, 1942), discuss the personal feud within the state's changing political environment. The controversial 1844 Democratic Party convention that resulted in Polk's presidential nomination is the subject of James N. Paul, *Rift in Democracy* (Philadelphia: University of Pennsylvania Press, 1957).

As president, Polk involved his cabinet in every major decision. An older study that remains important because of its focus on Polk's concern with sectional balance is H. Barrett Learned, "The Sequence of Appointments to Polk's Original Cabinet: A Study in Chronology, 1844–1845," *American Historical Review* 30 (1924): 76–83. Despite its title, a more recent source that addresses the composition of Polk's cabinet is Brian G. J. Walton, "James K. Polk and the Democratic Party in the Aftermath of the Wilmot Proviso" (Ph.D. diss., Vanderbilt University, 1968). An excellent study of Polk's vice president is John M. Belohlavek, *George Mifflin Dallas: Jacksonian Patrician* (University Park: Pennsylvania State University Press, 1977). The most recent biography of Polk's controversial secretary of state is Frederick Moore Binder, *James Buchanan and the American*

Empire (Selinsgrove, PA: Susquehanna University Press, 1994). Polk's secretary of war is the subject of Ivor D. Spencer, *The Victor and the Spoils: A Life of William L. Marcy* (Providence, RI: Brown University Press, 1959). The most important study of Polk's confidant and postmaster general is Clement L. Grant, "The Public Career of Cave Johnson" (Ph.D. diss., Vanderbilt University, 1951). James P. Shenton gives an excellent analysis of the influential secretary of the treasury in *Robert John Walker: A Politician from Jackson to Lincoln* (New York: Columbia University Press, 1961). George Bancroft, secretary of the navy and subsequently a diplomat, is the subject of several biographies, the most recent being Lilian Handlin, *George Bancroft: The Intellectual Democrat* (New York: Harper and Row, 1984).

More than any other subject, the completion of continental expansion dominates the literature about the Polk administration. The concept of Manifest Destiny and its concomitant expression of nationalism are often used to describe the U.S. quest for territorial expansion. Several studies explore the intellectual foundations of the concept. Albert K. Weinberg's seminal work, *Manifest Destiny: A Study of Nationalist Expansionism in American History* (Baltimore: Johns Hopkins University Press, 1935), argues that America's moral ideology justified expansion. Other broad descriptions of the intellectual justification for expansion include Arthur A. Ekirch, Jr., *Ideas, Ideals, and American Development: A History of Their Growth and Internationalization* (New York: Appleton-Century-Crofts, 1966); and Michael H. Hunt, *Ideology and U.S. Foreign Policy* (New Haven: Yale University Press, 1987). William H. Goetzmann, *When the Eagle Screamed: The Romantic Horizon in American Diplomacy, 1800–1860* (New York: John Wiley and Sons, 1966), explains that the expansionist impulse derived from European ideas, particularly those of grandeur and destiny. In *Empire on the Pacific: A Study in American Continental Expansion* (New York: Ronald Press, 1955), Norman A. Graebner focuses on the maritime aspects of U.S. expansion. Reginald Horsman, *Race and Manifest Destiny: The Origins of American Anglo-Saxonism* (Cambridge, MA: Harvard University Press, 1981), emphasizes the concept of racial superiority as the justification for expansion. Frederick A. Merk, *Monroe Doctrine and American Expansionism* (New York: Alfred A. Knopf, 1966), examines the American perception of European, particularly British, efforts to thwart Westward expansion. Merk is more critical of the motives for midcentury expansion in his *Manifest Destiny and Mission in American History* (New York: Alfred A. Knopf, 1963). An anthology of representative statements, both for and against U.S. expansion from 1844 to 1860, can be found in Norman A. Graebner, ed., *Manifest Destiny* (Indianapolis: Bobbs-Merrill, 1968). Three other works of particular interest to the reader are Michael A. Morrison, *Slavery and the West: The Eclipse of Manifest Destiny and the Coming of the Civil War* (Chapel Hill: University of North Carolina Press, 1997); Anders Stephenson, *Manifest Destiny: American Expansion and the Empire of Right* (New York: Hill and Wang, 1995); and Thomas R. Hietala, *Manifest Design: Anxious Aggrandizement in Late Jacksonian America* (Ithaca: Cornell University Press, 1985).

Westward expansion began long before Polk became president in 1845. Studies of the earlier period include Donald Jackson, *Thomas Jefferson and the Stoney Mountains: Exploring the West from Monticello* (Urbana: University of Illinois Press, 1981); and William Earl Weeks, *John Quincy Adams and American Global Empire* (Lexington: University Press of Kentucky, 1992).

Several other political notables of this time shed light on Polk's policies regarding the extension of U.S. boundaries. The memoirs of three other expansionists are Thomas Hart Benton, *Thirty Years View*, 2 vols. (New York: D. Appleton and Company, 1858); John Charles Frémont, *Memoirs of My Life* (New York: Belford, Clarke, 1887); and Charles Wilkes, *The Autobiography of Rear Admiral Charles Wilkes, U.S. Navy, 1798–1877*, ed., William J. Morgan (Washington, DC: Naval History Division, Department of the Navy, 1978). Biographies of other important persons include Irving H. Bartlett, *John C. Calhoun* (New York: W. W. Norton and Company, 1993); Frank Woodford, *Lewis Cass, the Last Jeffersonian* (New Brunswick: Rutgers University Press, 1950); Charles H. Ambler, *Thomas Ritchie* (Richmond, VA: Bell Book and Stationery Company, 1913); Oliver P. Chitwood, *John Tyler: Champion of the Old South* (New York: Russell and Russell, 1939); and Donald B. Cole, *Martin Van Buren and the American Political System* (Princeton: Princeton University Press, 1984).

The most comprehensive account of Polk's diplomacy can be found in David M. Pletcher, *The Diplomacy of Annexation: Texas, Oregon, and the Mexican War* (Columbia: University of Missouri Press, 1973). Howard Jones and Donald A. Rakestraw, *Prologue to Manifest Destiny: Anglo-American Relations in the 1840s* (Wilmington, DE: Scholarly Resources, 1997), provides the U.S. response to the perceived British threat to the continent. An equally important study is Wilbur D. Jones, *The American Problem in British Diplomacy, 1841–1861* (Athens: University of Georgia Press, 1974), in which the au-

thor examines Britain's foreign policy within the context of its domestic politics. An important documentary source for this period
is William R. Manning, ed., *Diplomatic Correspondence of the United
States: Inter-American Affairs, 1831–1860*, 12 vols. (Washington, DC:
Carnegie Endowment for International Peace, 1932–1939).

Polk arrived in Washington as "Oregon fever" was reaching its
zenith. A good overview of the Oregon Territory controversy is
found in Frederick Merk, *The Oregon Question: Essays in Anglo-
American Diplomacy and Politics* (Cambridge, MA: Harvard University Press, 1967). This collection of the author's previously published
essays traces the Oregon question from the late eighteenth century
through six sets of negotiations that culminated in the 1846 treaty.
Richard W. Van Alstyne examines the beginnings of the international rivalries over Oregon and its adjoining waters in "International Rivalries in the Pacific Northwest," *Oregon Historical Quarterly*
46 (1945): 185–218. Donald A. Rakestraw also tackles the Oregon
question in *For Honor or Destiny: The Anglo-American Crisis over the
Oregon Territory* (New York: Peter Lang, 1995).

From the U.S. perspective, Bernard DeVoto's *Year of Decision,
1846* (Boston: Houghton Mifflin, 1942) and *Across the Wide Missouri*
(Boston: Houghton Mifflin, 1947) illustrate the spread of American
culture and political ideas to the Oregon Territory by pioneers who
settled in the region. In a series of essays entitled "The Federal Relations of Oregon," *Oregon Historical Quarterly* 19 (1918): 89–133,
189–230, 283–331, Lester B. Shippee argues that the Oregon question had become a national concern as early as 1819. Robert G.
Cleland, "Asiatic Trade and the American Occupation of the Pacific Coast," in the annual report of the American Historical Association for 1914, demonstrates that interest in trade with East Asia
was the primary motive for the U.S. desire for Oregon. Daniel W.
Howe, "The Mississippi Valley in the Movement for Fifty-Four Forty
or Fight," *Proceedings of the Mississippi Valley Historical Association,
1912*, 99–116, claims that as the congressional debates on Oregon
proceeded, many legislators came to question the claim to all of
Oregon, thus prompting a settlement. Robert L. Schuyler, "Polk and
the Oregon Compromise of 1846," *Political Science Quarterly* 26
(1911): 443–61, demonstrates that the president always was willing
to compromise at 54° 40' despite his public rhetoric to the contrary.

To understand the basis of British interests in the territory, one
must turn to the Hudson's Bay Company and the classic study by
Edwin E. Rich, *Hudson's Bay Company, 1670–1870*, 3 vols. (New York:
Macmillan, 1961). Joseph Schafer's "The British Attitude toward

the Oregon Question, 1815–1846," *American Historical Review* 16 (1911): 273–99, which is based on British documents, demonstrates that after 1815 both the British and the United States had legitimate interests in Oregon that could only be resolved through compromise. Richard S. Cramer, "British Magazines and the Oregon Question," *Pacific Historical Review* 32 (1963): 369–82, reports that the major British publications supported the government's claim to the disputed triangle of territory above the Columbia River. Others argued that specific factors prompted Britain to settle the matter. Wilbur D. Jones in *Lord Aberdeen and the Americas* (Athens: University of Georgia Press, 1958) argues that Vancouver Island and the use of the Columbia River were more important to the British than any piece of the disputed land. Wilbur D. Jones and J. Chalmers Vincent in "British Preparedness and the Oregon Settlement," *Pacific Historical Review* 22 (1953): 353–64, argue that Aberdeen's adept use of military preparedness in 1846 prompted the United States to settle the issue. Thomas P. Martin, "Cotton and Wheat in Anglo-American Trade and Politics, 1846–1852," *Journal of Southern History* 1 (1935): 293–319, finds that British free-traders pressured their government to compromise on Oregon in hopes of gaining greater access to U.S. wheat and cotton. In his essay, "France as a Factor in the Oregon Negotiations," *Pacific Northwest Quarterly* 44 (1953): 69–73, John S. Galbraith argues that Aberdeen's concern over good relations with France determined much of his Oregon policy.

Many Americans viewed California as a more important acquisition than Oregon. Three volumes of Hubert Howe Bancroft's *History of California*, 7 vols. (San Francisco: The History Company, 1886–1890), provide a detailed account from 1825 to 1840 of events leading to the American occupation of the territory. A briefer account can be found in Reuben L. Underhill, *From Cowhides to Golden Fleece* (Stanford: Stanford University Press, 1946). Several specialized studies are worth noting. Robert G. Cleland, "The Early Sentiment for the Annexation of California: An Account of the Growth of American Interest in California, 1835–1846," *Southwestern Historical Quarterly* 18 (1914): 1–40, 231–60, describes the events and publications on the East Coast and in California that supported annexation. Magdelena Coughlin, "California Ports: A Key to Diplomacy for the West Coast, 1820–1845," *Journal of the West* 5 (1966): 153–72, argues that the desire for Pacific Coast ports was the driving force of the U.S. interest in California.

Werner H. Marti, *Messenger of Destiny: The California Adventures, 1846–1847, of Archibald Gillespie, U.S. Marine Corps* (San Francisco: Howell, 1960), details Gillespie's secret mission to John C. Frémont in 1846 and the ensuing Bear Flag revolt. Lester D. Engelson, "Proposals for California by England in Connection with the Mexican Debt to British Bondholders, 1837–1846," *California Historical Society Quarterly* 18 (1939): 136–48, considers the proposals made by private bondholders to the British government. Frank A. Knapp, Jr., analyzes the increasing concern over California in the Mexican press and congress between 1838 and 1847 in "The Mexican Fear of Manifest Destiny in California," in Thomas E. Comer and Carlos Casteñada, eds., *Essays in Mexican History* (Austin: University of Texas Press, 1958), 192–208. The activities of the U.S. consul in California, Thomas O. Larkin, are the subject of two essays: John A. Hawgood, "The Pattern of Yankee Infiltration in Mexican Alta California, 1821–1846," *Pacific Historical Review* 27 (1958): 27–37; and Rayner W. Kelsey, "The United States Consulate in California," *Academy of Pacific Coast History Publications* 1 (1910): 161–267. Larkin's official correspondence is available in John S. Bassett, ed., *The Larkin Papers: Personal, Business, and Official Correspondence of Thomas Oliver Larkin, Merchant and United States Consul in California* (Berkeley: University of California Press, 1964).

Although the U.S. annexation of Texas and the boundary dispute with Mexico served as the immediate causes for war in 1846, there existed several long-standing issues that contributed to the conflict. Regarding the annexation of Texas in 1845 one should see Jesse S. Reeves, *American Diplomacy under Tyler and Polk* (Gloucester, MA: Peter Smith, 1967, reprint of 1907 edition); Carlos Bosch García, "Dos diplomacias y un problema," *Historia Mexicana* 2 (1952): 46–65; Annie Middleton, "Donelson's Mission to Texas in Behalf of Annexation," *Southwestern Historical Quarterly* 24 (1924): 247–91; and Lota M. Spell, "Gorostiza and Texas," *Hispanic American Historical Review* 37 (1957): 425–62.

Several accounts offer a historical perspective on the causes of the Mexican War. George L. Rives, *The United States and Mexico, 1821–1848*, 2 vols. (New York: Scribner's, 1913), is a balanced and detailed treatment that is still useful for understanding relations between the two nations. Despite its anti-Mexican bias, Justin H. Smith's Pulitzer Prize-winning *The War With Mexico*, 2 vols. (New York: Macmillan, 1919) dominated American thought about the causes of the war for more than one half-century. Clayton C. Kohl,

Claims as a Cause of the Mexican War (New York: New York University Press, 1914), remains the standard treatment on an aspect of the causes of the war, which loomed large in Polk's war message. Frederick Merk, *Slavery and the Annexation of Texas* (New York: Alfred A. Knopf, 1972), explains the conflict between slaveryites and abolitionists over expansion into Texas. Texas diplomacy, particularly with European nations, is the subject of Joseph W. Schmitz, *Texas Statecraft, 1836–1845* (New York: Barnes and Noble, 1941). An important biography is Llerena Friend, *Sam Houston: The Great Designer* (Austin: University of Texas Press, 1954).

The Mexican perspective is provided by Kosefina Vásquez de Knauth, *Mexicanos y norteamericanos ante la guerra del 47* (México, D.F.: Sep Setenta, 1972); and Carlos Bosch García, *Historia de las relaciones entre México y los Estados Unidos, 1819–1848* (México, D.F.: Escuela Nacional de Ciencias Políticas y Sociales, 1961). Both share the common theme of U.S. responsibility for the war. Gene M. Brack, *Mexico Views Manifest Destiny, 1821–1846: An Essay on the Origins of the Mexican War* (Albuquerque: University of New Mexico Press, 1975), suggests that few Mexicans desired war, which is in sharp contrast to the view presented by Justin Smith. Wilfred H. Callcott, *Santa Anna: The Story of an Enigma Who Once Was Mexico* (Norman: University of Oklahoma Press, 1936), remains the most important work in English about Santa Anna.

There are several important works about the war itself. K. Jack Bauer, *The Mexican War, 1846–1848* (New York: Macmillan, 1974), is a well-researched, balanced treatment of military engagements and the occupation of Mexico. Bauer's *Surfboats and Horse Marines: U.S. Naval Operations in the Mexican War, 1846–1848* (Annapolis: Naval Institute Press, 1969) is a comprehensive account of the U.S. naval operations. David Lavender, *Climax at Buena Vista: The American Campaign in Northeastern Mexico, 1846–1847* (Philadelphia: Lippincott, 1966), describes the initial war campaigns. A good account of the conquest of Santa Fe and California can be found in Dwight L. Clarke, *Stephen Watts Kearny: Soldier of the West* (Norman: University of Oklahoma Press, 1961). James McCaffrey examines the life of the common soldier in *Army of Manifest Destiny: The American Soldier in the Mexican War* (New York: New York University Press, 1992).

Polk's wartime diplomacy is the subject of Anna K. Nelson, *Secret Agents: President Polk and the Search for Peace with Mexico* (New York: Garland, 1988). Nicholas Trist is the focus of several scholarly articles. Among the most important is Eugene K. Chamberlin, "Nicolas Trist and Baja California," *Hispanic American Historical*

Review 32 (1963): 49–63, in which Chamberlin blames Trist for failing to secure Baja California for the United States. In contrast, Ken-
neth M. Johnson exonerates Trist for not securing the peninsula in
"Baja California and the Treaty of Guadalupe Hidalgo," *Journal of
the West* 11 (1972): 328–47. In Thomas J. Farnham, "Nicholas Trist
and James Feaner and the Mission to Mexico," *Arizona and the West*
11 (1969): 247–60, Feaner, who served as Trist's courier in Mexico,
claims that he was responsible for persuading Trist to refuse Polk's
demand to return to Washington in late 1847. Two important studies that examine the treaty ending the Mexican War are Donald C.
Cutter, "The Legacy of the Treaty of Guadalupe-Hidalgo," *New
Mexico Historical Review* 53 (1978): 305–15; and Richard G. del Castillo, *The Treaty of Guadalupe-Hidalgo: A Legacy of Conflict* (Norman:
University of Oklahoma Press, 1990).

During the war, Mexico confronted two secessionist move-
ments, one on the Yucatán peninsula and one in its northern provinces. In "Secessionist Diplomacy of Yucatán," *Hispanic American
Historical Review* 9 (1929): 79–100, Mary W. Williams traces the efforts of the local Yucatecan regime to end its caste war in 1847–48
through secession from Mexico and annexation to the United States.
Louis De Armond, "Justo Sierra O'Reilly and Yucatán-United States
Relations, 1847–1848," *Hispanic American Historical Review* 31 (1951):
420–36, describes O'Reilly's invitation for U.S. annexation that provoked congressional debate, but nothing more. Justin H. Smith, "La
República de Rio Grande," *American Historical Review* 25 (1920): 660–
75, traces the abortive attempt at secession in northeastern Mexico
until the movement disappeared in 1847.

An excellent analysis of the American public's view of the war
is Robert W. Johannsen, *The Halls of Montezuma: The Mexican War in
the American Imagination* (New York: Oxford University Press, 1985).
The criticisms of Polk's wartime policies are the subject of John H.
Schroeder, *Mr. Polk's War: American Opposition and Dissent, 1846–
1848* (Madison: University of Wisconsin Press, 1973). Despite sec-
tional socioeconomic differences between the Northeast and the
South, each region was home to antiwar activists. See Kinley J.
Brauer, *Cotton versus Conscience: Massachusetts Whig Politics and
Southwestern Expansion* (Lexington: University of Kentucky Press,
1967); and Ernest M. Lander, Jr., *Reluctant Imperialists: Calhoun, the
South Carolinians, and the Mexican War* (Baton Rouge: Louisiana State
University Press, 1980).

Several studies focus on specific interest groups. In a classic essay, "In Re That Aggressive Slavocracy," *Mississippi Valley Historical*

Review 8 (1921): 13–79, Chauncy W. Boucher destroys the myth that a unified South provoked and supported the war. In contrast, William E. Dodd finds that an alliance between the West and the South was responsible for the prosecution of the war in "The West and the War with Mexico," *Journal of the Illinois State Historical Society* 5 (1922): 159–72. Gurston Goldin, "Business Sentiment and the Mexican War, With Particular Emphasis on the New York Businessman," *New York History* 33 (1952): 52–70, demonstrates that most businessmen opposed the war because it would encourage abolition and harm their profitable ties to the South. Clayton S. Ellsworth, "The American Churches and the Mexican War," *American Historical Review* 45 (1940): 301–26, shows that most religious groups, with the exception of Catholics and most New England Protestant denominations, supported the war. In his study of congressional voting on war issues, John R. Collins, "The Mexican War: A Study in Fragmentation," *Journal of the West* 11 (1972): 225–34, demonstrates that partisan and sectional fragmentation prevailed. In contrast to the antiwar sentiment, an "All-Mexico Movement" gained momentum in late 1847 and early 1848; it is the subject of John D. P. Fuller, *The Movement for the Acquisition of All Mexico, 1846–1848* (Baltimore: Johns Hopkins University Press, 1936).

In "The War with the United States and the Crisis in Mexican Thought," *The Americas* 14 (1957): 153–73, Charles Hale presents an excellent analysis of the Mexican liberals who admired U.S. institutions but could not repudiate them with the outbreak of war. Edward H. Moseley, "The Religious Impact of the American Occupation of Mexico City, 1847–1848," in Eugene Huck and Edward H. Moseley, eds., *Militarists, Merchants, and Missionaries: United States Expansion into Middle America* (Tuscaloosa: University of Alabama Press, 1970), shows that the U.S. occupation of Mexico had little impact upon religion, but it may have encouraged the liberals to seek political reform following the war.

Tensions along the Mexican border continued after the war ended. These issues are explored by William H. Goetzman in "The United States-Mexican Boundary Survey, 1848–1853," *Southwestern Historical Quarterly* 62 (1958): 164–90; and Joseph H. Park, "The Apaches in American-Mexican Relations, 1843–1861: A Footnote to the Gadsden Treaty," *Arizona and the West* 3 (1961): 129–43. The U.S. acquisition of additional Mexican territory is explained in the standard, but outdated, work by Paul N. Garber, *The Gadsden Treaty* (Philadelphia: University of Pennsylvania Press, 1923).

For a general discussion of U.S. policy toward Cuba in the midnineteenth century see Louis A. Pérez, Jr., *Cuba and the United States: Ties of Singular Intimacy* (Athens: University of Georgia Press, 1990), chapter 2. For a detailed account of the Narciso López expeditions see Herminio Portell Vilá, *Narciso López y su época*, 3 vols. (Havana: Imprenta Hermanos Tipografia, 1933–1958). For a general discussion of U.S. relations during the 1840s see Thomas M. Leonard, *Central America and the United States: The Search for Stability* (Athens: University of Georgia Press, 1992), chapter 2. An excellent analysis of the British presence on the isthmus is Mario Rodríguez, *A Palmerstonian Diplomat in Central America: Frederick Chatfield, Esq.* (Tucson: University of Arizona Press, 1964).

Among the major newspapers of the period are Baltimore's *Niles Weekly Register* and *Sun*; Boston's *Advertiser*; Nashville's *Democratic Statesman* and *Daily Republican Banner*; New Orleans's *Picayune*; New York City's *Evening Post, Journal of Commerce*, and *Herald*; and Washington, DC's *Globe, Madisonian*, and *National Intelligencer*. Two important journals, the *Democratic Review* and the *North American Review*, are equally important for their commentary.

Just as border controversies with Mexico lingered after the war, so too did U.S. sectional differences over the newly acquired territories. For an overview of the growing sectional divisions in the postwar period see David M. Potter, *Impending Crisis, 1848–1861* (New York: Harper and Row, 1976); and Michael Holt, *The Political Crisis of the 1850s* (New York: John Wiley, 1978).

Index

1/0 1

ISBN 0-8420-2646-0

90000 >

9 780842 026468